Achieving Traffic Safety Goals in the United States

Lessons from Other Nations

Committee for the Study of Traffic Safety
Lessons from Benchmark Nations

TRANSPORTATION RESEARCH BOARD
OF THE NATIONAL ACADEMIES

Transportation Research Board
Washington, D.C.
2011
www.TRB.org

Transportation Research Board Special Report 300

Subscriber Categories
Highways; pedestrians and bicyclists; administration and management; policy; safety and human factors

Transportation Research Board publications are available by ordering individual publications directly from the TRB Business Office, through the Internet at www.TRB.org or national-academies.org/trb, or by annual subscription through organizational or individual affiliation with TRB. Affiliates and library subscribers are eligible for substantial discounts. For further information, contact the Transportation Research Board Business Office, 500 Fifth Street, NW, Washington, DC 20001 (telephone 202-334-3213; fax 202-334-2519; or e-mail TRBsales@nas.edu).

Copyright 2011 by the National Academy of Sciences. All rights reserved.
Printed in the United States of America.

NOTICE: The project that is the subject of this report was approved by the Governing Board of the National Research Council, whose members are drawn from the councils of the National Academy of Sciences, the National Academy of Engineering, and the Institute of Medicine. The members of the committee responsible for the report were chosen for their special competencies and with regard for appropriate balance.
This report has been reviewed by a group other than the authors according to the procedures approved by a Report Review Committee consisting of members of the National Academy of Sciences, the National Academy of Engineering, and the Institute of Medicine.
This study was sponsored by the Transportation Research Board and the General Motors Foundation.

Typesetting by Circle Graphics.

Library of Congress Cataloging-in-Publication Data

Achieving traffic safety goals in the United States : lessons from other nations / Committee for the Study of Traffic Safety Lessons from Benchmark Nations, Transportation Research Board of the National Academies.
   p. cm.—(Transportation Research Board special report ; 300)
 Includes bibliographical references.
 ISBN 978-0-309-16065-0
 1. Traffic safety—United States. 2. Traffic accidents—United States—Prevention. 3. Motor vehicle driving—United States—Safety measures. 4. Strategic planning—United States. I. National Academies (U.S.). Committee for the Study of Traffic Safety Lessons from Benchmark Nations.
 HE5614.2.A5935 2010
 363.12'50973—dc22
                                                                                2010040353

THE NATIONAL ACADEMIES
Advisers to the Nation on Science, Engineering, and Medicine

The **National Academy of Sciences** is a private, nonprofit, self-perpetuating society of distinguished scholars engaged in scientific and engineering research, dedicated to the furtherance of science and technology and to their use for the general welfare. On the authority of the charter granted to it by the Congress in 1863, the Academy has a mandate that requires it to advise the federal government on scientific and technical matters. Dr. Ralph J. Cicerone is president of the National Academy of Sciences.

The **National Academy of Engineering** was established in 1964, under the charter of the National Academy of Sciences, as a parallel organization of outstanding engineers. It is autonomous in its administration and in the selection of its members, sharing with the National Academy of Sciences the responsibility for advising the federal government. The National Academy of Engineering also sponsors engineering programs aimed at meeting national needs, encourages education and research, and recognizes the superior achievements of engineers. Dr. Charles M. Vest is president of the National Academy of Engineering.

The **Institute of Medicine** was established in 1970 by the National Academy of Sciences to secure the services of eminent members of appropriate professions in the examination of policy matters pertaining to the health of the public. The Institute acts under the responsibility given to the National Academy of Sciences by its congressional charter to be an adviser to the federal government and, on its own initiative, to identify issues of medical care, research, and education. Dr. Harvey V. Fineberg is president of the Institute of Medicine.

The **National Research Council** was organized by the National Academy of Sciences in 1916 to associate the broad community of science and technology with the Academy's purposes of furthering knowledge and advising the federal government. Functioning in accordance with general policies determined by the Academy, the Council has become the principal operating agency of both the National Academy of Sciences and the National Academy of Engineering in providing services to the government, the public, and the scientific and engineering communities. The Council is administered jointly by both the Academies and the Institute of Medicine. Dr. Ralph J. Cicerone and Dr. Charles M. Vest are chair and vice chair, respectively, of the National Research Council.

The **Transportation Research Board** is one of six major divisions of the National Research Council. The mission of the Transportation Research Board is to provide leadership in transportation innovation and progress through research and information exchange, conducted within a setting that is objective, interdisciplinary, and multimodal. The Board's varied activities annually engage about 7,000 engineers, scientists, and other transportation researchers and practitioners from the public and private sectors and academia, all of whom contribute their expertise in the public interest. The program is supported by state transportation departments, federal agencies including the component administrations of the U.S. Department of Transportation, and other organizations and individuals interested in the development of transportation. www.TRB.org

www.national-academies.org

Committee for the Study of Traffic Safety Lessons from Benchmark Nations

Clinton V. Oster, Jr., School of Public and Environmental Affairs, Indiana University, *Chair*
Tony Bliss, Transport Division, Energy, Transport, and Water Department, World Bank
William A. Bronrott, Federal Motor Carrier Safety Administration
Troy E. Costales, Transportation Safety Division, Oregon Department of Transportation
Kent L. Cravens, New Mexico Senate
John J. Cullerton, Illinois Senate
Joseph A. Farrow, California Highway Patrol
Patrick S. McCarthy, Georgia Institute of Technology
Alison Smiley, Human Factors North, Inc., Toronto, Ontario, Canada
John S. Strong, College of William and Mary, Williamsburg, Virginia
Richard Tay, La Trobe University, Bundoora, Australia
Allan F. Williams, Insurance Institute for Highway Safety (retired)

Transportation Research Board Staff
Joseph R. Morris, Study Director

Preface

In recent decades nearly every high-income country has made more rapid progress than has the United States in reducing the frequency of road traffic deaths and the rate of deaths per kilometer of vehicle travel. As a result, the United States can no longer claim to rank highly in road safety by world standards. The gap between traffic safety progress in the United States and the other high-income countries has gained the attention of U.S. transportation and public safety administrators because it indicates that the United States may be missing important opportunities to reduce traffic deaths and injuries.

The Transportation Research Board (TRB) formed the Committee for the Study of Traffic Safety Lessons from Benchmark Nations to document the experience of other high-income countries in reducing traffic deaths and injuries and to examine the safety programs that contributed to the reductions, in particular, interventions to alter driving behavior and strategies to build public and political support for safety interventions. The committee included experts in safety research, public policy, evaluation, and public administration and members of state legislatures. The purpose of the committee's study was to identify traffic safety strategies that could succeed in the United States. The study was sponsored by TRB and by the General Motors Foundation.

The committee made use of the work of two TRB projects that compared international safety experiences: a paper commissioned in 2004 by the TRB Research and Technology Coordinating Committee, written by Walter Diewald, on highway safety experience in Australia and Europe; and TRB *Special Report 287: Improving Road Safety in Developing Countries: Opportunities for U.S. Cooperation and Engagement: Workshop Summary,* the 2006 report on the Workshop on Traffic Safety in Developing

Nations. The committee also received presentations at its meetings from Marilena Amoni and Jeffrey Lindley of the U.S. Department of Transportation, Fred Wegman of the Institute for Road Safety Research (Netherlands), Jim Reed of the National Conference of State Legislatures, Ian Johnston of Monash University, Peter Kissinger of the AAA Foundation for Traffic Safety, Barbara Harsha of the Governors Highway Safety Association, and Susan Herbel of Cambridge Systematics.

U.S. traffic deaths declined by 9.3 percent from 2007 to 2008 and by 9.7 percent from 2008 to 2009. These are among the largest annual declines on record. The number of traffic deaths in 2009, 33,808, was the lowest total since 1950. The U.S. economy entered a recession in 2007, and the decline in traffic deaths is consistent with the declines that occurred during past recessions, given the exceptional depth and duration of the recent recession. U.S. traffic fatalities increased when economic growth resumed after past recessions, and such an increase can be anticipated after the recent recession. Therefore, the experience of the past 3 years is not grounds for concluding that sustainable progress has been made on traffic safety. The severity of the problem and the gap in performance between the United States and other countries remain great.

In recognition that major changes in traffic safety practices will require political leadership and acceptance by the public, in the United States as in other countries, the study charge directs the committee to identify strategies to build public and political support. The committee did not propose a comprehensive solution to this political problem, but it recommends actions that it concluded are necessary, if modest, first steps in bringing about the needed changes. The committee believes that the improvements in safety management and legislative oversight that it recommends will lead to initial safety gains and increase the credibility of the responsible executive agencies in seeking legislative support and resources.

The report has been reviewed in draft form by individuals chosen for their diverse perspectives and technical expertise, in accordance with procedures approved by the National Research Council's (NRC's) Report Review Committee. The purpose of this independent review is to provide candid and critical comments that assist the authors and NRC in making the published report as sound as possible and to ensure that the report meets institutional standards for objectivity, evidence, and responsiveness to the study charge. The contents of the review comments and draft manuscript remain confidential to protect the integrity of the deliberative process. The following individuals participated in the review of this report: William G. Agnew, Corrales, New Mexico; Paul S. Fischbeck, Carnegie Mellon University, Pittsburgh, Pennsylvania; Barbara L. Harsha, Governors Highway Safety Association, Washington, D.C.; Douglas W. Harwood, Midwest Research Institute, Kansas City, Missouri; James H. Hedlund, Highway Safety North, Ithaca, New York; Robert E. Hull, Utah Department of Transportation, Salt Lake City; Ian Johnston, Monash University, Victoria, Australia; James B. Reed, National Conference of State Legislatures, Denver, Colorado; and David Shinar, Ben-Gurion University of the Negev, Beersheba, Israel.

Although the reviewers listed above provided many constructive comments and suggestions, they were not asked to endorse the committee's conclusions or recommendations, nor did they see the final draft of the report before its release. The review of this report was overseen by Johanna T. Dwyer, Tufts University, Boston, Massachusetts, and by C. Michael Walton, University of Texas, Austin. Appointed by NRC, they were responsible for making certain that an independent examination of the report was carried out in accordance with institutional procedures and that all review comments were carefully considered. Responsibility for the final content of this report rests entirely with the authoring committee and the institution.

Joseph R. Morris managed the study and drafted the final report under the guidance of the committee and the supervision of Stephen R. Godwin, Director, Studies and Special Programs. Suzanne Schneider, Associate Executive Director of TRB, managed the report review process. Norman Solomon edited the report; Janet M. McNaughton handled the editorial production; Juanita Green managed the typesetting and printing; and Jennifer J. Weeks, Editorial Services Specialist, prepared the prepublication manuscript for web posting, under the supervision of Javy Awan, Director of Publications. Nikisha Turman and Claudia Sauls assisted with meeting arrangements and communications with committee members.

Contents

Summary	1
1 Introduction	**11**
Traffic Safety Progress in the United States and Other Countries	15
National Strategies	19
Study Origin and Charge	21
Outline of the Report	32
2 World and U.S. Safety Trends	**36**
World Fatality Rate Trends	36
U.S. State Fatality Rate Trends	44
Sources of Differences in the Trends	45
Factors Affecting U.S. Fatality Rate Trends	58
3 National Safety Programs in Benchmark Countries and the United States	**68**
Common Elements of Benchmark Nations' Safety Programs	69
Examples of National Safety Programs	76
Nationally Organized Safety Management Reform Initiatives in the United States	102

4 Case Studies of Safety Interventions	**131**
Alcohol-Impaired Driving Prevention	134
Speed Control	151
Seat Belts	174
Motorcycle Helmet Laws	182
Highway Network Screening and Safe Road Design	191
5 Conclusions and Recommendations	**211**
Lessons from the International Comparisons	211
Management and Planning of Safety Programs	215
Technical Implementation of Countermeasures	229
Political Leadership and Public Support	239
Study Committee Biographical Information	**243**

Summary

The United States is missing significant opportunities to reduce traffic fatalities and injuries. The experiences of other high-income nations and of the U.S. states with the best improvement records indicate the benefits from more rigorous safety programs. Most high-income countries are reducing traffic fatalities and fatality rates (per kilometer of travel) faster than is the United States, and several countries that experienced higher fatality rates 20 years ago now are below the U.S. rate. From 1995 to 2009, annual traffic fatalities declined by 52 percent in France, 39 percent in the United Kingdom, 25 percent in Australia, and 50 percent in total in 15 high-income countries (excluding the United States) for which long-term fatality and traffic data are available, but by only 19 percent in the United States. Some U.S. states have fatality rates comparable to those of the countries with the safest roads; however, no state matches the typical speed of improvement in safety in other countries.

The experience of these benchmark nations indicates that the successful national programs function effectively at three levels of activity:

- *Management and planning:* Transportation, public safety, and public health administrators systematically measure progress toward quantitative objectives, direct resources to the most cost-effective uses, and communicate with the public and with elected officials to maintain their support.
- *Technical implementation of specific countermeasures:* A range of measures is employed for regulating driver behavior, maintaining effective emergency response, and ensuring safe design and maintenance of

roads. The techniques are generally of proven high effectiveness and often intensively applied.
- *Political support and leadership:* Commitment of elected officials ensures that resources are provided, administrators are held accountable for results of safety initiatives, and system users are held accountable for compliance with laws.

Among these three areas, the most critical needs for action in the United States today may be in management and planning. Improved management will ensure that the available resources are used to greatest effect and, over time, will foster political and public support by demonstrating that reduction in fatalities and crashes is an attainable goal. The benchmark nations' experience indicates that systematic, results-oriented management can produce safety progress with the tool kit of countermeasures that is available to the responsible agencies. The tool kit will vary among jurisdictions depending on basic legal constraints, community attitudes, road system and traffic characteristics, and resources.

The Transportation Research Board (TRB) undertook a study to identify the sources of safety improvements in other countries. Researchers do not have a complete understanding of the underlying causes of long-term trends in crashes and fatalities. Differences among countries are in part attributable to factors other than government safety policies. To identify keys to success, the TRB study committee examined specific safety programs for which quantitative evaluations are available and relied on the observations of safety professionals with international experience. The committee's conclusions, summarized below, identify differences between U.S. and international practices that can account for some differences in outcomes. The recommendations below, which are addressed to elected officials and to government safety administrators, identify actions needed in the United States to emulate the successes that other countries have achieved. The recommendations do not comprehensively address all aspects of traffic safety programs but rather address areas of practice that are highlighted by the international comparisons and for which credible evidence of effectiveness is available.

MANAGEMENT AND PLANNING

Conclusions

Successful national safety programs are more distinguished by the programs' management than by the particular interventions. The essential elements of the management model are the following:

- A systems perspective that integrates engineering design, traffic control, regulatory enforcement, and public health methods to identify and reduce risks;
- A plan that specifies goals and milestones, methods, and resource requirements and that constitutes a commitment for which the government agencies responsible for delivery may be held accountable; and
- Regular monitoring to identify problems and measure progress toward goals and ongoing evaluation to determine effectiveness of the actions taken. Monitoring allows feedback so that programs can be improved and reinforces accountability of program managers.

In the United States, management practices in traffic safety programs typically are deficient in elements of this ideal management model. Meaningful goals and milestones are not published, data systems do not adequately monitor effort or performance, program impacts are not scientifically evaluated, and initiatives are episodic and reactive rather than strategic. Lack of safety planning analytical tools inhibits planning and weakens the case for safety spending in the competition for public resources. Activities of the U.S. Department of Transportation (USDOT) and the American Association of State Highway and Transportation Officials over the past decade have emphasized state and local safety planning, management processes, and evaluation, yet it is unclear that many states are making significant progress in critical elements of safety management.

Comparison of management methods in other countries with those of the United States must take into account the decentralized structure of U.S. government. The U.S. federal government regulates vehicle safety and the safety of commercial truck and bus operations, but otherwise its involvement is indirect, through the rules of federal highway and traffic safety grant programs. State governments build and operate intercity roads; state police enforce traffic regulations mainly on major roads; and state laws and courts govern driver licensing, vehicle inspection, and traffic safety. Local governments independently operate local streets and roads, enact regulations, and provide police and courts. In contrast, most of the benchmark countries' governments are highly centralized; for example, a national police force may conduct most traffic enforcement. This difference complicates the introduction of management practices of other countries in the United States.

Recommendations

1. Congress should authorize and provide funding for three USDOT and state activities:
   - USDOT should cooperate with selected states in organizing, funding, evaluating, and documenting a series of large-scale demonstrations of important elements of safety management.
   - USDOT should work with the states in revising the National Highway Traffic Safety Administration (NHTSA) Uniform Guidelines for State Highway Safety Programs to ensure that these documents provide directly applicable and practical guidance for development of state programs.
   - USDOT, in cooperation with the states, should develop a new model for the state Strategic Highway Safety Plans that is more rigorous in specifying resource requirements and expected outcomes.

   The purposes of the recommended demonstrations would be (a) to document the functioning of a program conducted according to stringent and specific guidelines (e.g., the NHTSA Uniform Guidelines) and (b) to disseminate information on safety program management methods, problems, costs, and benefits to transportation agencies, officials, and the public through training, publications, and other media. Most U.S. state and local transportation safety agencies lack the institutional and technical capacities required to apply the management techniques observed in the benchmark countries. Communicating the concepts of safety management to the responsible agencies will require a greater level of effort than has been devoted to the task.

   A demonstration would concentrate on specific components of a state's safety program, which could be a category of countermeasure (e.g., a speed management program or corridor improvement program) or a management process (e.g., monitoring and evaluation or preparation of elements of the Strategic Highway Safety Plan). Demonstrations could be designed to show how states can apply the NHTSA Uniform Guidelines effectively. Most demonstrations would entail recruitment of local government cooperation and training of local highway departments and police. Demonstrations also would require intensive collaboration among the government agencies with safety responsibilities.

2. Congress should consider designating and funding an independent traffic safety evaluation and policy research organization to provide technical support in development of interventions and management methods, advise officials on policy, and reinforce accountability of the operating agencies to legislators and the public through performance evaluations.

3. Transportation agencies should take into account demonstrated competency and professional qualification in highway safety in their hiring and promotion decisions. Engineering schools and accreditation associations should set standards for safety competencies of engineers practicing in areas that affect highway safety. In addition, in-service training programs are needed, especially short courses designed for local government public works engineers.

COUNTERMEASURES

Conclusions

Safety officials in the benchmark nations have attributed progress to their implementation of comprehensive safety programs that include improvements in road design and traffic management; regulation of vehicle safety; regulation of driver behavior with regard to speed, alcohol and drug use, and seat belt and helmet use; restrictions on younger and older drivers; and reliable emergency response. These programs require consistent actions by legislators and by administrators responsible for roads, police, courts, and public health. Within this comprehensive framework, countries that have sought rapid declines in casualty rates have emphasized curbing high-risk driver behavior, especially speeding, drunk driving, and failure to use seat belts, by means of stringent laws, intensive public communication and education, and rigorous enforcement.

Two enforcement techniques aimed at driver behavior that have contributed to fatality reductions in the benchmark nations are automated enforcement of speed limits (i.e., detection and identification of speeding vehicles by means of automated cameras and speed-measuring devices installed in the roadway) and frequent roadside sobriety checks to enforce laws against alcohol-impaired driving. The objective of these techniques is general deterrence, that is, to make the risk of detection and punishment high enough to change the driving behavior of the population. Neither technique is in common use today in the United States because of legal restrictions, popular opposition, and cost considerations. Despite these constraints, the United States can learn important lessons from the benchmark nations' enforcement practices. They demonstrate that sustained and intensive enforcement, rationally organized and managed, can alter driver behavior sufficiently to produce worthwhile systemwide safety improvement.

As case studies of international differences, the committee compared five categories of countermeasures—alcohol-impaired driving prevention, speed control, motorcycle helmet laws, seat belt laws, and highway network screening (identifying and correcting high-hazard locations on the road network)—in the benchmark nations and the United States. Conclusions with regard to opportunities for more effective use of countermeasures are outlined below.

Prevention of Alcohol-Impaired Driving

- The two most evident differences between drunk driving countermeasures in the benchmark countries and those in the United States are the legal maximum blood alcohol content (BAC) limits and the intensity of enforcement efforts. The BAC limit is 0.8 g/L in the United States and 0.5 g/L or lower in Australia, Canada, Japan, and nearly every country in Europe except the United Kingdom and Ireland. The rate of roadside alcohol testing is about 1 test per 16 drivers per year in Europe and even higher in Australia. Complete U.S. statistics on testing frequency do not exist, but the U.S. rate probably is far lower.
- Effective programs to reduce alcohol-impaired driving include public health measures to combat alcohol abuse and efficient judicial procedures that include intensive follow-up on offenders. For follow-up, ignition interlocks are now recognized as an effective means to reduce recidivism.

- Programs of sustained, high-frequency sobriety testing in the benchmark countries have achieved reductions of 13 to 36 percent in the annual number of alcohol-involved fatal crashes. Evaluations of sobriety checkpoints in U.S. jurisdictions have reported comparable reductions. Widespread implementation of sustained, high-frequency sobriety testing programs in the United States at sobriety checkpoints could be expected to save 1,500 to 3,000 lives annually. There is evidence to indicate that lowering the legal BAC limit to 0.5 g/L, combined with more intensive enforcement, would reduce fatalities further.

Speed Control
- Successful speed management initiatives in other countries are of high visibility (through publicity and endorsement of elected officials), are long term (sustained for periods of years), target major portions of the road system, use intensive enforcement (e.g., automated enforcement and high penalties), sometimes use traffic-calming road features (such as narrow lanes and traffic circles that cause drivers to reduce speed), and monitor progress toward publicly declared speed and crash reduction objectives. No U.S. speed management program today is comparable in scale, visibility, and political commitment to the most ambitious programs in other countries.
- In countries that have such programs, typical results have been reductions in average free-flow speed of 3 to 4 mph and a 50 percent reduction in the incidence of speeding more than 6 mph over the limit. Officials in some countries credit these programs, after several years of sustained application, with reductions in fatalities on the order of 15 to 20 percent on the affected road system.
- If the results of the most rigorous speed management trials (not using automated enforcement) conducted in the United States could be reproduced and sustained throughout the country and benefits proportional to those reported in the benchmark countries resulted, 1,000 to 2,000 lives annually could be saved.
- The cost-effectiveness of conventional intensive speed enforcement strategies employed in the United States (e.g., short-term high-visibility enforcement campaigns that do not use automated enforcement) is uncertain. Evaluation of alternative enforcement strategies should be a research priority.

Motorcycle Helmet and Occupant Restraint Laws
- Laws in every benchmark country require motorcyclists to wear helmets. Thirty U.S. states lack such laws. If all states required helmet use, about 450 deaths annually would be avoided.
- France, Germany, the Netherlands, Sweden, the United Kingdom, Canada, Australia, and some U.S. states all report seat belt use rates by front seat occupants of more than 90 percent. The U.S. average in 2010 was 85 percent. If U.S. belt use were increased by 5 percentage points, about 1,200 lives would be saved annually. State enactment of primary seat belt laws is among the measures that have proved effective. A primary enforcement law is a state law authorizing police to stop a vehicle and issue a citation solely on the grounds of failure to use a seat belt.

Highway Network Screening
- Safety corridor programs constitute a more comprehensive approach to reducing the risk of travel on a particular road than traditional state highway hazard elimination programs, which often operated in isolation from other highway and safety functions. Corridor programs target routes with high crash frequencies and combine strengthened traffic law enforcement, publicity, and other measures with roadway physical improvements.
- Two new evaluation practices in use in several of the benchmark nations, road safety audits and road assessment programs, are bringing greater attention to the problem of upgrading the safety of road infrastructure. Road safety audits are formal, independent examinations of the safety of the design of new road projects. Road assessment programs are non-governmental initiatives that aim to increase public demand for safety and to make officials more accountable for the safety performance of highways by revealing and publicizing hazards.

Recommendations

1. State and local governments that seek to match the performance of the benchmark nations should recognize that additional resources for enforcement will be required. The level of enforcement can be raised by using existing resources more effectively; by increasing funding; and by adopting more cost-effective methods, in particular, automated

enforcement. Cost-effective enforcement methods maximize the impact of a given amount of law enforcement resources on crashes and fatalities.
2. The states and USDOT should give high priority to initiatives to encourage adoption of camera enforcement and regular use of sobriety checkpoints.
3. State officials and the federal government should act to preserve the existing universal helmet use laws by communicating the health, safety, and economic costs of repeal to legislators.
4. Each state should ensure that local police receive regular and substantial training in enforcement against impaired driving, speeding, and other high-risk driver behaviors.
5. The states and USDOT should transform the traditional practice of the hazard elimination program into a corridor safety improvement program that systemically identifies high-priority corridors and designs comprehensive safety improvement strategies for each corridor.

POLITICAL AND PUBLIC SUPPORT

Conclusions

Successful safety initiatives in the benchmark nations have had the advantage of genuine and active support of elected officials in almost all cases, although elected officials were not necessarily the originators. Sustaining the initiatives has depended on eventually gaining the trust of the public. International case studies and the experiences of U.S. states suggest that the following factors have been important in building support for rigorous safety programs:

- Public and political support has come about through long-term efforts of professionals, officials, and nongovernmental advocates. Safety programs in the benchmark countries and in the United States have long histories of evolutionary development and learning through experience.
- Creation of new high-level institutional structures has been a valuable step in the evolution of national programs. For example, in France a ministerial-level committee oversees the national traffic safety program.

- The programs have emphasized transparency with respect to goals and in public communications. Public statement of specific and credible goals is essential for accountability.
- Regular communication channels exist among the road safety agencies, police, and researchers, and forums exist for interaction of legislators with professionals and researchers.
- Public administrators and professionals often have been the initial leaders in educating and developing support among elected officials and the public.
- Most programs have used sustained, large-scale, and sophisticated social marketing (that is, the application of business marketing techniques to promote a social welfare objective) to amplify the deterrent effect of enforcement and to influence public attitudes toward high-risk behavior.

Recommendations

1. Each state legislature should require the responsible executive agencies to report regularly to it on progress in fulfilling the state's safety plan and success in meeting the plan's goals.
2. As a preliminary step to strengthening U.S. capabilities for application of social marketing to traffic safety, USDOT should conduct an in-depth review of methods and outcomes in other countries.
3. The national organizations of transportation and public safety officials, state legislators, and safety researchers should take every opportunity for organization of forums that bring together administrators, legislators, and researchers for exchange of information and views on traffic safety.
4. Public agencies should cooperate in the development of the United States Road Assessment Program, but the program must maintain independence, which is necessary for its effectiveness.
5. All states should enact the minimum framework of traffic safety laws that has been instrumental in achieving the gains that the most successful benchmark country safety programs have attained, including enabling legislation for automated speed enforcement.

1

Introduction

By some measures, the safety of road travel has improved greatly over the history of the automobile. Traffic deaths per kilometer of vehicle travel were five times higher in the United States in 1950 than today (National Safety Council 2007, 110–111; NHTSA 2010, 2). Per capita annual deaths of pedestrians and cyclists in road crashes declined by about two-thirds over the same period, although walking and bicycle trips per household have increased at least since the 1970s (FHWA 1983, 1, 6; FHWA 2010). However, because of growth in traffic, the health costs of automobile travel remain high. U.S. traffic deaths fluctuated between 40,000 and 44,000 annually from 1993 to 2007, then fell by 9.3 percent to 37,423 in 2008 and by an additional 9.7 percent to 33,808 in 2009, the fewest since 1949 (NHTSA 2010, 1). The exceptional percentage decline in deaths from 2007 to 2009 probably is largely a consequence of the recession that began in 2007.[1] About 262,000 persons suffered incapacitating injuries in traffic crashes in 2008 (NHTSA 2009, Table 54). Motor vehicle crashes caused 28 percent of all deaths among young people 1 to 24 years of age in the United States in 2006 (Heron et al. 2009, Table 10).

The lack of progress in reducing the highway casualty toll might suggest that Americans have resigned themselves to this burden of deaths and injuries as the inevitable consequence of the mobility provided by the road system. In other countries, public officials responsible for the roads have declared that this human and economic cost is neither inevitable nor

---

[1] As Chapter 2 describes, relatively large declines in deaths and in the fatality rate occurred during past recessions; therefore, it seems likely that the recession that began in 2007 is the major factor behind the recent trend. Traffic deaths increased with economic recovery after past recessions, and it is too early to determine whether the recent sharp decline represents a break from the long-term trend.

acceptable and have undertaken rigorous and innovative interventions to reduce crashes and casualties. In Europe, Australia, and Japan, annual numbers of deaths and death rates per kilometer of vehicle travel have declined dramatically. Nearly every high-income country is today reducing annual traffic fatalities and fatality rates faster than is the United States, and several countries where fatality rates per kilometer of travel were higher than in the United States 20 years ago are now below the U.S. rate.

Officials responsible for traffic safety in the countries with relatively good safety performance attribute this progress primarily to government traffic safety programs, including improvements in traffic control and road design, vehicle safety regulations, and willingness to enact and enforce stringent driver regulations regarding speed, alcohol and drug use, seat belt use, and restrictions according to driver age.

The gap between traffic safety progress in the United States and the other high-income countries deserves the attention of U.S. transportation administrators and the public because it indicates that the United States may be missing important opportunities to reduce traffic deaths and injuries. The Transportation Research Board (TRB) formed the Committee for the Study of Traffic Safety Lessons from Benchmark Nations to review the evidence on the factors that account for other countries' safety improvements and to recommend actions that would take advantage of the foreign experience and would fit in the U.S. context. The study committee's charge (defined in the task statement approved by the National Research Council) is as follows:

> This study will document the experience of nations such as Sweden, United Kingdom, Netherlands, and Australia in sharply reducing traffic deaths and injuries through safety programs designed to alter driving behavior. The study will focus on the strategies these nations used to build public and political support for such interventions.

The purpose of the committee's study was to identify traffic safety strategies that could succeed in the United States. However, comparative analyses of international traffic safety experience also have relevance outside the United States. With increased motor vehicle use worldwide, most dramatically in China, India, and other developing countries, traffic fatalities and injuries have become a major and rapidly growing global public health threat. The World Health Organization has estimated that 1.2 million deaths and 20 million serious injuries occur annually in road traffic crashes (TRB 2006, 1–9). Therefore, recognition of the successes that some countries have achieved should be of value internationally.

The charge calls on the committee to document the experience of other countries in reducing road traffic casualties. In fact, the international experience has been documented extensively in the reports on safety programs and management practices of a series of delegations of U.S. administrators to agencies in other countries, sponsored by the Federal Highway Administration (FHWA) and the American Association of State Highway and Transportation Officials (AASHTO) (FHWA 2009) and in reports of the Organisation for Economic Co-operation and Development (OECD) Working Groups on Speed Management (OECD and ECMT 2006a) and on Achieving Ambitious Road Safety Targets (OECD and International Transport Forum n.d.; OECD and International Transport Forum 2008). The latter OECD panel undertook a systematic benchmarking effort, soliciting reports from member states on fatality trends and on laws and safety initiatives concerning speeding, drunk driving, seat belt use, young drivers, pedestrians, and road infrastructure hazards. In 2004, TRB's Research and Technology Coordinating Committee commissioned a report that describes safety management methods used abroad and compares them with methods in U.S. states with successful safety programs (Diewald 2004). In 2006 the National Academies, with the sponsorship of the National Highway Traffic Safety Administration and the Centers for Disease Control and Prevention, convened a workshop on transferring the traffic safety technology of the high-income countries to developing nations (TRB 2006). The AAA Foundation for Traffic Safety, the Governors Highway Safety Association, and other organizations in the United States also are examining the international experience and developing programs to emulate international best practices. In 2009, FHWA and AASHTO began an initiative to develop a new national strategic highway safety plan through a series of workshops and other public events. The initiative, Toward Zero Deaths: A National Strategy on Highway Safety, reflects awareness of other countries' progress and methods on the part of U.S. safety administrators (FHWA n.d.).

The past reviews (summarized in Chapter 3) concur that successful national programs function effectively at three levels:

- Management and planning,
- Technical implementation of specific countermeasures, and
- Political support and leadership.

U.S. road and safety officials recognize the successes of other countries but face obstacles in transferring the strategies that other countries have used. Among the obstacles are the following:

- Decentralization: in most of the benchmark countries, regulation and enforcement are highly centralized, often the responsibility of a single national authority, whereas in the United States, 50 states and thousands of local jurisdictions are responsible for traffic safety and the operation of the highway system;
- Public attitudes that oppose measures common elsewhere: for example, in the United States, motorcycle helmet laws and speed enforcement using automated cameras often encounter active public opposition;
- Weak support for or opposition to rigorous enforcement in legislatures and among the judiciary, a reflection of these same public attitudes;
- The constitutional prohibition of unreasonable searches, which prevents U.S. police from conducting the frequent and routine driver sobriety testing without probable cause that is common practice in some other countries; and
- Resource limitations that prevent enforcement of the intensity common in other countries.

The obstacles are, to an extent, the product of differences in political systems and in the physical characteristics of transportation systems, and possibly of other social and cultural factors. However, a further important obstacle has been lack of technical capacities required to apply the systematic management practices that all previous reviews have identified as critical to the performance of the benchmark nations' safety programs. The committee has concentrated its attention on the obstacles to transferring successful practices of other countries to the United States, and the recommendations in Chapter 5 include proposals for steps toward overcoming the obstacles.

The term "benchmark nations" in this report refers to the group of high-income nations whose traffic safety practices have been commonly compared with practices in the United States. The past reviews concluded that governments in these countries have given high visibility and genuinely high priority to traffic safety initiatives and that these nations have achieved low absolute rates of traffic fatalities and steady progress in reducing rates. The countries most often cited in the literature reviewed by the committee include Australia, New Zealand, Canada, the Netherlands, Germany, Sweden, Finland, Norway, France, and the United Kingdom. These countries are not uniform in their practices or results, and information was more readily available for some than for others. In the descriptions of safety programs in Chapters 3 and 4, the countries chosen for comparison with the United States vary with the topic under discussion.

In this introductory chapter, the first two sections below summarize statistics on traffic fatality trends in the United States and other countries and observations from several sources, including the scanning tours of FHWA and AASHTO, on the programs of some of the benchmark countries. The third section explains how the committee understood and responded to its charge. The final section outlines the remainder of the report.

TRAFFIC SAFETY PROGRESS IN THE UNITED STATES AND OTHER COUNTRIES

Fatality rates per vehicle kilometer of travel have declined greatly in the high-income countries for at least the past 40 years (and in the United States, for as long as data have been available, since the 1920s). For six large high-income countries, Table 1-1 shows fatalities per vehicle kilometer in 1970 and 2008 and the percentage decline in the fatality rate during the period. In France, Germany, and Japan, an automobile trip in 1970 was 10 times more likely to result in a death than an average trip of the same length today. In the 1970s, the U.S. fatality rate was the lowest in the world, but because safety has improved more slowly in the United States than elsewhere, today most high-income countries have matched or gone below the U.S. rate. Among 17 high-income countries with annual data available for the period 1997–2008, the U.S. speed of improvement was the poorest: a 2.4 percent reduction in the fatality rate annually compared with

TABLE 1-1 Traffic Fatality Rates in Six Countries, 1970 and 2008

	Fatality Rate[a]		
	1970	2008	Percent Change
France	9.0	0.78	−91
Germany	7.8	0.65	−91
Great Britain	3.7	0.52	−86
Australia	4.9	0.65	−87
Japan	9.6	0.81	−92
United States	3.0	0.78	−74

[a]Fatalities per 100 million vehicle kilometers.
SOURCES: OECD n.d.; NHTSA 2010; OECD and International Transport Forum 2010.

6.9 percent in France, 6.4 percent in Germany, 5.5 percent in Japan, 4.3 percent in Australia, and 3.9 percent the United Kingdom (Figure 1-1).

Reducing the fatality rate has reduced total annual fatalities in most high-income countries in the past decade. For the six countries tabulated above, Table 1-2 shows the reduction in fatalities. While some other countries reduced deaths by nearly half in the period, in the United States the decline was only 11 percent as a result of slow progress in reducing crash rates. If the United States had been able to reduce fatalities per kilometer of travel by the same percentage each year as did the United Kingdom (which achieved one of the slower average annual reductions among the countries shown in Figure 1-1), 29,000 U.S. lives would have been saved in the 1997–2008 period.

The United States is larger and more diverse than any of the nations with which it is compared above, so a more meaningful comparison might be between other countries and U.S. regions with similar geographic characteristics (e.g., U.S. regions with population density and urbanization similar to those of European countries). Indeed, the fatality rate in the New England states about equals the rates in the best-performing countries abroad. However, no U.S. state has matched the median speed of improvement (a 5 percent annual reduction in the fatality rate) among the foreign countries shown Figure 1-1.

The causes of these disparities in highway safety experience among the high-income countries are not well understood. Government traffic

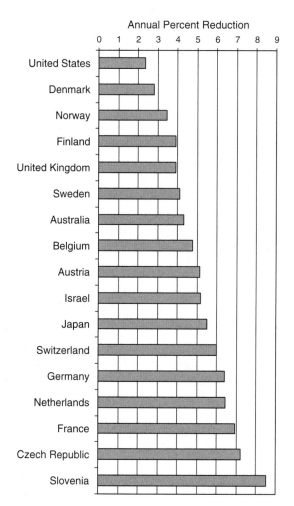

FIGURE 1-1 Average annual percentage reduction in fatalities per vehicle kilometer traveled, 17 countries, 1997–2008. Netherlands value is for 1997–2005. (SOURCES: OECD n.d.; OECD and International Transport Forum 2009; OECD and International Transport Forum 2010; NHTSA 2010.)

TABLE 1-2 Traffic Deaths in Six Countries, 1997 and 2008

	Traffic Deaths		Percent Change
	1997	2008	
France	8,400	4,300	−49
Germany	8,500	4,500	−48
United Kingdom	3,700	2,600	−29
Australia	1,800	1,400	−18
Japan	11,300	6,000	−46
United States	42,000	37,400	−11

NOTE: The United Kingdom includes Great Britain and Northern Ireland.
SOURCE: OECD n.d.

safety policies are a significant influence. However, research has shown that differences in demographic, geographic, and economic factors and in characteristics of vehicle fleets and transportation systems also affect international differences in crash rate trends, and evaluations designed to test the causal linkage between interventions and crash rates rigorously have been conducted too infrequently. Because crash risk varies with driver age, time of day, road characteristics, and other factors, it is possible for Country A to have a lower aggregate fatal crash rate than Country B and yet that a driver in Country B would always have a lower risk of a fatal crash than a driver in similar circumstances in Country A. For example, fatality rates on urban roads are generally lower than on rural roads worldwide. If Country A were predominantly urban and Country B rural, B could have lower fatality rates than A on both urban and rural roads and yet still have a higher total rate than A.

The convergence of national fatality rates to similar values in recent years (in the range of 0.6 to 1.0 fatality per 100 million vehicle kilometers) suggests the possibility that, as rates become lower, it becomes more difficult to obtain further reductions comparable in absolute terms with the reductions of earlier decades. From this point of view, the slow improvement of the U.S. fatality rate might not seem to be cause for concern, since the U.S. rate was already relatively low 15 years ago, and the other countries have simply been catching up to a level of performance that the U.S. achieved earlier. However, this interpretation of the trends is contradicted by the experience of several countries (including the United Kingdom, the Scandinavian countries, the Netherlands, West Germany, and Australia) that already had rates close to or lower than the U.S. rate in 1997 but nonetheless reduced their rates faster than did the United States in the past decade.

Chapter 2 presents a more detailed comparison of safety trends in the United States and other countries and among U.S. states. It also reviews research on the causes of differences in the trends.

NATIONAL STRATEGIES

Several of the countries that have achieved lower fatality rates and faster safety improvement than the United States also have undertaken rigorous, sustained, and carefully planned safety initiatives that are internationally recognized as innovative. Features of programs in four countries are given below as examples.

- **France** progressively strengthened its laws and enforcement efforts concerning seat belt use, drunk driving, and speeding during the 1990s. Then in 2002, the national government initiated a program for reducing fatalities by intensified enforcement, relying especially on automated speed enforcement coordinated with a public communication and marketing campaign. The initiative is centrally planned and administered; a central facility monitors the nationwide network of 2,300 automatic speed cameras, issues citations, and collects fines. It is supported by central data collection and analysis to guide management and measure results. The initiative has had sustained, high-level political support. At the beginning of his 2002 term, the president of France announced that traffic safety was among the top priorities of his administration, and a cabinet-level multiagency committee has met periodically to oversee the safety program. The program produced important reductions in average speeds throughout the road system (a two-thirds reduction in the fraction of vehicles exceeding speed limits by more than 10 km/h between 2001 and 2008). As noted in the preceding section, France has achieved one of the fastest rates of improvement in traffic safety in the past decade. Government analysts attribute a large share of the reduction to the enforcement program.

- **Australia** has a federal system of government, so major responsibilities for highway safety rest with the states, and innovative programs have emerged at the state level. The safety programs of the state of Victoria have received international attention. A series of formal plans has guided the Victoria program since 1990. The plans identify quantitative safety improvement targets, intervention strategies for meeting the targets, and requirements for interagency coordination. New regulations and enforcement strategies and added enforcement resources have targeted drunk driving, speeding, and oversight of new drivers. Speed limits in urban areas have been reduced, and automated speed enforcement is widely used. Random alcohol and drug testing of drivers is frequent, and the average driver can expect to be tested once every few years. Performance measurement is integrated with administration of the program. The program receives active support from elected officials, who make up the Ministerial Road Safety Council and Parliamentary Road Safety Council that oversee the state's safety program. Traffic safety has been, at least at times, a high-visibility political issue. Victoria achieved a greater percentage reduction in traffic fatalities than Australia as a whole over the period 1988–2004.
- **United Kingdom** traffic safety programs share some basic similarities with the programs in France and Australia: consequential national planning that incorporates targets and performance measurement, political visibility and high-level political support, and application of progressively more rigorous interventions over the past 20 years. As elsewhere, drunk driving and speeding have been important targets. A national blood-alcohol content (BAC) limit was enacted in 1967, 11 years before all U.S. states had such a limit. As in the United States, random alcohol testing of drivers is illegal; however, drivers in crashes and drivers stopped for traffic offenses may be tested. Laws and enforcement practices are largely uniform nationwide, although local government authorities have certain management responsibilities. Widespread deployment of automatic speed enforcement devices was coordinated and funded by a program of the national government from 2001 to 2007. Nongovernmental organizations, including the automobile clubs, were instrumental in starting the New Car Assessment Program (NCAP) and the Road Assessment Program (RAP) in the United Kingdom and other countries in the 1990s. These programs rate vehicles and road-

way segments for safety and publicize the ratings. The U.K. rate of fatalities per vehicle kilometer, among the lowest in the world, has been lower than the U.S. rate since 1990 and has continued to decline more rapidly than the U.S. rate. The speed of improvement over this period has been similar to those of the Scandinavian countries and Australia (Figure 1-1).

- **Sweden's** road safety program also is based on effective national planning and sustained political support and has emphasized control of drunk driving and speed. The driver BAC limit (0.02 percent) is among the lowest in the world, and random alcohol checks are conducted. The speed control program aims to reduce average speeds throughout much of the road network, and many speed limits have been reduced since the 1990s. In 1997, the Swedish Parliament established the Vision Zero policy to guide Swedish safety programs. It sets zero road fatalities and injuries as the appropriate goal of transportation programs and places responsibility on road authorities and vehicle regulators for designing a transportation system that is forgiving of the errors of drivers. In practice, Vision Zero has been interpreted to mean that road designs and traffic and vehicle regulations should favor injury prevention more strongly than conventional considerations would dictate—for example, lower speeds and more frequent property-damage crashes in return for fewer serious injuries. Safe design of the highway system has entailed various traffic-calming measures (road design features like narrow lanes and traffic circles that cause drivers to reduce speed) and rules to minimize conflicts between motorized and nonmotorized traffic. Sweden's fatality rate per kilometer of vehicle travel has been the lowest in the world for most of the past 20 years, and progress in reducing the rate has been faster than in the United States (Figure 1-1).

Programs of these benchmark nations are described in more detail in Chapter 3, where the sources of information for the above descriptions are cited.

STUDY ORIGIN AND CHARGE

Some past analyses have found deficiencies in U.S. traffic safety efforts at each of the three functional levels identified above: for unfocused management practices, for reliance on ineffective countermeasures, and for failure to sustain political and public support. These criticisms are relevant to the committee's charge because they are hypotheses about the sources of the differences in safety performance between the benchmark nations and the United States. The following three subsections cite examples of such criticisms. They describe the views of others and are not conclusions of the committee. The final subsection explains how the committee took into account these criticisms of U.S. practice in responding to its charge.

Unfocused Management

Most comparisons of U.S. and international safety efforts have noted differences among jurisdictions in safety program management practices. For example, the members of one of FHWA's scanning teams that observed safety programs abroad were struck by the results of greater application of measurement and evaluation as management tools in other countries (MacDonald et al. 2004, xiii):

> The scan team found examples in which the processes of setting priorities and making planning, investment, and management decisions are based on, or use, performance measures to a much greater extent than is typical in the United States. In those cases where performance measures were used as input to priority setting, the process represented a new level of organizational behavior.... Perhaps the most impressive application of performance measurement, in terms of showing how the process can influence governmental policy and budget determinations, was in the area of road safety. Impressive results in reducing fatalities and injuries have occurred in some of the sites the scan team visited through a comprehensive program of engineering, enforcement, and education.

Another comparison of safety management and planning in the United States and Australia, after noting "a sound and realistic plan" as one of the factors accounting for success of Australian programs, observes that "lack of progress reduces the FHWA [1998] strategic plan to little more than a publicity piece, since the results have so little relationship to the goals. During the eight years since the plan was announced, there has been little tracking of results, and almost no mid-course corrections to ensure that the goals are being met" (Tarnoff 2007, 22).

The 2008 report of the OECD Working Group on Achieving Ambitious Road Safety Targets, which compared programs of OECD nations, also emphasizes "a robust management system" as a critical factor distinguishing successful from unsuccessful programs (OECD and International Transport Forum 2008, 16–17; see also Box 3-4 in Chapter 3).

The FHWA report *Halving Roadway Fatalities,* on lessons for U.S. safety programs from the Victoria, Australia, program (written by one of the designers of the Australian program), similarly ranks management practices higher than any specific countermeasure among the critical factors accounting for Victoria's relative success in reducing fatalities (Johnston 2006, 16):

> Note that there is nothing [among the identified critical factors] about specific measures. The keys are knowing what the big problems are, selecting interventions known to be effective, and systematically implementing those for which political and community support can be garnered. Different packages of measures will have different aggregate impacts, require different levels of investment, and operate on different time frames, but many different packages will work.

In other words, according to this view, systematic, results-oriented, data-driven management can produce safety progress with the tool kit of countermeasures that is available to the responsible agencies. Jurisdictions that fail to make progress are those that lack adequate overall long-term management of their safety programs.

Any comparison of management methods in other countries with those of the United States must take into account the highly decentralized structure of U.S. government. The U.S. federal government regulates motor vehicle safety and the safety of commercial truck and bus operations, but otherwise its involvement is indirect, exercised through rules imposed on state and local government recipients of federal highway and traffic safety grants. State governments build and operate intercity roads; state police enforce traffic regulations mainly on major roads; state laws and courts govern driver licensing, vehicle inspection, speed limits, impaired driving, and other aspects of traffic safety. Local governments operate local streets and roads, enact local regulations, and provide local police and courts that enforce traffic laws within their jurisdictions.

In contrast, most of the benchmark countries' governments are relatively highly centralized; for example, a national police force may conduct most traffic enforcement. Australia's federal system has similarities to the U.S. structure, but no country's institutions match the thousands of U.S. entities with independent authority for public safety and for road maintenance and operation.

Ineffective Countermeasures

The committee's charge (given earlier in this chapter) asserts that interventions aimed at modifying driver behavior explain the relatively rapid declines in traffic fatalities that the benchmark nations have experienced. The most prominent behavior modification initiatives in these countries have targeted speeding and drunk driving. The managers of these programs attribute their success to a great extent to these interventions. For example, France's safety statistical agency estimated that three-fourths of the sharp reductions in fatalities and injuries on French roads between 2002 and 2005 resulted from a decline in speeds over the period induced by the speed control program begun in 2002 (CISR 2006, 6). With experiences like this in mind, the report of the OECD Working Group on Speed Management promised rapid reduction in fatalities through more effective regulation of driver behavior (OECD and ECMT 2006b, 3):

> Speeding . . . is the number one road safety problem in many countries, often contributing to as much as one third of fatal accidents and speed is an aggravating factor in the severity of all accidents. . . .
> Research indicates that coordinated actions taken by the responsible authorities can bring about an immediate and durable response to the problem of speeding. Indeed, reducing speeding can reduce rapidly the number of fatalities and injuries and is a guaranteed way to make real progress towards the ambitious road safety targets set by OECD/ECMT countries.

Similarly, a review of the history of road safety policy in France, written by a participant in the development of the policies, emphasized the power of behavior modification. The author attributes the large and rapid improvements in France and the other cases cited to government-organized campaigns of "psychological and media shocks" that combined stricter driver behavior rules (in particular with regard to speeding and drunk driving), stronger enforcement, and harsher penalties with well-funded and forceful public communication programs. The author concludes that this experience demonstrates that "all other things being equal, i.e., for a given population, road network, and vehicle fleet, the level of road crashes is in no way an incompressible figure and may vary considerably depending on the policies pursued by the authorities. An examination of crash trends shows that these may sometimes be rapidly cut by a quarter or a third, and even, in rare circumstances, by half" (Gerondeau 2006, 3).

In comparison, U.S. safety programs have been faulted for concentrating on vehicle and infrastructure improvements while underemphasizing measures to control unsafe behavior more effectively. In the assessment of one safety researcher (Evans 2004, 389–408), the lag between percentage reductions in fatality rates in the United States and reductions achieved in other countries in recent decades reflects a "dramatic failure of U.S. safety policy" (Evans 2004, 390). Under the failed policy, "U.S. safety priorities have been ordered almost perfectly opposite to where technical knowledge shows benefits are greatest" (Evans 2004, 389). In particular, the author argues, policy has concentrated on regulation of vehicle design and safety features, which are of lesser value, and has neglected countermeasures aimed at altering the driver behavior factors that are the major determinants of risk. A similar criticism by public health professionals labeled U.S. safety policy "a public health failure" for neglecting to take advantage of the potential for "immediate, large and sustained reductions of deaths and injuries" through more rigorous speed control (Richter et al. 2001, 176, 177).

Improving road safety by upgrading infrastructure and imposing safety design standards on new road construction (e.g., with regard to alignment, lane width, sight distance, and roadside clear zones) are central elements of the safety programs of the U.S. and state departments of transportation and of other nations' road authorities. However, statistical analyses of the factors related to differences in traffic safety among countries or states have failed to find a strong correlation between the level of infrastructure investment and crash rates or frequencies (Noland 2003; Kopits and Cropper 2005). One such study concluded that this finding shows that traffic safety policy has been misdirected: "Changes in [U.S.]

highway infrastructure that have occurred between 1984 and 1997 have not reduced traffic fatalities and injuries and have even had the effect of increasing total fatalities and injuries. This conclusion conflicts with conventional engineering wisdom on the safety benefits of 'improving' highway facilities and achieving higher standards of design. . . . Other factors, primarily changes in the demographic age mix of the population, increased seat-belt usage, reduced per capita alcohol consumption, and improvements in medical technology are responsible for the downward trend in total fatal accidents" (Noland 2003, 610).

The arguments of the researchers cited above regarding the relative effectiveness of categories of interventions highlight the difficulty of the problem of deciding on the best allocation of resources in the design of a long-term safety strategy. However, they cannot be regarded as definitive. Specific limitations of studies of the effect of infrastructure investment on safety are described in Chapter 2. Indeed, as Chapters 2 and 3 will describe, all strong statements about the causes of differences in safety trends among the high-income countries must be examined skeptically because data limitations seriously hamper historical research and because, even in the countries with the most advanced management systems, safety program evaluations often are lacking or are inconclusive.

These arguments also are not fully consistent with the philosophies of the safety programs in the benchmark nations with the best safety records, all of which incorporate safe vehicle design and safe infrastructure design in their comprehensive strategies. Examples mentioned in the preceding section are the principle that roadway design should be error-tolerant that is part of Sweden's Vision Zero framework and NCAP and RAP in the United Kingdom. The "sustainable safety" principles that are the guiding philosophy of the national road safety program in the Netherlands call for a systems perspective that seeks to optimize the performance of all components of the road transportation system, including infrastructure, vehicles, and drivers (OECD and ECMT 2006a, 228). The *Halving Roadway Fatalities* report on Australia's safety programs explains the mix of measures used in that country as follows (Johnston 2006, 15):

> While evaluation research has shown high levels of effectiveness for most of these measures, it would be wrong to assume that Australia's success turned entirely on the implementation of behavior-control measures. It is more

that, of all the measures in the traffic safety toolbox, legislation and intense enforcement, supported by public education to secure community support, are the types of interventions most likely to produce systemwide results in a short timeframe. Australia has also benefited greatly from improvements in vehicle and road infrastructure safety. Indeed, the strategic plans now emerging focus on the need for greater investment in creating and maintaining a safe system.

Australia's current safety plans (described in Chapter 3) have adopted a comprehensive framework known as the safe system approach, which is directed at attaining safer speeds, designing roads and roadsides more forgiving of human error, promoting use of vehicles with features that reduce the likelihood of a crash and injury severity in a crash, and providing aid and incentives to road users for responsible driving. The various safety interventions operate over differing timescales. As Chapter 3 will describe, this difference has influenced the safety strategies of the benchmark countries. Intense enforcement has been demonstrated to produce immediate benefits in a number of countries. Investments in safe infrastructure accrue over time as the investment program is carried out over many years. Similarly, vehicle design changes take greater effect as the vehicle fleet modernizes over time. Some of the benchmark countries, searching for the means to continue improvement after the immediate gains of intense enforcement have been achieved, have renewed emphasis on the longer-term strategies.

Lack of Political and Public Support

The study charge acknowledges that rigorous safety interventions depend on public and political support and directs the committee to examine how this support was built in the benchmark countries. Lack of support for road safety action has been cited as the underlying source of poor performance of U.S. programs. For example, the Insurance Institute for Highway Safety (IIHS) has commented as follows: "Motor vehicle crash deaths on U.S. roads exceed 40,000 annually. . . . Yet society responds with something akin to a collective shrug. . . . Traffic safety laws that are known to be effective—and that are implemented in other countries with little or no controversy—often are resisted by U.S. politicians" (IIHS 2002, 1–2). IIHS cites federal research funding as an indicator of the low priority that the public assigns to highway safety, noting that the National Institutes of Health's 2001 budget for dental research was five times the research budget of the National Highway Traffic Safety Administration. IIHS cites as well weak media coverage of traffic safety issues and the success of organized public opposition to such measures as motorcycle helmet laws and red light cameras as indications of low priority.

U.S. observers consistently have noted that the successful national programs rely on measures that are regarded in the United States as politically controversial or legally impermissible. State officials encounter public objection and interest group opposition to such measures as radar detectors, speed limit reductions, automatic speed and red light enforcement, helmet laws, seat belt laws, sobriety checkpoints, and reduced BAC limits. A summary of FHWA's international safety scanning tours compared U.S. attitudes and institutions with those in other countries as follows (Baxter et al. 2005):

> Partly because of cultural differences ... [other] countries may be more successful than the United States in implementing certain behavioral practices, such as seatbelt usage or prevention of impaired driving. Expectations about implementation may need to be adjusted because some countries can adopt practices at a national level that can be implemented only at a State or local level in the United States. Similarly, the political context in the United States may inhibit adoption of certain technologies that are more readily accepted in other countries, such as speed enforcement cameras.

A compendium of 22 invited papers on *Improving Traffic Safety Culture in the United States: The Journey Forward* (AAA Foundation for Traffic Safety 2007) addressed the question of cultural factors influencing traffic safety outcomes. The articles, by authors from diverse disciplinary backgrounds, do not present empirical analysis of the relation of cultural factors to safety performance or of the effectiveness of interventions intended to change cultural attitudes, although there are references to such research in another area (for antismoking campaigns). The summary document (Hedlund 2007) contains a list of 20 actions derived from the papers, which, the author proposes, could contribute to producing cultural change. These recommendations include better communication with the public, communication across professional disciplines, planning and management based on performance goals, design of intervention programs based on scientific evidence, and research on the determinants of risk and on the elements of effective programs. Nearly all these amount to more effective performance of management functions that are already part of every state traffic safety program.

More recently, the AAA Foundation for Traffic Safety and another transportation organization have proposed that the administration hold a White House conference on traffic safety as a means of lending high-level political support to transportation safety initiatives (AAA Foundation for Traffic Safety 2009).

That differences among societies in values and attitudes account for differences in traffic safety performance is a credible hypothesis, and a few studies have examined it empirically. A Belgian study examining why that country had one of the highest traffic fatality rates in Europe in 2000 found that the European countries have similar laws but nonetheless divergent results and noted a correlation between country fatality rates and an index of perceptions of the degree of corruption in public life. It concluded that "countries . . . where people are not convinced of the necessity of compliance with imposed measures, do not perform well in traffic safety improvement" and that public attitudes toward law-abiding behavior partly explain differences in the impact of traffic safety legislation (Vereeck and Deben 2003, 17, 21). An update of the Belgian study that used the same measure of attitudes toward authority concluded (on the basis of a statistical analysis of fatalities for 15 European countries for 1995–2002) that a major share of Belgium's relatively high rate of traffic fatalities per vehicle kilometer of travel could be explained by the country's higher alcohol consumption (which itself might be regarded as an indicator of social norms), but that Belgium's higher score on the index of perception of the degree of corruption in public life also appeared to account for an important part of the difference (Vrolix and Vereeck 2006). The authors explain that "[the Corruption Perceptions Index] was used as a proxy for the general attitudes and social norms of citizens towards traffic legislation and policy. . . . In countries where corruption figures are low . . . it is assumed that law-infringing behavior is less tolerated" (Vrolix and Vereeck 2006, 43).

A second empirical study examined correlations of traffic fatality rates per capita in 46 countries in 2007 with measures of quality of governance developed by the World Bank and with empirical measures of national cultural values taken from the sociology literature (Gaygisiz 2010). The study found that fatality rate correlates negatively with quality of governance, positively with cultural measures characteristic of traditionally hierarchical societies, and negatively with measures indicative of personal autonomy and egalitarianism. However, the simple correlations do not control for international differences in income, which is strongly correlated with fatality rate and with most of the cultural measures. The author concludes that "since cultural values . . . are almost impossible to change or would change very slowly . . . and the quality of governance seems to have both direct and indirect impact on traffic safety, the development programs aimed at the improvement of the governance quality of institutions may play an important role in changing the traffic safety conditions" (Gaygisiz 2010, 7).

The comparison of Australian and U.S. planning cited above concludes that "perhaps most important [in the United States] there has been little legislative support for the use of techniques that will ensure these goals [of the 1998 FHWA strategic safety plan] are met. There is little point in strategic planning without assurance of the needed underlying support" (Tarnoff 2007, 22). The case studies of implementation of specific countermeasures that are presented in Chapter 4 cite instances where measures of proven effectiveness that are applied in some U.S. jurisdictions are rejected in others because of controversy or active opposition. In other instances, inaction may be the result of lack of public demand or inattention on the part of responsible officials rather than active opposition.

Committee's Approach to Its Charge

The various hypotheses about the causes of international differences in traffic safety progress are not mutually exclusive. Opportunities undoubtedly exist in the United States to reduce the costs of road crashes through improvements at all three levels of safety programs: through management reforms, wider application of the highest-payoff interventions, and more consistent political support. Most probably, sustained progress will require competent application of the full range of available interventions in a balance that is appropriate to the individual characteristics of jurisdictions.

The task statement asserts that the benchmark countries' fatality rate trends are explained by their behavioral (i.e., anti–drunk driving and speeding) interventions. However, the committee's perspective has been that claims of the effectiveness of particular intervention programs or overall national strategies must be subjected to critical scrutiny. The claims that merit the greatest weight are those supported by rigorous and objective quantitative evaluation. In many instances such evaluations were not available. Therefore, as Chapter 2 explains, the committee concluded that the causes of trends in national rates are incompletely understood.

As described above, the benchmark countries typically attribute their successes to comprehensive and balanced strategies that seek to reduce risk through interventions involving vehicle and road design, pedestrians, and emergency medical services as well as driver behavior regulations. The committee did not interpret the study charge reference to altering driver behavior as ruling out investigation of the role of other categories of intervention in explaining international differences. The committee's examination of specific interventions in Chapters 3 and 4 covers occupant restraints, motorcycle helmets, and infrastructure improvements as well as antispeeding and anti–drunk driving campaigns (as case studies of methods rather than a comprehensive survey of interventions). The actions recommended in Chapter 5 include measures to improve the effectiveness of enforcement of antispeeding and anti–drunk driving laws as well as measures to strengthen infrastructure hazard elimination programs and occupant protection regulations. The recommendations regarding management practices are intended to increase the effectiveness of all categories of interventions.

The committee considered the charge to imply three questions that U.S. policy makers and transportation program administrators must answer to profit from the experience of other countries:

- What are the sources of the declines in highway injury rates in Europe, Australia, and the United States, and especially, what has been the contribution of government safety programs?
- What are the necessary elements of successful national risk reduction programs? These elements may include safety management systems, the specific interventions employed, structures of administrative oversight

and accountability, political support and leadership, and strategies for building public and political support.
- What institutional or social differences between the United States and other countries might affect the success of efforts to transfer safety practices, and can any of these factors be altered to create a U.S. environment more conducive to safety improvement?

This study has not definitively resolved the question of the sources of differences in national rates of improvement in traffic safety, and the committee has not attempted to outline a comprehensive program to replicate the successes of other countries in the United States. The results of the study are more modest: in comparing the safety programs of the United States and other countries, the committee found certain gaps in the United States in program elements that appear to be prerequisites for progress. The most critical of these gaps may be in the management and planning capacities that safety agencies require to direct safety programs toward attaining defined goals. The recommendations propose measures to begin to close these gaps as first steps toward a more successful U.S. safety program.

OUTLINE OF THE REPORT

The remainder of this report is organized as follows. Chapter 2 describes trends in traffic fatalities and crashes in other countries, the United States, and U.S. states and reviews studies of the forces driving these trends. Chapter 3 contains a summary of conclusions of past studies about key elements of the most successful traffic injury reduction programs in other countries, descriptions of programs in five countries (Australia, Canada, France, Sweden, and the United Kingdom), and descriptions of aspects of the organization of U.S. state and federal safety programs for comparison with the other countries' programs.

Chapter 4 compares practices in the United States and other countries and among U.S. states in five categories of safety intervention: control of drunk driving, speed control, seat belt regulations, motorcycle helmet regulations, and highway network screening and safe road design. These five areas were selected as case studies. The committee did not comprehensively survey all areas of safety practice. The selection of the interventions described in Chapter 4 was dictated mainly by the emphasis that the prominent benchmark countries place on these interventions in their accounts of their safety successes. The committee did not have independent means of verifying that these program areas are indeed the primary sources of other countries' progress. Among the areas the chapter does not examine are countermeasures aimed at distracted driving and aggressive driving (i.e., the complex of hazardous behaviors that includes speeding, illegal passing, tailgating, weaving, and ignoring signals), truck safety, driver training, vehicle safety rating, emergency medical services, and graduated drivers' licensing, some of which (e.g., graduated licensing) are areas of U.S. success and leadership.

Chapter 5 presents the committee's conclusions and recommendations. The conclusions identify the accomplishments of the benchmark nations, sources of success, and differences between U.S. and international practices. The recommendations, addressed to elected officials and to government safety professionals and administrators, identify actions needed in the United States to emulate the successes that other countries have achieved.

REFERENCES

Abbreviations

CISR	Comité Interministériel de la Sécurité Routière
ECMT	European Conference of Ministers of Transport
FHWA	Federal Highway Administration
IIHS	Insurance Institute for Highway Safety
NHTSA	National Highway Traffic Safety Administration
OECD	Organisation for Economic Co-operation and Development
TRB	Transportation Research Board

AAA Foundation for Traffic Safety. 2007. *Improving Traffic Safety Culture in the United States: The Journey Forward.* April.

AAA Foundation for Traffic Safety. 2009. Traffic Safety Culture Summit. *AAA Foundation for Traffic Safety E-Newsletter,* Sept. 25, 2009. http://www.aaafoundation.org/e-news/issue21/TSCS.cfm.

Baxter, J., M. L. Halladay, and E. Alicandri. 2005. Safety Scans—A Successful Two-Way Street. *Public Roads,* Vol. 69, No. 1, July–Aug., pp. 31–37.

CISR. 2006. Dossier de Presse. July 6.

Diewald, W. 2004. *Recent Highway Safety Experience in Australia and Several European Countries.* Staff working paper for TRB Research and Technology Coordinating Committee, Nov. 22.

Evans, L. 2004. *Traffic Safety.* Science Serving Society, Bloomfield Hills, Mich.

FHWA. 1983. Person Trip Characteristics: 1977 Nationwide Personal Transportation Study. Dec.

FHWA. 2009. International Technology Scanning Program. Updated June 26. http://international.fhwa.dot.gov/scan/.

FHWA. 2010. Introduction to the 2009 NHTS. http://nhts.ornl.gov/introduction.shtml.

FHWA. n.d. Toward Zero Deaths: A National Strategy on Highway Safety. http://safety.fhwa.dot.gov/tzd/.

Gaygisiz, E. 2010. Cultural Values and Governance Quality as Correlates of Road Traffic Fatalities: A Nation Level Analysis. *Accident Analysis and Prevention,* online prepublication, June.

Gerondeau, C. 2006. *Road Safety in France: Reflections on Three Decades of Road Safety Policy.* FIA Foundation for the Automobile and Society, May.

Hedlund, J. 2007. *Improving Traffic Safety Culture in the United States: The Journey Forward: Summary and Synthesis.* AAA Foundation for Traffic Safety, Dec.

Heron, M., D. L. Hoyert, S. L. Murphy, J. Xu, K. D. Kochanek, and B. Tejada-Vera. 2009. Deaths: Final Data for 2006. *National Vital Statistics Reports,* Vol. 57, No. 14, April 17.

IIHS. 2002. *Status Report.* Vol. 37, No. 10, Dec. 7.

Johnston, I. 2006. *Halving Roadway Fatalities: A Case Study from Victoria, Australia, 1989–2004.* Federal Highway Administration, April.

Kopits, E., and M. Cropper. 2005. *Why Have Traffic Fatalities Declined in Industrialized Countries? Implications for Pedestrians and Vehicle Occupants.* Policy Research Working Paper 738, World Bank, Washington, D.C., Aug.

MacDonald, D., C. P. Yew, R. Arnold, J. R. Baxter, R. K. Halvorson, H. Kassoff, K. Philmus, T. J. Price, D. R. Rose, and C. M. Walton. 2004. *Transportation Performance Measures in Australia, Canada, Japan, and New Zealand.* Federal Highway Administration, Dec.

National Safety Council. 2007. *Injury Facts 2007.*

NHTSA. 2009. *Traffic Safety Facts 2008.*

NHTSA. 2010. *Highlights of 2009 Motor Vehicle Crashes.* Aug.

Noland, R. B. 2003. Traffic Fatalities and Injuries: The Effect of Changes in Infrastructure and Other Trends. *Accident Analysis and Prevention,* Vol. 35, No. 4, July, pp. 599–611.

OECD. n.d. International Road Traffic Accident Database. http://www.swov.nl/cognos/cgi-bin/ppdscgi.exe?toc=%2FEnglish%2FIRTAD.

OECD and ECMT. 2006a. *Speed Management.* Joint Transport Research Centre.

OECD and ECMT. 2006b. *Speed Management: Summary Document.* Joint Transport Research Centre.

OECD and International Transport Forum. 2008. *Towards Zero: Ambitious Road Safety Targets and the Safe System Approach: Summary Document.* Joint Transport Research Centre.

OECD and International Transport Forum. 2009. *Trends in the Transport Sector 1970–2007.*

OECD and International Transport Forum. 2010. Press Release: A Record Decade for Road Safety: International Transport Forum at the OECD Publishes Road Death Figures for 33 Countries. Sept. 15.

OECD and International Transport Forum. n.d. Country Reports on Road Safety Performance. http://www.internationaltransportforum.org/jtrc/safety/targets/Performance/performance.html.

Richter, E. D., P. Barach, E. Ben-Michael, and T. Berman. 2001. Death and Injury from Motor Vehicle Crashes: A Public Health Failure, Not an Achievement. *Injury Prevention,* Vol. 7, pp. 176–178.

Tarnoff, P. J. 2007. Can We Stop Now? *Thinking Highways,* Vol. 2, No. 1, pp. 18–22.

TRB. 2006. *Special Report 287: Improving Road Safety in Developing Countries: Opportunities for U.S. Cooperation and Engagement: Workshop Summary.* National Academies, Washington, D.C.

Vereeck, L., and L. Deben. 2003. An International Comparison of the Effectiveness of Traffic Safety Enforcement Policies. *Proceedings, Hawaii International Conference on Social Sciences.* http://www.hicsocial.org:16080/Social2003Proceedings/.

Vrolix, K., and L. Vereeck. 2006. *Social Norms and Traffic Safety: A Cross Country Analysis in the EU-15.* Policy Research Center for Traffic Safety, Hasselt University, Belgium, March.

2

World and U.S. Safety Trends

Chapter 1 explained that the safety programs of other countries seized the attention of U.S. safety professionals and advocacy groups because of impressive declines in numbers and rates of traffic fatalities relative to U.S. experience. In this chapter, the first section compares traffic safety trends of the United States and other countries over the past 40 years. The second compares trends among U.S. states, since the performance of the best states might also be a useful benchmark for judging U.S. safety programs, along with the best performances among other countries. The third section reviews studies that used statistical methods to explain why some countries and states have performed better than others. The final section presents a more detailed characterization of the U.S. traffic safety problem, describing how risks differ among categories of roads, vehicles, regions, and drivers.

WORLD FATALITY RATE TRENDS

Nations differ greatly in traffic fatality rates (per capita and per vehicle kilometer) and in trends in rates over time. They differ also in practices with regard to driver and vehicle safety regulation and enforcement and road construction. The relative success of the different policies cannot be inferred by examining the aggregate fatality rate data alone because many factors other than government policies affect the trends. Nonetheless, the trends measure overall progress in reducing risk and naturally have led policy makers to ask whether lessons applicable to the less successful jurisdictions can be learned from the experiences of those that are more successful.

Most of the comparisons in this chapter are in terms of fatality rates per kilometer of vehicle travel. Comparisons of rates of injuries and total crashes would also be valuable, but comparable international data on these measures do not exist. Box 2-1 explains why rates per vehicle kilometer are useful measures for comparisons.

When fatality rates for high-income and low-income countries over many years are compared, a pattern emerges of rising per capita fatality rates in the earlier stages of motorization of transport, followed by falling rates in the later stages. Because motorization rises with income,

---

BOX 2-1

Measures for International Comparisons of Safety Performance

Some analysts have argued that total fatalities or casualties or per capita rates are more suitable measures than rates per vehicle kilometer for benchmarking safety performance or for defining safety goals. For example, the Organisation for Economic Co-operation and Development's Working Group on Achieving Ambitious Road Safety Targets avoids reporting crash rates per vehicle kilometer, explaining (OECD and International Transport Forum 2006, 8):

> The relative progress in road safety depends somewhat on what one uses as a measure of exposure to risk (i.e., population, registered vehicles, distance travelled). There has been a considerable debate in the past about which measure is most appropriate as an exposure measure. Those in the health sector prefer the use of population as the denominator since it permits comparisons with other causes of injury or with diseases. As the health and transport sector increase their level of co-operation, fatalities per 100 000 population are becoming more widely used.
>
> In the transport sector, it has been common, where data are available, to use fatalities per distance travelled (e.g. fatalities per million vehicle-kilometres) as a principal measure or fatalities per 10 000 vehicles. Fatalities per distance travelled has traditionally been favoured by road transport authorities as it implicitly discounts fatality rates if travel is increased.

(continued on next page)

BOX 2-1 *(continued)*
Measures for International Comparisons of Safety Performance

Objections to the use of rates per vehicle kilometer to measure safety have been strongly stated, for example as follows (Richter et al. 2001):

> The use of [deaths per vehicle mile] as the criterion implicitly endorses an ethically problematic paradigm that weighs the benefits of transportation—time saved—against the losses—deaths and injuries. If we use absolute numbers, we hold that individuals should not be sacrificed for collective benefits. . . . The use of time trends in [deaths per vehicle mile] within one mode of travel precludes examining alternative strategies based on shifts to public transport, a mode usually with much lower risks.

In this report, international and interstate comparisons are expressed in terms of rates per vehicle kilometer and of total numbers of fatalities. One of the goals of public policy concerning road safety is to reduce the risk of road travel. The road-using public expects government authorities to provide safe roads. Crash and fatality rates per unit use of the road system (e.g., per vehicle kilometer) are measures of this risk. (In contrast, few people would argue that reducing tobacco-related fatalities per cigarette smoked should be a goal of health policy.) Observing rates, and not just numbers of crashes, is essential in determining the effectiveness of most of the safety measures that road authorities have at their disposal. The reductions in total annual fatalities in the benchmark nations are the consequence of declining rates of fatalities per vehicle kilometer, not of declining use of the roads in those countries. This rate decline is therefore the phenomenon that must be understood if the United States is to take advantage of other countries' experiences.

The number of fatalities per vehicle kilometer is an imperfect measure of road travel risk. Data on rates for all crashes and for injury crashes by severity would be more useful in examining the effects of safety programs, but these data are not available on a consistent basis internationally. In addition, aggregate annual rates for entire national or state road systems hide important geographical and temporal differences.

fatalities per capita tend to increase with increasing income among countries with low to medium income per capita, and then to decline with increasing income among countries with medium to high average incomes (Figure 2-1). For example, from 1975 to 1998, reported road traffic deaths per capita declined by 43 percent in France and 27 percent in the United States but rose by 79 percent in India (1980–1998) and 243 percent in China (Kopits and Cropper 2005a, 170). In the poorest countries, only a small proportion of trips is by motor vehicle, and deaths are relatively rare. However, fatality rates per vehicle kilometer of travel are high for several reasons: the condition of infrastructure and vehicles may be poor; road users and authorities lack experience; and on roads where motor vehicles mix with many pedestrians and cyclists, deaths of pedestrians and cyclists are a large share of the total.

In wealthier countries, most trips are by motor vehicle, and thus deaths of persons who are not motor vehicle occupants are a smaller proportion of total traffic deaths than in low-income countries. Also, vehicle occupant fatalities per vehicle kilometer decline, presumably because infrastructure and vehicles become safer, drivers become more skilled, traffic regulation becomes more effective, and increasing vehicular congestion in cities

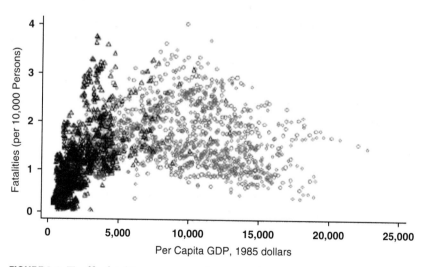

FIGURE 2-1 Traffic fatality rate per capita versus income, 88 countries, 1963–1999. (SOURCE: Kopits and Cropper 2005a; copyright, Elsevier; used with permission.)

slows speeds and thus reduces crash severities. Eventually fatalities per vehicle kilometer decline enough that fatalities per capita begin to fall. The negative correlation between degree of motorization and national traffic fatality rate is known as Smeed's law and has long been a subject of study and controversy (Adams 1987).

Fatality rates per vehicle kilometer have declined greatly in every high-income country in the past several decades (Figure 2-2a, Table 1-1), and the absolute disparity of rates among countries has lessened (Figure 2-3). A comparison of the U.S. experience with that of 15 other high-income countries for which 1975–2008 data are available shows that the U.S. fatality rate was less than half the aggregate rate in the other countries in 1975 but has been higher since 2005 (Figure 2-2c). Consequently, total annual traffic deaths in the 15 countries fell by 66 percent in the period, while U.S. deaths fell by only 16 percent. The U.S. fatality rate was among the best before 1990 but has been below the median rate of the group every year since 2001.

The roughly exponential shapes of the fatality rate time trends and the bunching of national fatality rates in the 0.6 to 1.0 range in recent years (Figure 2-3) suggest the possibility that, as rates become lower, it becomes more difficult to obtain further reductions comparable in absolute terms with the reductions of earlier decades. According to this interpretation of the trends, U.S. improvement has been slow because the U.S. rate was already low 30 years ago, and other countries have been able to improve more rapidly because improvement is easier when the starting point is a relatively high fatality rate. These curves suggest at least that some underlying universal phenomena have driven fatality rate trends toward convergence. It may be speculated that the improvement reflects a learning process by all the agents—drivers, nonmotorized road users, road authorities, health services, and law enforcement and public safety agencies—within the road transportation system as that system develops and matures in a country. In the 1960s, U.S. highways, vehicles, and travel patterns differed greatly from those of most of the benchmark countries. Today, the differences persist but have narrowed.

However, the experience of the past decade no longer appears to fit this description of convergence to similar, stable fatality rates. In a group of countries that includes the United Kingdom, Sweden, Norway, Finland,

World and U.S. Safety Trends **41**

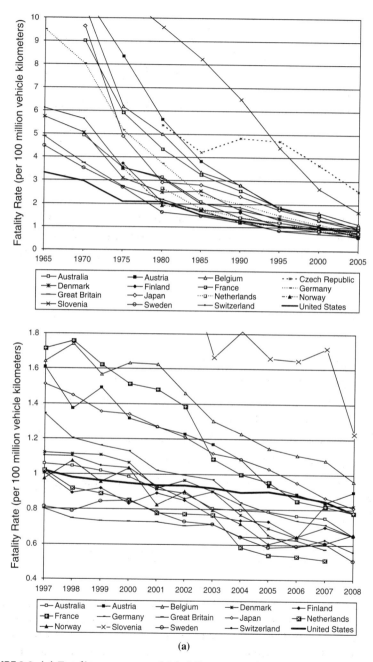

FIGURE 2-2 (*a*) Fatality rates per vehicle kilometer, selected high-income countries, 1965–2005 and 1997–2008. *(continued on next page)*

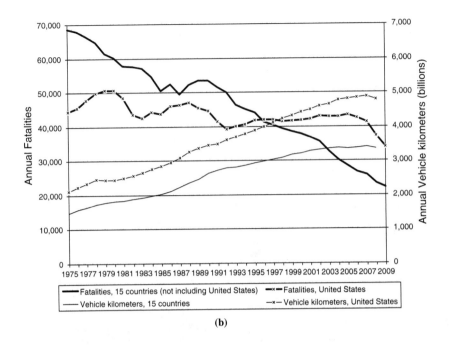

(b)

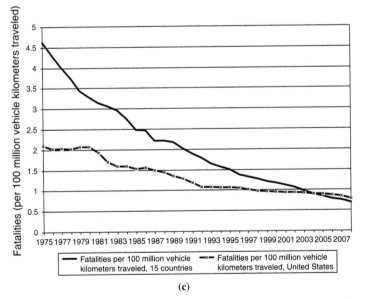

(c)

FIGURE 2-2 (*b*) Annual traffic fatalities and vehicle kilometers, United States and 15 other high-income countries, 1975–2009. (*c*) Fatalities per 100 million vehicle kilometers, United States and 15 high-income countries, 1975–2008.
NOTE: Countries included in Figures 2-2*b* and 2-2*c* are Australia, Austria, Belgium, Denmark, Finland, France, Germany, Great Britain, Israel, Japan, Netherlands, Norway, Slovenia, Sweden, and Switzerland. (SOURCES: OECD n.d.; OECD and International Transport Forum 2010.)

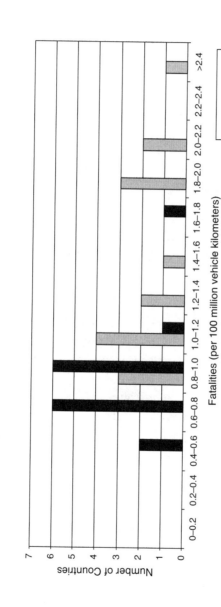

FIGURE 2-3 Distribution of fatality rates of 16 high-income countries, 1994 and 2007. NOTE: Countries are as in Figure 2-2, including the United States. (SOURCE: OECD n.d.)

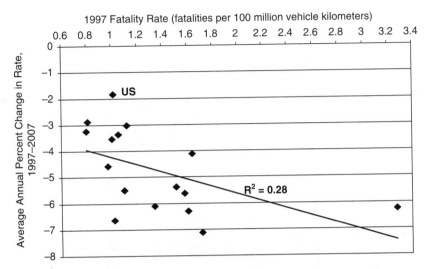

FIGURE 2-4 Fatality rates of 16 countries: average annual percentage change for 1997–2007 versus 1997 rate. NOTE: The countries included are as in Figure 2-2. (SOURCE: OECD n.d.)

the Netherlands, Switzerland, West Germany, and Australia, the fatality rate per vehicle kilometer was close to or lower than the U.S. rate in 1997, yet each achieved a greater percentage improvement in its rate than did the United States in the 1997–2007 period (Figure 2-2a). In this period, every high-income country shown in Figure 2-2 has reduced its fatality rate by a greater percentage than has the United States. Improvement in fatality rate in the decade is only weakly correlated with the level of the 1997 rate among high-income countries (Figure 2-4).

U.S. STATE FATALITY RATE TRENDS

If fatality rate trends can be used as indicators of jurisdictions with relatively successful government safety programs, then comparisons of trends among the U.S. states might have at least as much relevance as comparisons of the United States with other countries. The states independently manage their traffic safety programs [although with a degree of central control through federal-aid highway program rules and National Highway Traffic Safety Administration (NHTSA) regulations] and are diverse with respect to demographics, geography, and transportation system characteristics.

The pattern of fatality rates among the states in some ways mirrors that of the high-income nations. The 2007–2008 average rate varied among the states from below 0.5 deaths per 100 million vehicle kilometers in Massachusetts and Rhode Island to 1.3 in Louisiana and 1.4 in Montana (Figure 2-5). Similar to the distribution of national rates, the distribution of state fatality rates (Figure 2-6) shows a shift toward lower rates and a bunching of rates in the 0.6 to 1.0 range over the past decade. The rates of four states (Massachusetts, Rhode Island, Minnesota, and New Jersey) were lower in 2008 than that of any of the countries of Figure 2-2.

It is in the speed of improvement in highway safety that the experience of the states differs from performance abroad. Few states could match the 4 to 6 percent annual reductions in fatality rates that many high-income nations achieved in the period 1994–2008 (Figure 2-7). Figures 2-8 and 2-9 show fatality rate trends for selected states that improved more slowly (Figure 2-8) and more rapidly (Figure 2-9) than the U.S. average in the past decade. The five states included in Figure 2-8 are those with the smallest percentage declines in the period among all states with above-average 2008 fatality rates, excluding states with fewer than 300 traffic deaths in 2008. The five states included in Figure 2-9 are those with the greatest percentage declines in the period among all states with below-average 2008 fatality rates, excluding states with fewer than 300 traffic deaths in 2008.

SOURCES OF DIFFERENCES IN THE TRENDS

Safety researchers have attempted to understand the sources of differences in safety performance among countries and among the U.S. states by looking for correlations between crash frequencies or rates and the characteristics of the jurisdictions (including road conditions, safety policies, and demographic and economic factors) that are suspected to influence crash risk. A second research approach to this question is to measure the impacts of particular safety interventions directly and then to judge whether the measured program effects are large enough to explain the overall trends. Studies taking the latter approach to evaluate safety programs in France, Australia, and the United Kingdom are described in Chapter 3.

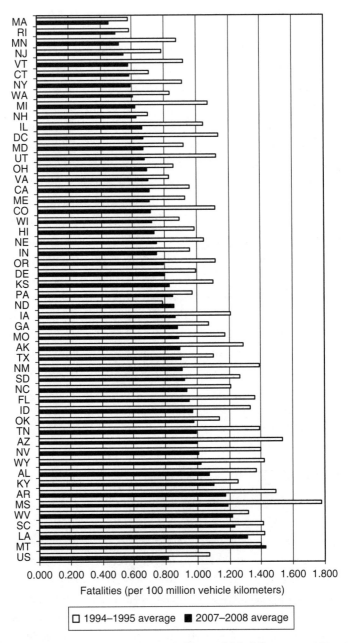

FIGURE 2-5 State fatality rates per 100 million vehicle kilometers, 1994–1995 and 2007–2008. (SOURCE: NHTSA n.d.)

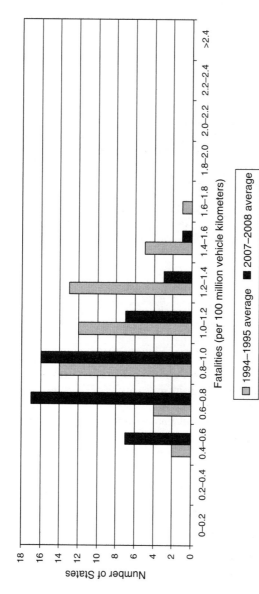

FIGURE 2-6 Distribution of U.S. state fatality rates, 1994–1995 average and 2007–2008 average.
(SOURCE: NHTSA n.d.)

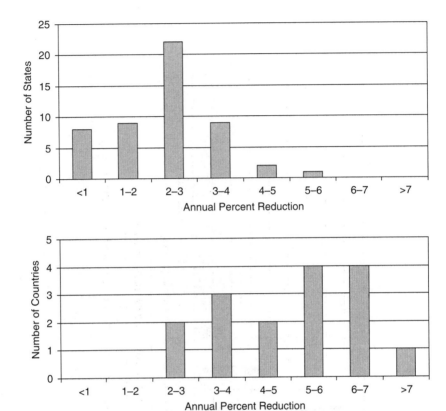

FIGURE 2-7 Distribution of average annual percent reductions in fatality rates of U.S. states (*top*) and of 16 high-income countries (*bottom*), 1994–2008.
NOTE: In bottom graph, countries are as in Figure 2-2, including the United States. Values for Great Britain and Netherlands are for 1994–2007.
(SOURCES: NHTSA n.d.; OECD n.d.)

In general, the statistical studies take the following factors into consideration in their crash risk models:

- Traffic characteristics, including the mix of pedestrians and vehicle types sharing the roads, the degree of congestion, and speeds;
- Demographics: higher crash rates are expected among younger populations;
- Land use: urban and rural areas may have differences in risks;
- Road design standards and maintenance standards;

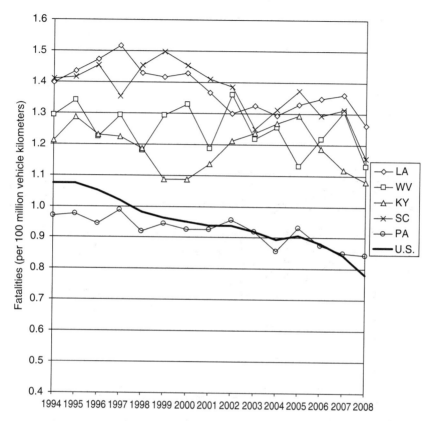

FIGURE 2-8 Fatality rates, selected states with 2008 rate higher than the U.S. average and with smaller than average rate declines since 1994. (Source: NHTSA n.d.)

- Motor vehicle characteristics and condition, including the average age of the fleet and the presence of passenger restraints;
- Prevalence of alcohol abuse in the population of the jurisdiction;
- Driver behaviors: the prevalence of drunk driving, the rate of seat belt use, speed, and respect for speed and other traffic laws;
- Quality of medical services; and
- Government safety policies, including vehicle and road design standards, traffic regulations, enforcement practices, and education and communication activities, which may influence all of the factors listed above.

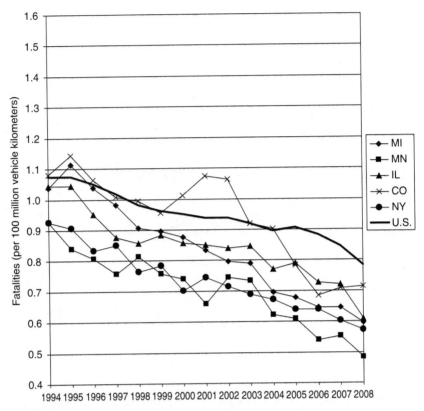

FIGURE 2-9 Fatality rates, selected states with 2008 rate lower than the U.S. average and with greater than average rate declines since 1994. (Source: NHTSA n.d.)

The high-income countries are diverse with respect to geography, population density, and transportation habits. These differences affect the risks that road users confront. As one example, in Japan and the Netherlands, pedestrians and cyclists make up a greater share of all persons killed in crashes than in the United States (Table 2-1 and Figure 2-10).

Although exposure data are not available, it is likely that the differences shown in the table and figure primarily reflect differences in exposure: a much larger share of all road travel occurs on roads where motor vehicles are mixed with high volumes of bicycle travel in the Netherlands than in the United States. Such differences are likely to

TABLE 2-1 Fatalities by Category of Road User (Percentage of Total Traffic Fatalities)

	Japan 2005	Netherlands 2007	United States 2007
Motor vehicle occupants	40	46	74
Bicycle riders	12	24	2
Motorcycle and moped riders and passengers	17	8	13
Pedestrians and other nonoccupants	31	12	12

SOURCES: Cabinet Office 2006, 9; SWOV n.d.; NHTSA 2008.

affect trends in fatality rates, but in complex ways. Trends will be affected by changes in transport habits (e.g., trends in the relative use of bicycles and motor vehicles), and the differences will affect the relative magnitudes of the impact of various interventions. For example, the emphasis in the Netherlands on pedestrian and bicycle safety reflects the high share of deaths in those user categories.

The three studies summarized below are diverse with respect to the jurisdictions and time spans that are analyzed, but all asked the same basic

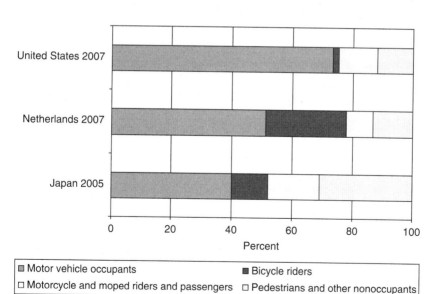

FIGURE 2-10 Percentage of total fatalities by category of road user.
(SOURCES: Cabinet Office 2006, 9; SWOV n.d.; NHTSA 2008.)

questions, and certain common themes emerge from their conclusions. The three studies are as follows:

- A World Bank study of safety trends in 32 nations worldwide over a 38-year period;
- A study by the Insurance Institute for Highway Safety that analyzed the sources of differences in the fatality rates of the 50 U.S. states during a single time period; and
- A second study of differences among the U.S. states over 13 years, focusing on the role of road investment on traffic fatalities.

Sources of Differences Among Country Fatality Rates

The World Bank study analyzed statistically the trend of declining fatality rates in the high-income countries (Kopits and Cropper 2005b; Kopits and Cropper 2008). The World Bank has been engaged in road safety in developing countries for 30 years and is committed to scaling up its initiatives. This activity will require an appreciation of the factors that have driven safety improvements in high-, middle-, and low-income countries and the linkages between economic development and road safety.

In the study, fatalities of motorized vehicle occupants and road fatalities of pedestrians and bicyclists per vehicle kilometer are related to socioeconomic, demographic, and transportation system characteristics. The data are annual pedestrian and vehicle occupant fatalities and vehicle kilometers for 32 high-income countries for 1964–2002, obtained primarily from the Organisation for Economic Co-operation and Development's International Road Traffic Accident Database. In the summary country data tabulated (for 28 countries and for 1970–1999 for most countries), the median reduction in the fatality rate was 83 percent for pedestrian fatalities and 72 percent for occupant fatalities. The median fraction of total deaths that were deaths of pedestrians was 22 percent in 1999. In the United States, the fatality rate reductions were 76 percent for pedestrians and 66 percent for occupants, and 14 percent of 1999 deaths were pedestrians.

The main results of the fatality rate analysis were as follows:

- The decline of the pedestrian fatality rate can be explained largely by increasing income (a 10 percent increase in income reduces the pedestrian fatality rate by 6 percent on average). This relationship is reasonable: with increasing income, a larger share of trips is taken by motor vehicle, and pedestrian and bicycle density on roads will tend to decline. The occupant fatality rate shows no significant relationship to income (in an analysis that considers only income and a time trend as explanatory variables), although it declines significantly over time.

- When the socioeconomic and demographic variables are included in the analysis, the variation in the occupant fatality rate is explained by changes in the proportion of drivers under age 24, alcohol abuse, traffic density, and the number of doctors per capita.
- The decline in the youth population in the countries studied can explain nearly 30 percent of the decline in the occupant fatality rate in the period. The ratio of the population aged 15 to 24 years to total population over 15 declined by 20 to 30 percent in most countries in the sample between 1970 and 2000. The clearest conclusion drawn from the study is that the aging of the population in the high-income countries in the past 30 years has been a major contributor to reduced fatality rates.
- Reduction in excessive alcohol consumption (measured in the model by the death rate from cirrhosis of the liver) reduces the occupant fatality rate. The effect is statistically significant but small, accounting for only a few percent of the rate decline over the period in most countries. The study did not have data reflecting any differences in rates of drunk driving independent of rates of alcohol consumption.
- In countries and years in which the number of motor vehicles grows slowly, the occupant fatality rate tends to be lower. However, this effect is small, accounting for only a few percent of the variation in fatality rates. This variable was intended to capture the impact of having a high proportion of inexperienced drivers on the road. The small effect seems surprising, since one plausible explanation of the apparent general pattern of convergence of accident rates shown in Figure 2-2 is that it is a learning phenomenon—that is, newly motorizing countries must learn over time how to operate their highway systems safely.
- Increasing the mileage of the road network, with all other factors held constant, improved safety in the 1960s, but by the 1990s expanding the network had no significant safety effect.
- Increasing physicians per capita (a measure of the quality of medical services) reduces the fatality rate.

The analysis has certain limitations. Policy-related characteristics (e.g., improvements in road quality, in vehicles, and in emergency medical services, and driver behavior regulation) could only be represented by rough indirect measures. For example, vehicle and road quality improvements are represented by time trends, with uniform effects for all countries, so the analysis yields little insight on the effects of quality improvements. Constructing better measures of these factors would be difficult but might allow this kind of analysis to shed more light on the importance of policy interventions.

The World Bank study findings are consistent with those of an earlier statistical comparison of traffic fatalities among OECD countries using annual data for 21 countries from 1980 to 1994, which related deaths in each year in a country to demographic characteristics, vehicles per capita, and alcohol consumption per capita (Page 2001). Fatalities were found to increase with the percentage of young people in the population, alcohol consumption, and percentage of the population employed, and to decrease with the percentage of the population that is urban. The author proposes that the difference between a country's actual trend in fatalities over the period and the trend predicted by the statistical model is an indicator of the effectiveness of the country's safety interventions. Because the analysis does not include data on safety effort, conclusions from its results concerning the effectiveness of country safety programs are speculative. Interpretation of the statistical results is problematic because data on vehicle kilometers of travel were not included in the analysis.

Sources of Differences Among Fatality Rates of States and Local Areas

The Insurance Institute for Highway Safety study used statistical methods to search for causes of the disparity in highway fatality rates among U.S. states (O'Neill and Kyrychenko 2006). As described above (and shown in Figure 2-5), the states with the highest rates have more than twice as many fatalities per kilometer of travel as the states with the lowest rates.

The data examined were total fatalities and passenger vehicle occupant fatalities per billion vehicle miles of travel for 3 years combined (2001 to 2003) in each of the 50 states. The study tested whether the differences in fatality rates (annual state total traffic fatalities per vehicle mile) among the states could be accounted for by differences in characteristics of the populations and transportation systems: population density, the percentage of the population that is urban, percentage age 16 to 20, median income, percentage with college degree, school spending per pupil, highway traffic density, and average vehicle age. For example, since rural road fatality rates are higher than urban rates nationwide, a state with a high percentage of urban travel would have a lower total fatality rate than a more rural state, even if the two states had identical rates on urban roads and on rural roads.

The analysis showed that most of the variation in fatality rates among the states could be explained by differences in these characteristics and that statistical models using the characteristics could fairly accurately predict the fatality rate ranking of each of the states. States with a higher percentage of urban population, higher population density, higher traffic density, higher incomes, and fewer young people had lower fatality rates. The authors conclude that "crash death rates are strongly influenced by factors unrelated to highway safety countermeasures. Death rates should not be used . . . to assess overall highway safety policies, especially across jurisdictions. There can be no substitute for the use of . . . scientific evaluations of highway safety interventions that use outcome measures directly related to the interventions" (O'Neill and Kyrychenko 2006, 307).

The study shows how demographic factors influence state-level accident rates, but its results are not conclusive on the question of whether differences among the states in safety policies have affected their relative success in improving highway safety, and the study certainly is not intended to imply that safety policies do not matter. The inclusion of policy-related factors (e.g., the quality of the state's roads or the intensity of enforcement) in the statistical analysis might reveal that such factors account for a measurable share of the fatality rate differences among the states.

The second study of differences among the states (Noland 2003) focused on how improvements in road infrastructure have affected traffic fatalities and injuries and considered the effects of demographics, seat belt use, alcohol consumption, and quality of medical services. Road improvements have always been an important element of U.S. safety programs. Roads built to high design standards (for example, the Interstates) have lower average fatality rates than roads of lower classes, so the expectation has been that upgrading the road system would improve safety.

The study used data on annual injuries and fatalities and on various explanatory factors for each of the 50 states for 1985–1997. Road infrastructure was measured by data on lane miles by lane width and road class, excluding local roads. The statistical analysis also considered measures of seat belt use (belt use rates reported by NHTSA and whether a primary seat belt use law was in effect), demographics (state population by age cohort), quality of medical services (infant mortality rate and hospitals per square mile), and per capita alcohol consumption.

The study concluded that there are no consistent safety benefits from improving road infrastructure, as measured by extent, functional class, and lane width. Adding lane miles increased fatalities. Upgrading the functional class distribution had little effect on fatalities or injuries. A higher percentage of arterial and collector lanes with widths of 12 feet or greater was associated with an increase in fatalities and injuries. The author notes that all of these conclusions conflict with engineering conventional wisdom about the safety effects of geometric improvements but are consistent with other statistical studies. For example, an earlier statistical study (Fridstrøm and Ingebrigsten 1991, 370) using county-level data in Norway found that when traffic expands and road capacity remains constant, casualty crashes increase by only half the increase in traffic and so the crash rate declines, but when traffic volume and road capacity both expand at the same rate, crash rates are unchanged.

This study, as did the World Bank study, used very approximate measures of some of the explanatory factors because no direct measure was available. The analysis did not use vehicle kilometers of travel as an explanatory variable because, the author explains, vehicle kilometers are highly correlated with population, which was included. The omission of vehicle kilometers from the model means that a plausible alternative explanation for the findings cannot be excluded—that is, that a larger stock of infrastructure is observed to be related to higher fatalities because more infrastructure indicates more travel rather than because more infrastructure increases the risk of travel.

The age distribution of the population was found to have a large effect. When the percentage of the population between ages 15 and 24 years increases, fatalities and injuries increase. When the percentage of the population over age 75 increases, fatalities and injuries decrease, perhaps because this age cohort travels less by road. An increase in seat belt use and the existence of a primary seat belt law both are found to reduce fatalities, but seat belt usage does not affect injuries. Lower alcohol consumption reduces fatalities but not injuries.

Improvement in the quality of medical services, as approximated by the infant mortality rate in the state, reduces fatalities but does not have a significant effect on injuries. This result reinforces the conclusions of other research (Zwerling et al. 2005), which found by a different analysis method that, when crash severity is controlled for, persons injured in rural crashes have a lower chance of survival than persons injured in urban crashes, and that this difference accounts for an important share of the difference between urban and rural fatality rates. The largest positive effects (as indicated by the numbers of 1985 fatalities that would have been avoided if the 1997 values of the variables had prevailed) in the Noland study were for seat belt use, age distribution, and alcohol consumption.

The two U.S. studies summarized above are representative of numerous studies that have used data on fatality or casualty frequency in multiple U.S. states over a period of years to assess statistically the effects of particular interventions (e.g., seat belt laws) or to explore the possible causes of interstate differences in casualty frequency and rate. Another recent study in this group (Babcock and Gayle 2009) includes a literature review. In general, the studies find that external factors (e.g., demographic and travel characteristics) account for a large share of variation in casualties over time and among states and that a large share of interstate and temporal variation is unexplained by the factors considered. Some studies conclude that specific interventions are effective, but the effects usually appear to be small in comparison with the overall variation among states and over time.

Concluding Observations

None of the studies offers a satisfactory comprehensive explanation for the general pattern of declining and converging fatality rates among countries and among the U.S. states shown in Figures 2-2 and 2-6.

However, a small number of factors appear to be important in driving the trends:

- The aging of the populations of the high-income countries has reduced fatality rates.
- Increasing congestion appears to reduce rates, presumably through its effect on speed.
- Higher alcohol consumption and alcohol abuse in the general population lead to higher traffic fatality rates.
- Higher seat belt use decreases fatalities.
- Improved quality of medical services reduces fatality rates. The most important effect may be the speed and quality of emergency medical services, but the statistical studies were not refined enough to isolate this aspect of medical systems.

A lesson that all the studies support is that differences in national- or state-level rates are imperfect indicators of successful safety policies, because differences in these rates reflect to a great extent differences in fundamental demographic, economic, and geographical circumstances. Therefore, to find the best international models for the United States to emulate and to draw the right conclusions from these models, detailed examinations of specific policies and programs—how they were implemented and the results they produced—will be needed.

FACTORS AFFECTING U.S. FATALITY RATE TRENDS

The previous sections identified characteristics of populations (especially the age distribution) and highway systems (including the distribution of traffic between urban and rural areas, which is an indicator of congestion, speed, and timeliness of emergency response, and the mix of kinds of motorized and nonmotorized vehicles and pedestrians on the roads) that influence fatality rates and trends. As an aid to interpreting U.S. trends, this section describes coincident trends in population age distribution, the urban and rural distribution of travel, and the mix of size and types of vehicles on the roads. Chapter 4 will describe the U.S. incidence of high-risk behaviors (drunk driving, speeding, and failure to use occupant protection) that also influence trends and differences among countries.

Demographics

Research summarized in the previous section showed that countries with aging populations experience declines in highway fatality rates. U.S. drivers aged 16 to 20 years are involved in fatal crashes more than twice as frequently, per licensed driver in the age group, than drivers over age 35 (Figure 2-11). In the period 1997 to 2001, the fatal crash involvement rate per kilometer driven for drivers aged 16 to 20 years was 5 times the rate for drivers aged 45 to 54 years, and the rate per kilometer driven for drivers older than 75 years was nearly 4 times greater than the rate for drivers aged 45 to 54 years (GAO 2003, 18). Similar patterns probably hold in other countries.

The median age of the U.S. population is lower than in most other high-income nations. This characteristic probably tends to elevate the U.S. fatality rate in comparison with other countries. However, the rate of aging of the U.S. population is in the middle of the range for high-income countries (Figure 2-12); therefore, differences in the rate of aging probably

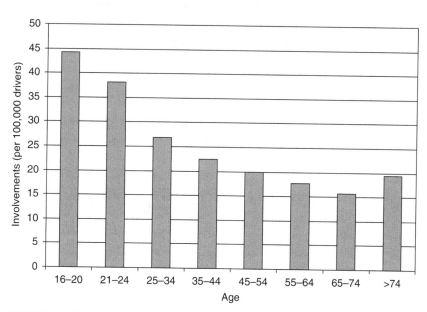

FIGURE 2-11 Driver involvements in fatal crashes, per 100,000 licensed drivers, by age, United States, 2008. (SOURCE: NHTSA 2009, 100.)

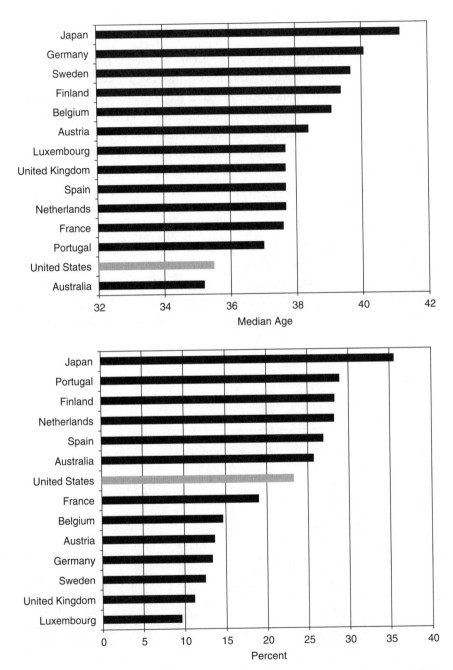

FIGURE 2-12 Median age in 2000 (*top*) and percentage change in median age between 1975 and 2000 (*bottom*) for various countries. (SOURCE: United Nations 2002, Annex III.)

do not explain much of the difference between the United States and other countries in the rate of decline of crash rates in recent decades.

Urban and Rural Travel

One factor that can explain part of the variation in fatality rates across U.S. states is differences in the distribution of travel by road type and by urban versus rural setting. Fatality rates per vehicle kilometer are 2 to 3 times higher on roads in rural areas than on urban roads of similar design and function (Figure 2-13). Fatality rates on secondary roads (the collector and local classes in Figure 2-13) are 1.5 to 3 times higher than on roads built to Interstate highway standards (limited-access divided highways) (FHWA n.d.).

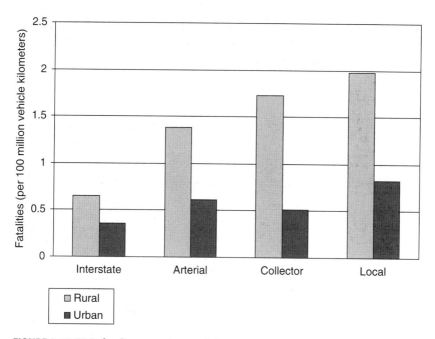

FIGURE 2-13 U.S. fatality rates by road class, 2007. NOTE: Arterials are roads designed to carry relatively high traffic volumes, usually at high speed. Local roads provide direct access to developed property and serve local trips; most are designed for relatively low volumes and low speeds. Collector roads are intermediate in function and design between local roads and arterials. (SOURCE: FHWA n.d.)

Since the states differ in the fraction of travel that is urban and in the distribution of travel by road class, the differences in fatality rates shown in Figure 2-13 account for part of the variation in fatality rates across states. In particular, rural states tend to have high fatality rates. Some states in which both rural and urban rates are lower than the national averages have total rates above the national average because a high proportion of their travel is rural. Similar differences in the mix of travel by road type and land use, and trends over time in this distribution, probably account for some part of observed international differences in fatality rates and trends.

The important policy problems are to determine why these differences by road type exist and what can be done to reduce fatality rates in the higher-risk road segments. Part of the difference in risk presumably relates to speeds (e.g., urban Interstates are more subject to congested, slower-speed operations) and to slower emergency response on rural roads. There may be other systematic differences among road classes in the frequency of alcohol-impaired driving, seat belt and helmet use, mix of vehicle types, and driver age distribution.

Vehicle Mix

The mix of vehicles in the United States has been changing over time and differs from that in many other countries. For example, in the United States, travel by light trucks (a category that includes light vans and sport-utility vehicles) has been growing more rapidly than that for passenger cars. The number of passenger cars involved in fatal crashes each year has been falling, while the number of light trucks involved increased from at least the 1970s until 2005 before beginning to decline. The number of motorcycles involved in fatal crashes increased sharply through 2008 (Figure 2-14). Motorcycle occupant fatalities declined from 2008 to 2009.

Whereas fatal involvement rates for cars and light trucks have been falling, motorcycle fatal involvement rates have risen sharply since the late 1990s. NHTSA reports that the fatal crash involvement rate of motorcycles nearly doubled between 1998 and 2005 (from 14.1 to 27.8 involvements per 100 million motorcycle vehicle kilometers), then declined moderately by 2008 (to 23.0 involvements per 100 million vehicle kilometers). In the 1998 to 2008 period, the fatal involvement rate declined for cars by 30 percent (from 1.2 to 0.8 involvements per

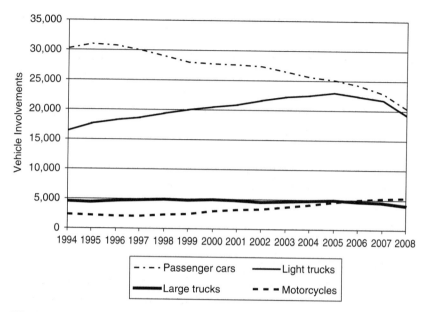

FIGURE 2-14 Number of vehicles involved in fatal crashes, by vehicle type, United States, 1994–2008. (SOURCE: NHTSA 2009, 17.)

100 million vehicle kilometers), for light trucks by 26 percent (from 1.4 to 1.0 involvements per 100 million vehicle kilometers), and for large trucks by 29 percent (from 1.6 to 1.1 involvements per 100 million vehicle kilometers). Thus in 2008, NHTSA reports that the motorcycle fatal involvement rate was 29 times the rate for cars. Estimates of vehicle kilometers of travel of motorcycles are much more uncertain than for other vehicle classes because motorcycles make up only a small fraction (less than 1 percent) of all vehicles on the roads. Consequently, the reliability of the estimated trend of motorcycle fatal involvement rate per vehicle kilometer is unknown. The 1998–2008 increase in motorcycle fatal involvements per registered motorcycle was only 15 percent (NHTSA 2009, 17).

The Business Cycle

A 1984 study by a NHTSA analyst showed that U.S. traffic fatalities over the period 1960–1982 correlated closely with trends in population, employment, and unemployment, once adjustments were made for the

1973–1974 oil embargo and for the imposition of the 55-mph speed limit. The correlation raised the question of whether any of the slowdown in the growth of fatalities since the late 1960s could be attributed to the new federal highway safety programs introduced in the 1960s and 1970s. An update of the analysis (Partyka 1991) found that the model fit to the 1960–1982 data predicted future fatalities poorly: the number of fatalities in 1983–1989 steadily declined compared with the level that extrapolation of the historical relationship with population and employment would predict. (The gap was 19,000 fewer fatalities in 1989.) When the original model was refit to data for 1960 to 1989, some correlation remained, but it was much weaker ($R^2 = .64$ versus .98).

In the 1991 update study, the author speculates that over half of the 1980s decline in fatalities relative to the prior trend might be attributable to the effects of the increase in the use of seat belts and the decrease in the incidence of drunk driving between 1983 and 1989. The author estimates that 9,700 fewer traffic deaths occurred in 1989 than if belt use and drunk driving had remained at 1983 levels. The study results suggest that external economic factors are important in explaining safety trends, and in particular trends over shorter time periods, but do not by themselves fully account for long-term safety trends.

U.S. traffic deaths declined by 9.3 percent from 2007 to 2008 and by 8.9 percent from 2008 to 2009 (NHTSA 2009; NHTSA 2010). These annual declines were two of the largest on record. The U.S. economy entered a recession in 2007, and the declines are consistent with experience in past recessions. The largest annual declines in U.S. traffic fatalities in the period 1971–2007 all occurred in the recession years of the period: 7.0 percent in 1991, 9.9 percent in 1982, and 16.4 percent in 1974 (the latter from the combined effects of recession and the oil embargo). U.S. traffic fatalities increased when economic growth resumed after these past recessions. In the 15 high-income countries shown in Figure 2-2b (not including the United States), total fatalities declined by 9.0 percent from 2007 to 2008 and by 5.6 percent from 2008 to 2009, somewhat less than the U.S. annual declines. The employment impact of the recession that began in 2007 was more severe in the United States than in most other high-income countries: the number of unemployed increased by 102 percent between 2007 and 2009 in the United States, compared with 29 percent in the other

European Organisation for Economic Co-operation and Development member countries (OECD 2010). The significance of these short-period traffic safety trends is difficult to interpret, especially since data on traffic volumes in the period are not available for most countries. As Figure 2-2*b* shows, U.S. annual vehicle kilometers traveled declined from 2007 to 2008; this was the first annual decline since 1980. U.S. vehicle kilometers traveled rose by 0.2 percent from 2008 to 2009 (NHTSA 2010).

Concluding Observations

Differences in demographics, in the urban-versus-rural distribution of road travel (and the associated distribution of travel by congested and uncongested conditions), in the distribution of travel by road class, and in the mix of vehicle types using roads can account for a portion of the differences in fatality rates between the United States and other countries and among the U.S. states. However, these factors may not explain a large share of differences in trends in fatality rates over the past decade or two. Economic cycles and isolated shocks, such as the 1970s energy crisis, can affect the crash rate trend in the short run.

The age distribution of the population is an external factor that is not directly affected by transportation policies, and road designs and the urban-versus-rural distribution of travel change only slowly. However, interventions can be targeted to the segments of road use that are associated with high risk. For example, licensing and testing requirements can target younger and older drivers, and highway network screening to identify and treat high hazard locations can reduce crashes on roads with high crash rates, provided the treatments selected are guided by sound research and evaluation.

REFERENCES

Abbreviations

FHWA	Federal Highway Administration
GAO	General Accounting Office
NHTSA	National Highway Traffic Safety Administration
OECD	Organisation for Economic Co-operation and Development
SWOV	Institute for Road Safety Research (Netherlands)

Adams, J. G. U. 1987. Smeed's Law: Some Further Thoughts. *Traffic Engineering and Control*, Feb., pp. 70–73.

Babcock, M. W., and P. G. Gayle. 2009. State Variation in the Determinants of Motor Vehicle Fatalities. *Journal of the Transportation Research Forum*, Vol. 48, No. 3, Fall, pp. 77–96.

Cabinet Office. 2006. *White Paper on Traffic Safety in Japan 2006: Abridged Edition*. Oct. http://www8.cao.go.jp/koutu/taisaku/h18kou_haku/english/wp2006-1.pdf.

FHWA. n.d. Fatality Rate by Road Function Class Table. http://safety.fhwa.dot.gov/speedmgt/data_facts/.

Fridstrøm, L., and S. Ingebrigsten. 1991. An Aggregate Accident Model Based on Pooled, Regional Time-Series Data. *Accident Analysis and Prevention*, Vol. 23, No. 5, pp. 363–378.

GAO. 2003. *Highway Safety: Research Continues on a Variety of Factors That Contribute to Motor Vehicle Crashes*. March.

Kopits, E., and M. Cropper. 2005a. Traffic Fatalities and Economic Growth. *Accident Analysis and Prevention*, Vol. 37, pp. 169–178.

Kopits, E., and M. Cropper. 2005b. *Why Have Traffic Fatalities Declined in Industrialized Countries? Implications for Pedestrians and Vehicle Occupants*. Policy Research Working Paper 738. World Bank, Aug.

Kopits, E., and M. Cropper. 2008. Why Have Traffic Fatalities Declined in Industrialized Countries? Implications for Pedestrians and Vehicle Occupants. *Journal of Transport Economics and Policy*, Vol. 42, Part 1, Jan., pp. 129–154.

NHTSA. 2008. *Traffic Safety Facts 2007*.

NHTSA. 2009. *Traffic Safety Facts 2008*.

NHTSA. 2010. *Highlights of 2009 Motor Vehicle Crashes*. Aug.

NHTSA. n.d. Fatality Analysis Reporting System Encyclopedia: Fatalities and Fatality Rates by State, 1994–2008. http://www-fars.nhtsa.dot.gov/States/StatesFatalitiesFatalityRates.aspx.

Noland, R. B. 2003. Traffic Fatalities and Injuries: The Effect of Changes in Infrastructure and Other Trends. *Accident Analysis and Prevention*, Vol. 35, No. 4, July, pp. 599–611.

OECD. 2010. Labour Force Statistics (MEI): Harmonised Unemployment Rates and Levels (HURs). http://www.oecd.org/topicstatsportal/0,3398,en_2825_495670_1_1_1_1_1,00.html.

OECD. n.d. International Road Traffic Accident Database. http://www.swov.nl/cognos/cgi-bin/ppdscgi.exe?toc=%2FEnglish%2FIRTAD.

OECD and International Transport Forum. 2006. *Country Reports on Road Safety Performance*. July.

OECD and International Transport Forum. 2010. Press Release: A Record Decade for Road Safety: International Transport Forum at the OECD Publishes Road Death Figures for 33 Countries. Sept. 15.

O'Neill, B., and S. Kyrychenko. 2006. Use and Misuse of Motor Vehicle Crash Death Rates in Assessing Highway Safety Performance. *Traffic Injury Prevention,* Vol. 6, No. 4, Dec., pp. 307–318.

Page, Y. 2001. A Statistical Model to Compare Road Mortality in OECD Countries. *Accident Analysis and Prevention,* Vol. 33, No. 3, May, pp. 371–385.

Partyka, S. C. 1991. Simple Models of Fatality Trends Revisited Seven Years Later. *Accident Analysis and Prevention,* Vol. 23, No. 5, pp. 423–430.

Richter, E. D., P. Barach, E. Ben-Michael, and T. Berman. 2001. Death and Injury from Motor Vehicle Crashes: A Public Health Failure, Not an Achievement. *Injury Prevention,* Vol. 7, pp. 176–178.

SWOV. n.d. Casualties by Mode of Transport. http://www.swov.nl/uk/research/kennisbank/inhoud/00_trend/01_monitor/casualties_by_mode_of_transport.htm.

United Nations. 2002. *World Population Aging: 1950–2050.* Department of Economic and Social Affairs, Population Division.

Zwerling, C., C. Peek-Asa, P. Whitten, S. Choi, N. Sprince, and M. Jones. 2005. Fatal Motor Vehicle Crashes in Rural and Urban Areas: Decomposing Rates into Contributing Factors. *Injury Prevention,* Vol. 11, pp. 24–28.

3

National Safety Programs in Benchmark Countries and the United States

This chapter describes safety practices in other countries that have been credited with producing substantial and rapid reductions in highway deaths. Also described are examples of U.S. efforts at the national level to develop the capabilities that appear to be important in other nations' programs. The first section below summarizes several past international surveys of safety programs by the U.S. Department of Transportation (USDOT) and others that attempted to define the common features of successful programs. The reviews have been influential in drawing attention in the United States to the methods and the successes in other countries. The second describes the features of selected major initiatives in France, Australia, Sweden, and the United Kingdom to illustrate the general features that the past reviews identified. The third describes several recent national-level initiatives to strengthen and reform U.S. traffic safety programs, some of which were influenced by awareness of practices in other countries. These include USDOT-sponsored multistate demonstrations of anti–drunk driving and speed control campaigns and new approaches to safety planning in the states promoted by USDOT and by the American Association of State Highway and Transportation Officials (AASHTO), as reviewed in reports of USDOT and the National Cooperative Highway Research Program (NCHRP). These sources provide a basis for comparison of U.S. state and federal safety programs with those of other countries and indicate the challenges of applying methods used in other countries in the U.S. context.

COMMON ELEMENTS OF BENCHMARK NATIONS' SAFETY PROGRAMS

Chapter 1 cited reports of several U.S. expert groups, sponsored by USDOT and AASHTO, that have surveyed traffic safety practices in other countries with the goal of identifying the essential components of successful programs. At least 10 such groups in the past decade have studied aspects of safety programs or of general management practices (e.g., performance measurement) that are essential elements of safety programs (FHWA 2009c). Boxes 3-1, 3-2, and 3-3 present lists of components as compiled in these reports. These U.S. syntheses highlight largely the same program elements as the comparison of international practices by the Organisation for Economic Co-operation and Development (OECD) Working Group on Achieving Ambitious Road Safety Targets (Box 3-4).

A detailed specification of the elements of road safety management is provided in the World Bank's *Country Guidelines for the Conduct of Road Safety Management Capacity Reviews and the Specification of Lead Agency Reforms, Investment Strategies and Safe System Projects* (Bliss and Breen 2009). The guidelines define a process for countries receiving World Bank assistance to follow in creating a program that reduces traffic casualties. They are based on the recommendations of the United Nations' *World Report on Road Traffic Injury Prevention* (Peden et al. 2004) and on in-depth analyses of safety program organization in seven countries (summarized in the document). The guidelines strongly emphasize the essential step of identifying a lead agency in government and endowing it with the necessary powers, resources, and responsibility. The lead agency is to "guide the national road safety effort, with the power to make decisions, manage resources and coordinate the efforts of all participating sectors of government" (Bliss and Breen 2009, 16).

The generalization that emerges from the past analyses is that successful programs must function effectively at three levels:

- Management and planning: Transportation, public safety, and public health administrators systematically measure progress toward quantitative objectives, direct resources to the most cost-effective uses, coordinate programs across agencies, and communicate with the public and with elected officials to maintain their support. Management commitment (in terms of attention and resources) is sustained and consistent.

BOX 3-1

Lessons from a Decade of Safety Scanning Tours

A summary by Federal Highway Administration (FHWA) safety professionals of the experience of more than a dozen FHWA–AASHTO safety scanning tours conducted over the past decade highlighted five lessons that U.S. states can apply to improve highway safety (Baxter et al. 2005):

1. A top-down commitment by the political leadership is essential for reducing fatalities. Leadership is required to provide direction, accountability, and resources.
2. A "safe systems" approach—that is, identifying the causal factors of crashes in the jurisdiction so that specific strategies can be implemented in response—is a valuable method of planning the program of countermeasures to be applied. This approach will often lead to multidisciplinary countermeasure strategies (e.g., combining actions to change driver behavior with road design improvements).
3. A collaborative process of planning and implementation, reaching out to all relevant agencies and to interested nongovernmental groups, contributes to success. In the United States, this lesson implies that collaboration between the states and local governments, allowing local input to planning and providing local governments with training and assistance, will be vital.
4. Successful national safety strategies are based on a "business approach"; that is, management entails defining objectives, quantifying results, and showing cost-effectiveness.
5. Innovative concepts developed abroad would have safety payoffs if applied in the United States. Examples include the European and Australian Road Assessment Programs and road designs on the principle of the "self-organizing roadway" that are being applied in some European countries—features such as intersection roundabouts that naturally induce drivers to operate their vehicles in a safer manner.

BOX 3-2

Steps to Better Safety Management Through Performance Measurement

A 2004 FHWA–AASHTO scanning tour of Australia, Canada, Japan, and New Zealand observed the use of performance measures in transportation planning and decision making. The study panel concluded that "transportation agencies in the countries visited use performance measures for setting priorities and making investment and management decisions to a greater extent than is typical in the United States" and that "the most impressive application of performance management [was] in road safety, where it was used to identify strategies to reduce fatalities" (MacDonald et al. 2004, ii). The panel attributed these countries' success in reducing road fatalities primarily to systematic management practices founded on goal setting, quantitative performance evaluation, and accountability for results (MacDonald et al. 2004, 60).

The panel identified eight steps that were common to the approaches to safety management in the countries visited (MacDonald et al. 2004, 60–67):

1. Understand the problem. Successful safety programs rely on systematic data collection, analysis, and research to understand the most important crash causes and risk factors on the country's roads.
2. Establish institutional leadership, responsibility, and accountability. Success was associated with direct engagement of the most senior level of government administration and close coordination among the responsible agencies, including transportation agencies, police, and courts.
3. Define desired outcomes. Successful programs have established quantitative targets for total casualties and for specific categories

(continued on next page)

BOX 3-2 *(continued)*
Steps to Better Safety Management Through Performance Measurement

of risks (e.g., high crash frequency locations, young drivers, alcohol-related crashes).

4. Identify performance indicators. Indicators are measures of the desired ultimate outcomes (reduced fatalities, injuries, and crashes) and measures of organizational outputs that are expected to lead to these outcomes (e.g., numbers of enforcement actions taken, frequency of violations of speed limits and other road regulations).
5. Compare performance with experiences of other jurisdictions. Benchmarking is an aid in setting goals and revealing potential problems.
6. Implement a systematic safety data collection and analysis process. Information systems in successful countries were geared toward providing continual and timely monitoring of performance indicators and evaluating the effectiveness of implemented actions.
7. Develop a safety plan and integrate it into agency decision making. Plans in the countries studied define the safety problem, performance targets, and organizational responsibilities and evaluate a range of strategy options for reaching targets. The plans are developed with public input.
8. Monitor effectiveness of implemented actions. Transportation officials in the countries visited had good information on the injury reduction achieved by each implemented strategy.

BOX 3-3

Critical Success Factors

The 2006 FHWA publication *Halving Roadway Fatalities* was inspired by FHWA's 2004 Pacific scanning tour on performance measurement and written by an Australian expert on that country's safety methods. It identifies the following critical success factors and enabling circumstances in the highway safety program of the Australian state of Victoria (Johnston 2006, 17):

1. A sound and realistic plan: The plan must identify and focus on the major problems, propose interventions known to be effective, set objective targets, and provide for monitoring of progress and public accountability.
2. Political and bureaucratic leadership: Committed political leadership must be supported by leadership from each agency responsible for implementing the plan.
3. Integrated implementation: Integrated, coordinated implementation by the various agencies with responsibilities under the plan is an essential ingredient of the Victorian success story.

Beyond these critical factors, the following enabling circumstances in Victoria contributed to the success of the safety program:

- A history of success with interventions based on legislation and enforcement helped create a political willingness to act.
- Relationships have long existed between the traffic safety research community and policy makers, which facilitated planning and created a climate in which scientific evaluations of interventions are routine.
- Extensive public education traffic safety programs have been instrumental in sustaining community concern for road safety and support for effective interventions.
- The media historically have been supportive of effective interventions, which has facilitated political willingness to act.

> BOX 3-4
>
> ## Achieving Ambitious Road Safety Targets
>
> The OECD Working Group on Achieving Ambitious Road Safety Targets compiled reports in uniform format from 39 member states on traffic safety performance and trends, road safety problems, and the content of safety program (OECD and International Transport Forum n.d.). This information supported a comparative analysis of common institutional features of successful safety programs, summarized in the report as follows (OECD and International Transport Forum 2008d, 16–17):
>
>> **Improving Key Institutional Management Functions**
>> Because road safety performance is determined by institutional capacity to implement efficient and effective interventions, targets will be most readily met if a robust management system can be established. This system should have a clear focus on producing agreed results. Results are dependent on interventions which are in turn dependent on institutional management functions. . . . Much of the day to day discussion concerning road safety centres only on interventions. Addressing all parts of the management pyramid [results, interventions, and institutional management functions] brings in such important and often neglected issues as institutional ownership and functional capacities for road safety policies, a safety performance framework for delivery of interventions and accountability for results.
>>
>> The following seven institutional management functions are critical determinants of a country's capacity to achieve results:
>>
>> - Results focus—a strategic focus that links the delivery of interventions with subsequent intermediate and final outcomes. This requires government to designate a lead agency to work with other agencies to:
>>   – Develop management capacity to understand a country's road safety issues.

> - Provide a comprehensive strategy with intermediate and outcome targets.
> - Deliver interventions and target achievements.
> - Review performance.
>
> - Coordination of the key agencies to develop and deliver road safety policy and strategy.
> - Effective legislation to enable desired results to be delivered.
> - Adequate funding and well targeted resource allocation for interventions and related institutional management functions.
> - Promotion of road safety within government and the broader community.
> - Robust and systematic monitoring and evaluation to measure progress.
> - Proactive research and development and knowledge transfer programmes which actively influence improvement in interventions, institutional management functions and performance monitoring.
>
> Above all, the commitment to a results focused approach to road safety management has a critical role in determining the achievement of a country's road safety ambition and related targets.

- Technical implementation of specific countermeasures: A range of measures is employed for regulating driver behavior (for example, enforcement techniques to control speed and drunk driving), maintaining effective emergency response, and incorporating hazard reduction in the design and maintenance of roads. The techniques are generally of proven high effectiveness and often intensively applied.
- Political support and leadership: Elected officials and their appointees establish safety as a priority, provide the necessary legal framework and resources, and hold public-sector managers accountable for results. A degree of public acceptance of the need for rigorous countermeasures has been gained, and system users expect to be held accountable for compliance with laws and regulations.

EXAMPLES OF NATIONAL SAFETY PROGRAMS

Authorities in several countries have summarized their road safety programs by means of timelines showing policy actions and coincident changes in fatalities (Figure 3-1). However, as Figure 2-2 in Chapter 2 shows, declines in fatality rates have been nearly universal; therefore, the assertion that the policy milestones marked on the graphs caused the fatality declines would be more convincing if the links between specific policy changes and specific results could be shown directly. For example, did introduction of more rigorous speed enforcement efforts lead to a measured reduction in speeds, and did lower speed lead to a reduction in the kinds of crashes associated with speeding?

The first two subsections below describe two cases, new safety policies in France since 2002 and in Australia since 1990, where these links are relatively well documented: changes in high-level policy in a national or regional comprehensive safety program led to changes in strategies, resources, and countermeasures applied, and ultimately to changes in injury frequency. As the summaries of evaluations below will indicate, even in highly regarded safety programs, quantitative evaluation of effects of policies is not as systematic or conclusive as would be ideal; also, the committee obtained little information on program expenditures in the benchmark countries. Nonetheless, study of cases where these links are clearest will provide the most useful insights on the changes needed in U.S. practices to produce safety improvement. The final two subsections describe safety programs in Sweden and the United Kingdom. Road fatality rates in those two countries are among the lowest in the world over the past several decades, and both conduct significant national safety strategic planning and monitoring activities.

France

From 1970 to 2008, vehicle kilometers of travel on roads in France increased 200 percent (from 182 billion to 550 billion annually) and highway fatalities declined by 74 percent (from 16,400 to 4,300) (OECD n.d.; OECD and International Transport Forum 2010); consequently, fatalities per vehicle kilometer declined by 91 percent. The rate of 0.78 fatalities per 100 million vehicle kilometers of motor vehicle travel in 2008 was equal to the rate in the United States but remained higher than that in several high-income countries. France has achieved among the steepest declines in fatality rate in the past decade of the OECD countries for which data are available, reducing fatalities per vehicle kilometer by 6.9 percent per year in the 1997–2008 period, compared with 2.4 percent per year in the United States (see Figure 1-1 in Chapter 1). Total fatalities fell by 49 percent from 1997 to 2008, including a 21 percent reduction from 2002 to 2003.

Program Evolution and Planning

During the 1990s, laws and enforcement efforts against unsafe driver behavior were strengthened. In 1992 a point system was introduced that imposed license suspensions for accumulated infractions. The legal limit for a driver's blood alcohol content (BAC) was lowered to 0.7 grams per liter in 1994 and to 0.5 in 1995. Starting in 1994, license points were assessed for failure to wear seat belts. Speeding penalties were increased and speed enforcement intensified in the late 1990s. Highway safety had become an increasingly visible political issue during this period (Documentation Française 2006; OECD and ECMT 2006a, 6).

The earlier efforts were substantially reinforced after the president of France announced in 2002 that road safety would be one of the priority initiatives of his new term of office. Political sponsorship at the highest level allowed prompt action on a plan for reducing crashes by intensified enforcement that government agencies had been developing for a period of years (Documentation Française 2006; OECD and ECMT 2006a, 3). Political commitment has been sustained. The Interministerial Committee on Road Safety that directs the program has twice-yearly meetings chaired by the prime minister. It sets government policy on highway safety with the participation of the two national police agencies, the transportation agency, the justice ministry, the health ministry, and the safety statistical agency.

The centerpiece of the initiative is an automated speed limit enforcement system. One thousand radar and camera apparatuses were in operation by 2005, 1,850 by 2007, and 2,300 by April 2009. Two thousand additions were planned between 2008 and 2012 (Documentation Française 2006; CISR 2006, 6; OECD and International Transport Forum 2008a; Carnis 2008; ONISR 2009a). Sites that had high frequencies of speed-related crashes and that met other criteria were identified as locations for automated speed enforcement. Most sites are on undivided

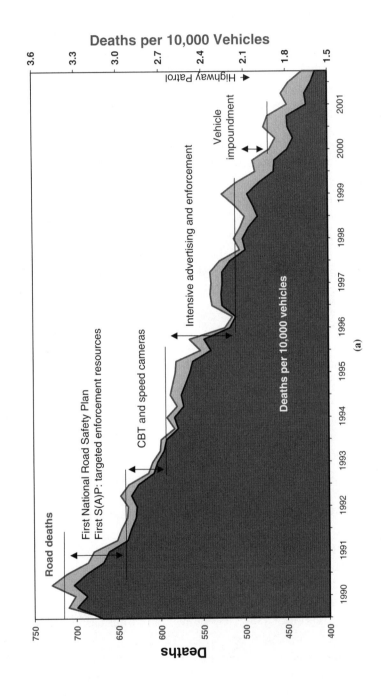

(a)

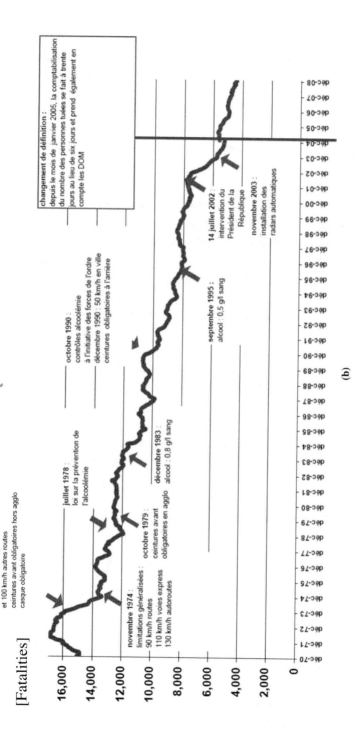

FIGURE 3-1 Safety policy timelines: (*a*) New Zealand and (*b*) France. [SOURCES: Fitzgerald 2002 (New Zealand), reproduced courtesy of the New Zealand Transport Agency; *La Sécurité Routière en France: Bilan de l'Année 2008*, ONISR 2009, p. 15 (France), reproduced with permission.]

roads with two-way traffic (ONISR 2005, 4). Both fixed and movable cameras are deployed. A national speed enforcement center monitors the enforcement devices via a dedicated telecommunication network, issues citations, and collects fines.

The other principal measures in the current French initiative are increased penalties for drunk driving and for failure to use seat belts or motorcycle helmets, introduction of a probationary 6-month license for new drivers, and a road safety infrastructure improvement program. The selection of emphasis areas was guided by analyses that showed that speed and alcohol were contributing factors in large shares of fatal crashes (Raynal 2003; ONISR 2005, 6).

France's annual traffic safety review highlights interventions aimed at driver behavior. However, the report acknowledges (ONISR 2008, 22) that among the most effective available interventions are improvements to infrastructure, citing in particular treatment of roadside obstacles and separation (e.g., by barriers) of opposing lanes on high-volume two-lane roads. It does not describe the extent of such improvements in France.

A safety-motivated infrastructure program that is documented is roundabout installation at road junctions. The number of roundabouts in France increased from 10,000 in 1993 to 30,000 in 2008, and roundabouts continue to be installed at an average rate of 1,000 per year (Scrase 2008; Guichet 2005). French evaluations indicate that installing a roundabout at an intersection reduces the rate of injury crashes by at least 50 percent, and studies in the United States and other countries have reported similar benefits (Fuller 2008). A benefit–cost evaluation of the French roundabout program has not been conducted (Scrase 2008, 3), but these intersection improvements and programs to reduce roadside hazards and install lane separation probably have contributed to the reduction in France's fatality rate.

Performance Monitoring

The chronology of actions alone does not reveal what role the recent safety initiative has played in producing the downward trend in road fatalities. The general trend has been established for decades and the principal measures of the initiative were not in full force until 2004, whereas the sharpest 1-year reduction in fatalities was from 2002 to 2003. However, data are available that allow a more detailed examination of program impacts. France has strong capabilities for evaluating the effects of safety countermeasures by means of its centralized, nationwide program of monitoring of highway crashes, speeds, and enforcement activities. Data are rapidly collected, analyzed, and published; for example, monthly reports on traffic injuries and fatalities and three-times-yearly reports on speed trends by road class and vehicle type are published shortly after the end of the reporting periods (ONISR 2009b).

Enforcement data document the substantial increase in effort after the start of the 2002 initiative. Speeding citations, which had increased 31 percent from 2000 to 2003, nearly doubled from 2003 to 2004, the result of the automated enforcement system. The total of license point penalties assessed increased 44 percent in 2004 compared with 2003, and license suspensions for accumulated points penalties increased 87 percent. These increases were largely the result of speed enforcement; the number of alcohol tests administered increased only 5 percent in 2004 (OECD and ECMT 2006a; ONISR 2005; ONISR 2008).

Speed data appear to show the results of stepped-up enforcement. The percentage of light vehicles in free-flowing traffic exceeding the speed limit by more than 10 km/h from 2000 to 2008 was as follows (ONISR 2006b; ONISR 2009a; ONISR 2010):

Year	Percentage More Than 10 km/h over Limit	Year	Percentage More Than 10 km/h over Limit
2000	36	2005	19
2001	36	2006	15
2002	34	2007	14
2003	27	2008 (8 months)	12
2004	21	2009	10

Measurements for monitoring speed trends are taken independently of measurements for enforcement and at locations not in proximity to cameras.

The overall level of enforcement effort, growth in enforcement effort over the past decade, and progress in the degree of compliance with traffic laws have been substantial. For example, moving violations cited increased by 166 percent, license suspensions by 137 percent, and alcohol tests by 31 percent from 1998 to 2007. Vehicle kilometers of road travel increased by 11 percent over the period. The alcohol test rate was 279 tests per thousand drivers in 2007 (Table 3-1). The increasing rate of positive alcohol tests in spite of increased testing frequency is attributed to better targeting of testing with respect to location and time (ONISR 2008, 166).

TABLE 3-1 Enforcement Level of Effort in France, 1998 and 2007

	Number (thousands) 1998	Number (thousands) 2007	Percent Change, 1998–2007	Number per 1,000 Drivers, 2007
Total moving violations cited	4,884	12,972	+166	322
Speed limit violations	1,084	8,098	+647	201
Failure to wear seat belt	635	407	−36	10
Driver's license suspensions for impaired driving, speeding, or points	110	261	+137	6
Alcohol tests	8,178	11,230	+29	279
Preventive test (i.e., not subsequent to crash or violation)	6,836	8,941	+31	222
Positive tests	167	376	+125	9
Fatalities	8.49	4.62	−49	
Licensed drivers		40,322		

NOTE: Citations include those issued by the two national police forces, which have jurisdiction on all roads and streets and account for most enforcement activity. Citations by municipal police are not included.
SOURCE: ONISR 2008, 14, 165–168, 172.

Seat belt and motorcycle helmet use rates are among the highest in the world. Belt use by front seat occupants is 98 percent overall, 99 percent on autoroutes, and 97 percent in urban areas. Helmet use is 89 to 99 percent depending on the road class (ONISR 2008, 135, 161, 202). These relatively high rates presumably reflect enforcement effort.

The intensity of enforcement is evidently considerably higher in France than in the United States, although comparison is difficult because U.S. jurisdictions generally do not monitor enforcement systematically or comprehensively. France's capability for collection, analysis, and publication of nationwide data on intermediate outputs and measures of enforcement effort is integral to its safety program and is in marked contrast with U.S. practices. Intermediate output measures of enforcement efforts are measures of behavior change caused by the enforcement (e.g., changes in speed and in belt use in response to enforcement). An intermediate output measure for a road infrastructure improvement program would be quantities of kinds of safety-enhancing features installed (e.g., numbers of roundabouts replacing intersections).

As an illustrative comparison, the state of Pennsylvania reports that in 2008, at all sobriety checkpoints and roving patrols targeting impaired driving conducted by state and local police, there were 227,000 "motorist contacts" (i.e., drivers stopped and observed by police), a rate of 26 motorists contacted per 1,000 licensed drivers (PennDOT n.d., 16; FHWA 2009b, Table DL-1C). Most motorists contacted would not have been administered alcohol tests. The French rate (Table 3-1) of 222 drivers per 1,000 subjected to preventive alcohol tests (i.e., tests not subsequent to a crash or citation) is 10 times the Pennsylvania rate of motorist contacts. In New York State in 2007, 64 speeding tickets per 1,000 licensed drivers were issued by state and local police (New York State Governor's Traffic Safety Committee 2008, 22). Perhaps surprisingly, in view of the extent of its automated speed control system, the French rate was only three times higher, 201 tickets per 1,000 drivers. The rate of ticketing for failure to wear seat belts in 2007 was higher in New York than in France (41 per 1,000 drivers in New York versus 10 in France), probably reflecting the high rate of belt use in France (98 percent for front seat occupants compared with 83 percent in New York in 2007).

Evaluations

The safety statistical agency has estimated that 40 percent of the reduction of fatalities in 2003 (Chapelon 2004) and 75 percent of the total reduction in casualties from 2002 through 2005 (CISR 2006, 6; ONISR 2006a) can be attributed to speed reductions over the period. The speed and enforcement data suggest that the speed reduction was the result of the enforcement effort. Reduced drunk driving, increased use of seat belts, a slowing of the rate of traffic growth, and unidentified factors also are reported to have contributed to the fatality decline (Chapelon 2004). The estimates of the effect of the speed control program were not based on analysis of the correlation between changes in speed and changes in fatalities on French roads in the period of introduction of the program. Rather, they were derived from a speed-versus-fatalities relationship extracted from a review of the accident research literature, which was then applied to the observed change in speed on French roads in the period (ONISR 2006a, 44).

Summary Observations

At least four circumstances seem to have been key to France's recent successful effort to reduce traffic fatalities. First, the program has received sustained high-level political direction. Second, centralization of administration, together with the parliamentary system of government, allows the government to act quickly and on a nationwide scale to implement policies and coordinate activities among agencies and to plan and carry out a consistent long-term strategy. Third, the government's ability to take effective action has been facilitated by strong capabilities for data collection, evaluation, research, and planning. The speed and efficiency of data collection are an example of the advantages of centralization.

Finally, public attitudes and public communication probably have been major factors in the outcome of the program. With 2,300 cameras on 950,000 km of roads, the French automatic speed enforcement network is not very dense, yet the overall enforcement effort has produced a worthwhile change in driver behavior. Substantial publicity has accompanied the speed camera program and is believed to have amplified its effect. To recruit support, the government has undertaken an outreach program aimed at businesses affected by work-related traffic casualties, awards grants to numerous private safety advocacy organizations, and provides technical assistance to local authorities (ONISR 2008, 27). Polling is reported to show strong public support of automated enforcement (OECD and ECMT 2006a, 9). The points system penalties are believed to be an effective deterrent because large numbers of drivers who have received speeding citations now face the threat of license suspension if cited again.

Australia

Australia has achieved fatality rate reductions typical of the high-income countries and greater than those attained in the United States in the past decade. The fatality rate per kilometer of travel, more than 50 percent higher than the U.S. rate in the 1970s, has been lower than the U.S. rate since 2001 (see Figure 2-2 in Chapter 2). Traffic fatalities fell from 1,767 in 1997 to 1,441 in 2008, an 18 percent decline, while traffic grew by 33 percent in the period (OECD n.d.; OECD and International Transport Forum 2010).

Primary responsibility for the road system and for road safety falls on the states and territories in Australia. The recent state safety plans harmonize with a national road safety strategy developed jointly by the states and territories and the national government in 2001 through the Australian

Transport Council. The council's 2009–2010 Action Plan highlights a safe system framework, which requires that safety programs direct actions at the four objectives of safer speeds, safer roads and roadsides, safer vehicles, and safer road users (Australian Transport Council 2008).

Victoria Safety Program Evolution and Planning

The state of Victoria in southeastern Australia, whose capital is Melbourne, achieved a greater percentage reduction in traffic fatalities than the nation as whole in the period 1988–2004 (Johnston 2006, 7). The state's safety program has influenced the views of U.S. transportation administrators on the possibilities for major reductions in traffic fatalities. The panel that conducted FHWA's 2004 Pacific scanning tour on transportation performance measures made the following observation (MacDonald et al. 2004, 45):

> [P]erhaps the most impressive application of a performance-based planning and decisionmaking process of any site visited . . . [is] Victoria's road safety program. The program has existed for many years, providing the opportunity to identify through absolute numbers and trends what impact it has had in achieving safety goals.

FHWA published its short report, *Halving Roadway Fatalities*, with a description of the Victoria experience and lessons for the United States (Johnston 2006), to publicize the case to a nonspecialist audience.

The genesis of the current approach to highway safety, according to the FHWA report, was in the "public outcry" that followed a sharp rise in highway fatalities in the late 1980s. State government ministers were compelled to become directly involved in addressing the problem. More or less continual high-level political support, driven by public demand for improvement and by "the personal beliefs of the ministers," is reported to have been an essential element of the program from that time (Johnston 2006, 8–9).

The state's first formal traffic safety strategy was developed in 1990. Its three elements were an inventory of the safety interventions available as well as measures that would require legislation to implement; a quantitative target for reduction in fatalities; and identification of needs for interagency coordination among the highway agency, the police, the justice department, and the state-monopoly highway injury insurance agency.

As in all the Australian states, a single state police agency is responsible for all enforcement.

From 1990 to 1992, a series of laws and regulations strengthened enforcement. Random alcohol testing for drivers was greatly increased (the test rate today is 300 per 1,000 licensed drivers annually). The penalty of immediate license suspension for a second drunk driving offense was established. The use of cameras for speed enforcement was introduced, and drivers were penalized points toward license suspension for speed camera violations. For new drivers, the probationary period for new licenses was increased to 3 years and a blood alcohol limit of zero was set for the first 3 years of a new license. Finally, a permanent program of public education was established to inform the public about safety measures and to build public support for safety (Johnston 2006, 9–10).

A similar series of events occurred in the late 1990s. After declining in the early 1990s, the annual fatality trend had again leveled off, and a new government declared that reducing fatalities was a priority. In 2000–2004, new regulations lowered the urban speed limit, increased penalties for speeding, and required interlock devices on vehicles of repeat drunk drivers. The state greatly increased the density of the speed camera system and began random driver testing for drug use. Subsequently, fatalities resumed a downward trend. Although the new measures and public information campaigns emphasize driver behavior controls, the safety program also involves safety-enhancing infrastructure improvements (Johnston 2006, 10–11).

The state's 2002–2007 strategic plan committed to a 20 percent reduction in annual deaths and serious injuries over the term of the plan and promised specific initiatives in 17 program areas, including speeding, drunk driving, road infrastructure, vehicle occupant protection, postcrash trauma treatment, older and younger drivers, community involvement, and crash information systems (State Government of Victoria 2001). Implementing, enforcing, and providing public information about the new 50-km/h speed limit in urban areas were major components of the strategy. The fatality reduction target was exceeded (State Government of Victoria 2008, 4). The current plan calls for reducing annual fatalities by 6 percent during the period 2008–2017. The major initiatives are to be a requirement for all new vehicles registered in the state to be equipped with electronic stability control and head-protecting devices (e.g., side curtain air bags), new media campaigns, a new graduated licensing system, a substantial infrastructure investment program aimed at reducing crash risks, and stepped-up enforcement aimed at drug-impaired driving and other priority targets. The state describes its comprehensive strategy, involving improvements in the safety of roads, vehicles, and users, as the safe system approach (State Government of Victoria 2008).

Program plans and progress reports on the various initiatives are published periodically during the life of each strategic plan. Funding has been provided in part by the Transport Accident Commission, the state's injury insurance enterprise.

Performance Monitoring

The 2004 U.S. scanning tour panel was impressed especially by the Victoria safety program's use of performance measures, that is, quantitative targets established for enforcement actions and outputs and for reductions in crashes and fatalities. The panel's report gives examples of the use of performance measures:

- Commitment to a quantitative goal (e.g., the 20 percent improvement goal in the 2002–2007 strategic plan) as part of a strategic plan that defines the initiatives that will be used to reach it;
- Regular benchmarking of the state's safety experience by comparison with other Australian states and other countries;
- The applications of the highway agency's Road Crash Information System, which provides timely information on high crash frequency locations by type of crash, regular updates on crash frequencies and other performance measures, and information on the progress of projects in the safety program; and
- Regular evaluation of the impacts of each element of the safety program. For example, systematically collected speed data in Melbourne allow the state police to track in detail the effectiveness of speed cameras and other enforcement measures in implementing the new reduced urban speed limits.

In the state of South Australia, the transport department publishes periodic summary reports on performance indicators for level of enforcement effort and outcomes relating to speed, alcohol- and drug-impaired driving, and seat belts. For example, the 2007 report's monitoring measures on impaired driving enforcement include the following (Wundersitz et al. 2009):

- Number of alcohol tests administered, 678,000;
- Alcohol tests per 1,000 licensed drivers, 632; and
- Illegal BAC detected (percent of tests), 0.9.

The state's safety program emphasizes driver behavior controls, including measures against impaired driving and control of speed through lowering speed limits and strengthening enforcement in cities with the use of speed cameras. It also espouses the safe system approach, using engineering measures to make roads more forgiving (State Government of South Australia 2008). Some performance indicators relevant to this program are not included in the periodic reports; for example, roadside seat belt use surveys are not regularly conducted, and historical data on vehicle speeds do not exist. In 2007, the state began a systematic program of speed measurement to observe the effects of its speed reduction countermeasures (Wundersitz et al. 2009, 60). The South Australia performance indicators report is noteworthy not only for the high level of enforcement intensity it documents but also as an illustration of the kind of routine performance monitoring that is considered necessary in support of the management of Australian safety programs.

Evaluations

Victoria's safety program and its record of fatality reduction are a compelling success story. However, to understand the basis of the safety improvement record and to learn from it, the evidence on how the enforcement program changed speeding, drunk driving, and other high-risk behaviors and on how changes in behavior affected the frequency of casualties in crashes linked to these behaviors must be examined. The effects of the safety initiatives in Victoria and of similar measures in the state of Queensland have been estimated in a series of statistical analyses conducted at the Monash University Accident Research Centre.

For the earlier phase of the Victoria program, an evaluation study supported by the state and by the automobile club estimated the contributions of safety interventions and external factors to changes in the frequency of serious casualty crashes between 1983 and 1996 by means of regression analysis based on monthly data (Newstead et al. 1998). Most of the decline was between 1988 and 1992, the period during which the new safety programs were introduced. The factors considered and the estimated percentage point contributions to the overall 43-percent reduction in serious casualty crash frequency between 1988 and 1996 are as follows:

- Speed camera operation (measured by the number of speeding tickets issued), 11;
- Television advertising targeting speeding (based on a measure derived from television ratings), 6;
- Drunk driving enforcement (the combined effect of numbers of roadside breath tests conducted and the volume of media publicity with a theme of drunk driving), 10;
- Alcohol sales (which declined substantially over the period), 10;
- Unemployment rate (which increased over the period), 10; and
- Highway black spot (i.e., high hazard location) treatments (cumulative number of locations treated since 1988), 6.

The percentage point impacts of the individual factors do not add to the total 43 percent because the cumulative effects are multiplicative. The analysis credited all road safety programs together with a 29 percent reduction and external factors (changes in alcohol sales and unemployment) with a 19 percent reduction. The effect of high hazard location treatments was estimated by judgment rather than in the regression analysis. The estimated 16 percent decline in fatalities in Victoria attributable to the multiyear speed enforcement and publicity program is comparable with the estimate for the French speed program, cited in the previous section, of a 20 percent reduction after 3 years. This analysis illustrates the importance of monitoring of enforcement effort as well as of crashes in evaluating and managing the safety program.

A second study evaluated the effect of new speed enforcement initiatives in Victoria in 2001 to 2003, during the period in which the speed limit on local streets was lowered from 60 to 50 km/h (D'Elia et al. 2007). In the same period, the hours of operation of speed cameras were increased, the speed detection threshold on the cameras was lowered, and advertising was increased. The method was generally similar to that of the 1998 study: a set of regression analyses related monthly crashes on each of several road categories to a set of external socioeconomic factors and the presence or absence of the countermeasure package. The study concluded that the package reduced the total of casualty crashes during the period by 3.8 percent. The effect was concentrated in metropolitan Melbourne and in speed zones with 60-, 50-, and 40-km/h speed limits. Estimates of effects in shorter time periods indicated that the reduction in casualty crashes was increasing throughout the 2001–2003 period.

With regard to the impact of the most recent efforts, the Victoria government asserts that the strategy laid out in the 2002–2007 safety plan "has played a vital part in substantially reducing the state's road toll and has prevented some 580 deaths" (State Government of Victoria 2008, 4). This estimate appears to be derived by extrapolating the pre-2002 death rate rather than by the quantitative techniques of the earlier evaluations.

The effect of the similar package of safety measures in the Australian state of Queensland also has been evaluated (Newstead et al. 2004). The intervention package was to include increased hours of operation of speed cameras; an increase in publicity (although the data show that advertising weighted by audience ratings actually was lower in the treatment period than previously); and an increase in on-road police enforcement against drunk driving, speeding, and failure to wear seat belts. By using a statistical analysis technique similar to those of the Victoria studies, the Queensland study estimated that the package had reduced the number of fatal and severe injury crashes in the state by 13 percent during the initial application period of December 2002 through January 2004. The analysis estimated the individual effects of the components of the intervention package and found that the largest effect was attributable to increased use of speed cameras. The doubling of total hours of speed camera enforcement as part of the intervention package was associated with a 9 percent decrease in fatal and serious injury crashes.

These statistical analyses would have provided greater insight if impacts of the countermeasures on driving speeds and on driver BAC, as well as on casualty crashes, had been estimated. Ideally, such analyses would be done routinely and frequently, rather than at multiyear intervals, as part of the management oversight of the programs. A more detailed examination of how each state's philosophy of following evidence-based strategies has worked in practice (for example, how evidence is used to adjust safety programs in progress) also would be valuable. The evaluations of program effectiveness appear to have been conducted at irregular intervals, and it is not clear how their results have affected the evolution of the safety programs.

Sweden

Sweden's rate of traffic fatalities per vehicle kilometer has been among the lowest of the OECD countries for as long as data have been available and has been lower than the U.S. rate since the late 1970s. The 2008 rate was 0.51 fatalities per 100 million vehicle kilometers, compared with 0.78 in the United States and 0.70 for the 15 non-U.S. OECD countries shown in Figure 2-2b. Sweden also has reduced its rate faster than the United States in the past decade (Figure 1-1). A small country (population of 9 million) with low population density outside the urban centers, Sweden is in some respects more comparable geographically with Canada and Australia than with the large European countries.

Vision Zero has been the philosophy guiding road safety programs since it was established by act of the parliament in 1997. The policy sets zero road fatalities and injuries as the appropriate goal of transportation programs and places responsibility on road authorities and vehicle regulators for providing a transportation system that is forgiving of the errors of drivers. The same act of parliament set a goal of a 50 percent reduction in annual traffic deaths by 2007 (Breen et al. 2007, 4–5). The actual reduction was 7 percent (from 541 to 471), while road travel increased 17 percent (from 67 billion to 78 billion vehicle kilometers) (OECD n.d.).

In practice, Sweden has adopted enforcement strategies common in the benchmark nations. Priorities are control of alcohol-impaired driving and of speed. An automated speed enforcement system has been installed nationwide, and speed limits are being selectively reduced. Seven hundred speed cameras in operation in 2006 were estimated to prevent 16 deaths annually (Breen et al. 2007, 26). Expansion of the system is under study, and a plan for selective speed limit reductions is being developed (OECD and International Transport Forum 2008b, 3). High-frequency alcohol testing is carried out. The rate was 380 tests per 1,000 licensed drivers in 2006 (Breen et al. 2007, 53), higher than in France. The legal BAC limit is 0.2 grams per liter (0.02 percent), the lowest in Europe.

The Vision Zero philosophy has led to emphasis on road design. Safety is a primary design criterion. Roads are to be built or reconstructed with features that ensure low casualty risk, and safety considerations play a major role in determining the selection of infrastructure investment projects. Safe design of the highway system has entailed various traffic-calming measures and rules to minimize conflicts between motorized and nonmotorized traffic. For example, roundabouts are replacing simple intersections with traffic lights, pedestrians and cyclists are separated from motor vehicles by barriers, opposing lanes are divided by barriers, and alignments incorporate features to force driver attentiveness (e.g., gentle curves in place of long straightaways). A total of 1,500 km of roads of the 2+1 lane design (a three-lane road on which opposing directions have access to the center lane in alternation) has been built since 1998 (Johansson 2007). In general, designs are meant to discourage risky behavior and inattention and to mitigate the consequences of driver errors.

Present road and safety plans provide a substantial budget for safety-related capital improvements to roads, including intersection and shoulder modifications and median barriers (OECD and International Transport Forum 2008b, 4). Budget increases have also allowed installation of the speed camera system and an increase in safety research (Breen et al. 2007, 20).

The Vision Zero strategy also encompasses vehicle design. Motor vehicle manufacturing is an important industry in Sweden. New vehicle safety standards are largely determined uniformly within the European Union. More than half of new cars sold in Sweden meet the highest level of the European occupant protection rating scheme (Breen et al. 2007, 27–28).

Planning emphasizes setting and measuring progress toward targets for intermediate outputs. The targets include kilometers of road with median barriers installed, average traffic speeds, proportion of drivers involved in fatal crashes who are alcohol-impaired, proportion of vehicle occupants wearing seat belts, proportion of motorcyclists wearing helmets, and proportion of total travel that is in vehicles meeting the European four-star crashworthiness rating (OECD and International Transport Forum 2008b, 13). Planning includes projections of the reductions in deaths that are expected from meeting each of the intermediate targets. In this way the plan presents a credible pathway to attaining the overall casualty reduction goal by means of a program of interventions. Sweden has a well-developed system for monitoring these intermediate output measures (Breen et al. 2007, 55–56).

Provisions for external review reinforce accountability of the program managers. A government entity, the Traffic Inspectorate, has been created as an independent review agency responsible for examining and issuing reports on the road authority's safety program (Breen et al. 2007, 22). The government in 2007 invited an independent panel of international experts to review its road safety program and recommend improvements (Breen et al. 2007). The expert panel followed a program review protocol developed by the World Bank. The panel report, while acknowledging Sweden's leadership in safety program management and results, points out gaps and inadequacies in planning and management and recommends improvements.

In summary, the Swedish traffic safety program shows similarities to that of France: it is centralized, enforcement is at a high level of intensity, and capabilities are strong for targeting and monitoring of intermediate outputs. Sweden has not achieved the rapid rate of decline in the fatality rate that France has experienced, but the absolute rate has been much lower than in France throughout the past 30 years. As in France, increased resources for enforcement together with automation have coincided with a continued decline in the fatality rate.

United Kingdom

The historical crash experience of the United Kingdom is similar to that of Australia, the Netherlands, and the Scandinavian countries: the fatality rate per vehicle kilometer was higher than in the United States in the 1970s and earlier and close to the U.S. rate in the 1980s; since the late 1980s the rate has been lower than in the United States, and it is still declining more rapidly than the U.S. rate (Figure 2-2). The 2008 rate was 0.52 deaths per 100 million vehicle kilometers. Traffic deaths in 2008 were 2,600, a 29 percent decline from 1997 (OECD and International Transport Forum 2010).

Laws and enforcement practices are largely uniform nationwide, although Scotland has autonomy in certain matters and local government authorities have management responsibilities. The police force is national, but with decentralized administration. The national government manages a £27 million/year traffic safety publicity program, organized around the THINK! campaign (DfT 2008a, 178).

Programs to achieve quantitative safety goals are proposed as part of safety planning in the United Kingdom. The first official target, announced in 1987, called for a one-third reduction in road accident casualties by 2000 (DfT 2008b, 176). In fact, casualties of all severities rose by 3 percent in the period, but fatalities fell by 33 percent, while traffic grew by 33 percent (DfT 2008b, 102). The current target, first declared in 2000, is a 40 percent reduction in deaths and serious injuries in road accidents by 2010 compared with the average for 1994–1998. The trend through 2007 suggests that this target will be met, although the percentage reduction in deaths probably will be considerably smaller (DfT 2008b, 5).

A 2000 research study by the U.K. Transport Research Laboratory demonstrated, by using U.K. data, how a plan could be developed on the basis of quantitative estimates of gains expected from specific planned interventions (Broughton et al. 2000). The 2000 study estimated historical relationships between particular safety initiatives and changes in crash frequency in the United Kingdom and applied the relationships in a hypothetical plan to project the safety impact of future safety measures that the authors judged to be feasible and consistent with government policy. In practice, planning targets do not appear to be tied explicitly to projected gains from interventions (DfT 2007; Broughton and Buckle 2008). Nonetheless, progress toward the plan is regularly reviewed, and commitments have been made to increase enforcement and take additional measures to maintain progress toward the goals (DfT 2007, 3–5; DfT 2008b, 5).

A major new safety initiative planned is a fundamental reform in driver training and licensing practices, supported by results of new research on the relationship of training to the crash record of young drivers (OECD and International Transport Forum 2008c, 11; DfT 2007, 33–35).

As in all the benchmark countries, speed control is a major enforcement priority. Penalty points for speeding have been increased recently, and the use of speed zones is being expanded (OECD and International Transport Forum 2008c, 3–4). Speed enforcement cameras have been in use since 1992 (DfT 2008b, 176). In 2006, 1.96 million speeding citations were issued (Fiti et al. 2008, 6), a rate of 58 citations per 1,000 licensed drivers (DfT 2009b, 12) (Table 3-2), about the same as the rate of speed-

TABLE 3-2 Enforcement Level of Effort in Great Britain, 1999 and 2006

	Number (thousands) 1999	2006	Percent Change, 1999–2006	Number per 1,000 Drivers, 2006
Total motoring offenses dealt with by police, excluding parking offenses	3,722	4,355	+17	129
Speed limit violations	995	1,960	+97	58
Failure to wear seat belt		232		7
Driving license disqualifications for specific offenses or points	190	192	+1	6
Alcohol screening breath tests (England and Wales only)	765	602	−21	18
Positive tests	94	106	+12	3
Fatalities	3.42	3.17	−7	
Licensed drivers	31,400	33,700	+7	

SOURCES: Fiti et al. 2008, 8, 22, 36, 38; DfT 2009b, 12; DfT 2008b, 102.

ing citations in New York State and about one-fourth the rate in France. Nearly 90 percent of speeding offenses cited are identified by cameras (Fiti et al. 2008, 15).

A nationwide speed survey is conducted periodically, and annual reports are published on speeds and congestion. (No such report exists in the United States at the federal level, and only a few states have similar data.) The 2009 report showed that from 1998 to 2008, the percentage of cars exceeding the speed limit (by any margin) declined consistently on roads posted at 30 mph and on divided highways other than motorways but changed little on other roads (DfT 2009a, 40). On motorways, 18 percent of vehicles exceeded the speed limit by more than 10 mph (16 km/h); on undivided roads with a 60-mph posted limit, 2 percent exceeded the limit by more than 10 mph (16 km/h) in 2007 (DfT 2008c, 21).

Speed cameras are installed at 5,500 sites (DfT 2008c, 23). Under a management and funding arrangement introduced in 2000, the cameras were paid for from speeding fine revenue through a fund controlled by the national government and overseen by an independent board. The assent and cooperation of local government authorities were required to install and operate speed cameras (PA Consulting Group and UCL 2005, 2–18). This arrangement funded expansion of the system. Since 2007, speed camera funding has been integrated with the general national safety program, and local authorities are responsible for camera deployment and operation (Fiti et al. 2008, 15).

A 2005 study evaluated the effect of the U.K. safety camera program in the period 2000–2004 (PA Consulting Group and UCL 2005). Safety cameras include speed cameras and red light cameras, but 93 percent of offenses identified by the cameras are for speeding (Fiti et al. 2008, 15). The method of the U.K. study differs from that of the evaluations of the French and Australian speed control programs described in the previous sections, which estimated impacts over an entire national or regional road system. In contrast, the U.K. study estimated impacts confined to camera sites. A site is defined as a stretch of road in proximity to a camera installation, which varies in length depending on the type of camera installation (50 meters for a red light camera, 400 to 1,500 meters for a fixed speed camera, and 3 to 10 km for a two-camera site that measures vehicle travel time between two cameras). All camera installation sites were chosen according to defined criteria with regard to casualty risk. The total of deaths and serious injuries at all camera sites is on the order of 1 percent of the nationwide total (PA Consulting Group and UCL 2005, 39; DfT 2007, 9).

The 2005 study estimated that the frequency of serious injuries and deaths was reduced by 42 percent at the camera sites, over and above the nationwide trend of a 3.5 percent per year reduction in frequency of deaths and serious injuries. That is, the analysis assumed that the camera installations were not influencing the national trend. Total fatalities were reduced by an estimated 100 per year and serious injuries by 1,745 per year. Average speed at sites dropped 6 percent after introduction of cameras, and incidence of speeding fell by 91 percent at sites with permanent cameras (PA Consulting Group and UCL 2005, 5–6). The study estimates the total cost to the government of installing and operating the camera enforcement system (not allowing for fine receipts) as £175 million over 2000–2004 (PA Consulting Group and UCL 2005, 81).

This estimated change in casualty frequency does not allow for the effect of regression to the mean. Sites selected because they have unusually high crash frequencies in a period are likely to have more nearly average crash frequency in a subsequent period. The study estimated that at urban sites, regression to the mean accounted for about three-fourths of the reduction in fatalities and serious injuries, after allowing for the nationwide trend (PA Consulting Group and UCL 2005, 154–155).

The legal per se BAC limit is 0.08 percent, the same as in the United States and Canada and higher than in any other high-income country. A BAC limit was first enacted in 1967, 11 years before all U.S. states had such a limit. As in the United States, random alcohol testing is not allowed. By law, police can test any driver involved in an accident and can administer a roadside breath test to any driver who has committed a moving traffic offense or who is reasonably suspected to have used alcohol (DfT 2008b, 37). The frequency of roadside screening breath tests (tests following a moving traffic offense or accident or conducted because of suspicion of alcohol use) for England and Wales in 2007 was 21 per 1,000 licensed drivers, 1/10th the rate in France and 1/30th the rate in South Australia. The government periodically conducts scientifically designed roadside surveys to measure the prevalence of alcohol impairment among all drivers (DfT 2008c, 33, 43, 54, 57). Limited surveying has been conducted to measure the prevalence of drug-impaired driving (Jackson and Hilditch 2010, 24–28).

Seat belt use is high, as is the case throughout Europe. According to the 2007 survey, 94 percent of car drivers, 95 percent of front seat passengers, and 69 percent of adult rear seat passengers wear belts. The front seat use rate has been constant since belt use was made mandatory in 1983 (DfT n.d.).

Safer infrastructure is one of the 10 themes of the government's current national road safety strategy. According to the summary of infrastructure programs in the most recent progress report on the strategy (DfT 2007, 43–47), the emphasis of infrastructure safety is on reducing hazards at spot locations and in corridors on existing facilities. The progress report does not describe a philosophy of rethinking basic road design principles from the point of view of safety, as the Swedish Vision Zero documents propose. Local authorities are responsible for maintenance and safety improvements on local roads. Local spending and safety results are regularly monitored by the national government. According to the safety strategy progress report, an analysis of local spending for specifically safety-motivated improvements in infrastructure concluded that these investments are earning a 300 percent rate of return. Such specifically safety-related projects on local roads (£135 million in 2005) amount to only a small percentage of total road infrastructure spending.

A demonstration project undertaken in 1997–2003 illustrates the philosophical approach to traffic safety that has been adopted by U.K. planners and administrators, which parallels practices described above in other countries, particularly Australia and Sweden. It is also a useful example of the conduct of a large-scale demonstration. The Gloucester Safer City project (DfT 2001; Mackie and Wells 2003) was a 5-year urban traffic safety demonstration partially funded with a £5 million competitively awarded grant from the national government. The objective was to demonstrate how safety could be improved within the area of an entire small city (population 100,000) by a comprehensive urban traffic safety management program, guided by a strategic plan and by ongoing monitoring and supported by adequate resources.

The project began with analysis of road safety problems in the city: the distributions of types, locations, and causes of crashes; in addition, traffic volumes and speeds were mapped. A project plan stating the safety improvement objective—to reduce casualties by at least one-third by 2002 compared with the baseline period of 1991 to 1995—and the methods to be used was produced.

The organizing principle of the intervention strategy was to establish and enforce a road hierarchy; that is, to force through traffic off local streets and onto main roads by means of traffic calming and other traffic management measures. Traffic-calming measures included introduction of features such as speed bumps and road narrowing that induce drivers to slow down.

Speed enforcement by means of cameras and police patrols was increased. The rate of issue of speeding tickets quadrupled during the project compared with the previous rate. Other measures included reductions in speed limit on selected roads, antiskid treatments at intersections, modification of the timing of traffic signals to reduce pedestrians' waits before crossing, and installation of additional crossings and other improvements for pedestrians and bicyclists. Interventions were designed and implemented on an areawide basis. The traffic interventions were reinforced by educational activities, publicity, and arrangements for regular consultation with community interest groups and citizens.

The project incorporated an independent evaluation by the Transport Research Laboratory. The budget for evaluation was £1 million, 20 percent of the national government's contribution. The method of the evaluation was to compare changes in crash casualty frequencies in Gloucester with changes over the same period in a group of similar cities chosen as controls. The project was estimated to have reduced the frequency of casualty crashes by 24 percent and the frequency of crashes resulting in death or severe injury by 37 percent, compared with the frequencies expected in the absence of the program. The evaluation also documented the planning, administrative, and public communications processes used in the project and lessons from these experiences.

Nongovernmental organizations have been prominent in the development of U.K. safety policies. Motorist organizations were instrumental in establishing the Road Assessment Program and the New Car Assessment Program in the United Kingdom and in other countries since the 1990s. These programs rate vehicles and roadway segments for safety and publicize the ratings (Castle et al. 2007, 1). The Parliamentary Advisory Council for Transport Safety (PACTS) is a private nonprofit organization that promotes safety for all modes of transportation. The council was founded in 1982 as an outgrowth of the campaign for the compulsory use of seat belts in the front of vehicles. Its broad membership includes 100 members of Parliament as well as public agencies, companies, and advocacy groups. Its intended audience is members of Parliament and other public officials. PACTS advocates adoption of research-based solutions and serves as an independent source of technical information and advice for members of Parliament (PACTS 2008).

U.K. rates of citation for all moving violations and for speeding and the rate of driver alcohol testing are far below those in France, and the alcohol testing rate is much lower than in Sweden and Australia. Citations for speeding offenses increased 97 percent from 1999 to 2006, but citations for all other offenses declined, and the rate of alcohol testing declined (Table 3-2). Because U.K. roads have been relatively safe by world standards for many years, it is perhaps understandable that interventions on the scale of those in France (where the fatality rate per vehicle kilometer has been twice the British rate throughout the past 30 years) would not be undertaken; however, historical fatality rates in Australia and Sweden are much more similar to the U.K. rate. According to the 2005 evaluation summarized above, the camera enforcement system has not had dominant impact on the overall casualty rate. Despite the apparent disparities in enforcement practices and outcomes, the U.K. fatality rate (per vehicle kilometer) has maintained its ranking as among the lowest in the world, and the U.K. rate has continued its decline, falling 28 percent from 1997 to 2007.

Summary Observations on National Safety Programs

The summary of past international reviews of safety programs in the first section of this chapter observed that the successful programs must function effectively at three levels: management and planning, technical implementation of countermeasures, and maintenance of political and public support. The benchmark country safety programs described above appear to share some practices in each of these three areas, although some differences are evident as well. Their practices in each area have contrasts with those in the United States, as the next section of this chapter will illustrate. Generalization from brief examination of four national programs must be tentative; however, the following observations are also supported by the past international reviews.

With regard to management, among the most evident common characteristics of the national programs is their capacity for systematic measurement of level of effort (e.g., alcohol tests administered, violations cited, judicial outcomes, and safety capital expenditures) and intermediate outputs (including speed distributions, seat belt use rates, roadway conditions, and, less consistently, impaired driving prevalence). The prompt and regular compilation, analysis, and publication of this information are indicative of the overall management philosophy in the programs. Management appears publicly committed to producing measurable results and possesses a realistic and technically sophisticated grasp of the relationship of results to level of effort. Monitoring is incomplete in some areas even in the most advanced programs. For example, prevalence of impaired driving among all drivers on the road does not appear to be measured as routinely as is prevalence of speeding.

Evaluations that use statistical or experimental techniques to measure the effects of interventions are conducted, but they are occasional, and the planning documents reviewed do not describe how results of evaluations are used in setting and adjusting program goals or in allocating resources. Only rarely are evaluations undertaken that estimate the contribution of each of the elements of a national (or state) safety program to the overall safety trend over a period of years. [Analyses of this kind include the 1998 Victoria study (Newstead et al. 1998) summarized above and a study undertaken for Norway (Elvik 2005).]

As a result of gaps in evaluation, even the most advanced benchmark countries lack a comprehensive, quantitative understanding of the major factors that have been driving trends in their traffic casualties. Therefore, it is difficult for outside observers to identify which elements have been critical to success. The evaluations of national speed control programs cited above illustrate this uncertainty. Evaluations in France and Australia appear to show that systemwide automated enforcement (together with publicity and other program measures) has produced a systemwide reduction in speed and a consequent reduction in casualties that is a major contributor to the favorable national traffic safety trend. Evaluations of automated speed enforcement in the United Kingdom and Sweden [and in Norway (Elvik 2005, 22)] do not report large systemwide speed effects and hence attribute only a small share of the national casualty reduction to speed control. Ongoing evaluation of the impacts of actual interventions will be needed to resolve such uncertainties.

With regard to countermeasures, the striking characteristic of the four countries' programs is the intensity of enforcement. Systematic U.S. data are not available for comparison, but citations for speeding and roadside tests for alcohol impairment may be 3 to 10 times more frequent in some of the benchmark countries than in the United States. Enforcement intensity in the United Kingdom appears to be intermediate between intensity in Australia, France, and Sweden and that in the United States. The United Kingdom nonetheless has a very low fatality rate, and the speed with which the fatality rate has been reduced is comparable with that of Sweden and Australia.

Publicity campaigns in the four countries appear to be intense, sustained, integrated with the overall traffic safety strategy, and based on a foundation of research, and they are reputed to have reinforced the impact of enforcement and other safety measures. The committee did not conduct a detailed comparison of the structure or content of publicity campaigns of the United States with those of the benchmark countries; such a comparison would be worthwhile.

Finally, with regard to political and public support, certain institutional features that appear to be typical of safety programs in the benchmark nations probably have contributed to their effectiveness. The features include centralization of most aspects of the programs; the parliamentary structure of government (which, in at least some cases, allows the ministries preparing plans to make firm multiyear commitments to strategies and resources); and a history of effective communication among program administrators, researchers, and elected officials. Nongovernmental organizations have influenced safety program development in the United Kingdom, but their importance in other countries is less evident.

Because of the sparse documentation available to the committee, the roles that public demands and leadership from elected officials played in the development of the benchmark countries' safety programs are unclear in most cases. In Victoria, Australia, a series of public outcries reportedly led to political pressure for action. However, in France, safety initiatives had been developing for a period of years at a lower level when the president decided to make safety a high-visibility political issue, and the speed enforcement system, the centerpiece of the French initiative, was guided by a plan that had been prepared earlier in the ministry. In other countries and in U.S. states, leadership by the executive agency in presenting credible proposals for safety initiatives and in educating elected officials was essential in stimulating action. Government traffic safety programs have sought to earn public and political support over time through transparency with regard to goals and methods and through demonstrated results.

NATIONALLY ORGANIZED SAFETY MANAGEMENT REFORM INITIATIVES IN THE UNITED STATES

Box 3-5 outlines the components of a comprehensive U.S. state and local government traffic safety program, as defined in AASHTO's model strategic safety plan (AASHTO 2005). The objectives of the comprehensive program are safe drivers, safe roads, safe vehicles, and efficient emergency

BOX 3-5

Elements of a Comprehensive Traffic Safety Program

AASHTO's Strategic Highway Safety Plan (AASHTO 2005) is an outline of a model plan for state government programs to reduce traffic deaths and injuries. The plan is organized in terms of 19 goals grouped into five plan elements. Most of the goals correspond to categories of interventions. The outline provides a definition of the scope of state and local government traffic safety activities.

AASHTO Strategic Highway Safety Plan Elements and Goals
1. Drivers (regulation of driver licensing and motorist behavior, publicity to change attitudes and behavior)
   - Instituting graduated licensing for young drivers
   - Ensuring that drivers are fully licensed and competent
   - Sustaining proficiency in older drivers
   - Curbing aggressive driving
   - Reducing impaired driving
   - Keeping drivers alert
   - Increasing driver safety awareness
2. Special users (measures to reduce risks to pedestrians and bicyclists)
   - Making walking and street crossing safer
   - Ensuring safer bicycle travel
3. Vehicles (state regulations concerning safe maintenance of vehicles and use of safety equipment such as helmets; the federal government regulates the safety of vehicle designs)
   - Improving motorcycle safety and increasing motorcycle awareness
   - Making truck travel safer
   - Increasing safety enhancements in vehicles

(continued on next page)

> **BOX 3-5** *(continued)*
> **Elements of a Comprehensive Traffic Safety Program**
>
> 4. Highways (roadway design and maintenance and traffic control to reduce the risk of injury and death)
>   - Reducing vehicle–train crashes
>   - Keeping vehicles on the roadway
>   - Minimizing the consequences of leaving the road
>   - Improving the design and operation of highway intersections
>   - Reducing head-on and across-median crashes
>   - Designing safer work zones
> 5. Emergency medical services: enhancing emergency medical capabilities to increase survivability
> 6. Management (management systems required to support the interventions)
>   - Improving information and decision support systems
>   - Creating more effective processes and safety management systems
>
> The AASHTO plan elements do not cover actions in the legislative or judicial branches. NHTSA's Uniform Guidelines (NHTSA n.d. a) include three guidelines—on codes and laws, judicial and court services, and prosecutor training—concerning the legal framework and ensuring that courts are competent to adjudicate traffic safety cases.

medical services. This structure parallels the comprehensive safety programs of other countries described above, for example, Australia's safe system framework.

As Chapter 1 observed, the decentralized structure of U.S. government is the source of significant organizational differences between U.S. safety programs and those of most of the benchmark nations. Box 3-6 outlines the division of responsibilities among levels of government for regulation and administration of traffic safety.

BOX 3-6

Federal, State, and Local Government Executive Agency Functions Related to Traffic Safety

Organization	Major safety-related responsibilities
Federal agencies	
Federal Highway Administration (U.S. Department of Transportation)	Design standards for new and rehabilitated state highways built with federal aid; safety capital improvement grants to states
National Highway Traffic Safety Administration (U.S. Department of Transportation)	New vehicle safety standards; federal traffic safety grants to states for speed control, anti–impaired driving, seat belt promotion, and other programs
Federal Motor Carrier Safety Administration (U.S. Department of Transportation)	Direct federal regulation of commercial truck and bus safety; oversight of state regulation and enforcement
National Transportation Safety Board	Independent advisory agency that investigates major transportation accidents
State government agencies (some may be organized as subunits of a state department of transportation)	
State highway agency	Construction and maintenance of state highways (including major intercity roads, as well as many minor roads in some states)

(continued on next page)

BOX 3-6 *(continued)*
Federal, State, and Local Government Executive Agency Functions Related to Traffic Safety

Organization	Major safety-related responsibilities
State government agencies *(continued)*	
Public safety agency, including state police	Enforcement of traffic and safety laws on state roads, emergency response
Vehicle registration and driver licensing agency	Motor vehicle registration, vehicle inspection, driver licensing
State highway safety office	Management or coordination of programs concerning driver behavior (occupant protection, impaired driving, and speeding); administration of NHTSA safety grants
Local government agencies	
Public works department	Construction and maintenance of local streets and roads
Police department	Enforcement on local streets and roads
Emergency medical response service	Ambulance service at crashes

Note: Associations of state officials or of state agencies, which are private nonprofit organizations, perform important functions including defining best practices and program guidelines; supporting training, professional development, and research; and representing collective views of members to the federal government. They include AASHTO, the Governors Highway Safety Association (state highway safety offices), the Commercial Vehicle Safety Alliance (truck safety enforcement officials), the American Association of Motor Vehicle Administrators, and the International Association of Chiefs of Police.

The legislative and judicial branches, not shown in the table, perform the essential functions of enacting safety laws and of trying accused offenders and overseeing penalties for offenders, respectively.

The list of involved agencies and the summaries of responsibilities are not comprehensive.

Aside from motor vehicle safety regulation (which is a direct federal responsibility), U.S. federal government involvement in traffic safety is indirect. It influences state and local governments' road and safety programs most strongly through the rules it imposes on recipients of federal highway and traffic safety grants. The federal government also provides information, training, and research in support of state and local government traffic safety activities. State governments build and operate the major intercity roads and highways (and more extensive portions of the road system in some states); maintain state police that enforce traffic regulations; operate the criminal and civil courts; and have the authority to enact laws concerning driver licensing, vehicle inspection, speed limits, impaired driving, seat belt and motorcycle helmet use, and other aspects of traffic safety. Local governments operate local streets and roads, enact local traffic regulations (e.g., with regard to speed zones), and provide local police who enforce traffic laws within their jurisdictions and local courts with authority over minor offenses.

Examples of U.S. activities organized at the national level and aimed at strengthening the capabilities of state and local agencies in planning, management, and evaluation of traffic safety programs are described in this section. The activities are the following:

- Two USDOT demonstration programs, the National Highway Traffic Safety Administration (NHTSA) Strategic Evaluation States Initiative (SESI), a 2002–2005 demonstration of intensive enforcement against alcohol-impaired driving; and the Demonstration Projects on Setting and Enforcing Rational Speed Limits, jointly sponsored by FHWA and NHTSA in seven states in 2001–2006;
- State safety plans, as influenced by the federal requirement for each state to prepare a Strategic Highway Safety Plan (SHSP) and by AASHTO guidelines on safety planning;
- The Uniform Guidelines for State Highway Safety Programs concerning speed management and impaired driving (these are two of the 18 guidelines that NHTSA has prepared, as required by federal law, to aid the states in conducting programs funded by federal safety grants); and
- New quantitative analysis aids for safety planning.

The purpose of examining these activities is to allow comparisons of U.S. practices with those of other countries. An understanding of how practices differ is necessary in drawing lessons from safety practices elsewhere. This section focuses on management practices and on federal government efforts to support state programs; the case studies in Chapter 4 compare applications of specific countermeasures in the United States and other countries.

USDOT-Sponsored Safety Strategy Demonstrations

Two recent USDOT-sponsored multistate projects were intended to demonstrate comprehensive strategies aimed at controlling the high-risk driver behaviors, speeding and drunk driving, that have high priority in the benchmark nations' initiatives. The experience of these projects indicates problems that USDOT has faced in attempting to provide leadership on safety.

Strategic Evaluation States Initiative

In 2002, NHTSA undertook a project, SESI, to demonstrate how states could organize statewide anti–drunk driving programs incorporating certain components that NHTSA believed were critical to success. NHTSA recruited 15 states to participate, which together account for more than half of U.S. alcohol-related traffic fatalities. The states agreed to organize programs under NHTSA guidance and to submit reports on their activities. The requirements were as follows (Syner et al. 2008):

- The participating states agreed to conduct high-visibility, multiagency enforcement operations, on a sustained, year-round schedule, covering substate jurisdictions that account for at least 65 percent of all alcohol-related fatalities. The states agreed to participate in the National Impaired Driving Enforcement Crackdown, a preexisting NHTSA annual program that organizes a nationwide 2-week period of stepped-up enforcement, and to sustain a relatively high level of enforcement by staging crackdowns at least monthly for at least a year. Saturation patrols and, in some states, sobriety checkpoints were used in enforcement.
- The lead state agencies agreed to secure commitments from local law enforcement agencies that they would participate in enforcement and to provide guidance to the local agencies on enforcement methods.

- States agreed to cooperate with NHTSA in media campaigns to publicize the anti–drunk driving initiatives. NHTSA produced advertisements and paid for advertising synchronized with crackdowns.

NHTSA summarized the results of SESI in a report on three states, which, NHTSA cautions, "does not represent a formal, scientific evaluation" (Syner et al. 2008, 6). The three (West Virginia, Georgia, and Alaska) were chosen from among the 15 participants because their programs were judged to be strong. The report describes the procedural aspect of SESI, that is, the organization of the programs in the states, but does not evaluate the impact on safety.

The summaries of the states' programs and NHTSA's conclusions illuminate the problems that the states' safety improvement efforts confront and suggest directions for strengthening federal efforts to promote best practices. The following observations are among the lessons that the report's description of the initiative suggests:

- A functioning statewide anti–drunk driving program, even on a modest scale, requires a major coordination effort. NHTSA highlights, as a principal accomplishment, the improved communication and coordination among state and local law enforcement agencies and among state agencies with public safety responsibilities brought about by participation in SESI. It was necessary for each state lead agency to recruit local police force participation; incentives (e.g., reimbursement for police overtime shifts) were offered in at least some cases. Georgia reported commitments from 587 law enforcement agencies in the state to participate in the annual crackdowns. Success also required that each local police agency coordinate enforcement crackdowns with local courts and prosecutors to gain their support and to allow them to prepare for the increased workload.
- Officers in some local forces were found to lack basic training in anti–drunk driving enforcement techniques. The NHTSA report concluded that providing local police training is an essential element in organizing statewide programs.
- Applying a standard program model uniformly in all states is not possible. The states differ greatly in population density, roadway extent, and traffic volumes; in their laws; and in state and local government organizational structure. For example, some states used sobriety

checkpoints during enforcement crackdowns, while others, presumably because state law does not sanction this method, did not.
- Resource constraints significantly limit the level of effort that states are able to devote to stepped-up enforcement. Consequently, the increase in effort during the demonstration appears overall to have been small. For example, 30 person-hours of enforcement per week were added in Anchorage, a city of 270,000. (However, West Virginia reported substantially increasing statewide enforcement over the program period.) The NHTSA summary contains little information on level of effort or expenditures, but only modest funding appears to have been available in the states to pay for increased policing or for state-level coordination, training, and publicity. Even if the interventions used were potentially effective, the increase in the level of effort during the demonstration might have been insufficient to produce measurable safety effects.

NHTSA has sponsored a retrospective evaluation of an earlier anti–drunk driving demonstration program, conducted in 2000–2003 with seven participating states (Fell et al. 2008). The research solicited information from each state on numbers of enforcement activities conducted (sobriety checkpoints and saturation patrols) and media budgets. Arrests for driving while intoxicated were obtained from Federal Bureau of Investigation crime statistics. Impact measures were derived from NHTSA's Fatality Analysis Reporting System database. The statistical analysis concluded that the program reduced fatalities in four of the seven states. This kind of evaluation is valuable; however, incorporating evaluation into the design of demonstration projects would produce more detailed and definitive insight into the relation of the methods and the level of effort to outcomes.

Setting and Enforcing Rational Speed Limits
In a second project, NHTSA and FHWA recruited participants in seven states to demonstrate and evaluate an integrated approach to speed management. In test sites in each state, posted speed limits were revised (apparently more often raised than lowered) on the basis of engineering studies of each site that considered prevailing speed, pedestrian activity, crash history, and other factors. Then a program of strict enforcement was instituted, supported by local publicity campaigns. The judiciary were

informed of the program. Each demonstration included data collection and evaluation. The participants and demonstration sites were as follows (FHWA n.d. a; FHWA 2005):

Participant	Site
Mississippi Department of Transportation	Major arterial highway in Gulfport
Massachusetts Governors Highway Safety Bureau	Residential collectors in Natick
Connecticut State Police	Secondary roads in Hebron
Tippecanoe County, Indiana, Highway Department	Two-lane county roads
City of Taylor, Michigan, Police Department	City streets and freeway connector
South Central Planning and Development Commission, Louisiana	Urban and rural roads in two parishes
Virginia Department of Transportation	Freeway bypass in Martinsville

Organization of the program began in 2001, and the demonstrations were conducted at most sites from 2003 through 2005. Each demonstration was of small scale; the USDOT contribution was $150,000 to $400,000 at each site. The demonstrations typically involved several miles of streets or roads in a local area and 4 to 18 months of special enforcement. Most involved a single local jurisdiction.

No summary report of the program has appeared. Evaluations were published by NHTSA for the Mississippi demonstration (Freedman et al. 2007) and by the evaluation researchers for the Virginia (Son et al. 2007), Indiana (Tarko 2008), and Massachusetts (Knodler et al. 2008) demonstrations. A brief summary of the Connecticut results was published by the state legislative research office (Fazzalaro 2006). Each site had a different evaluator, and the evaluations varied in method and sophistication.

All the evaluations estimated the impact of the demonstrations on speeds. Some examined crash data, but the scale of the demonstrations was such that a safety impact would not have been measurable unless it had been very large. The evaluations reported small but apparently significant speed impacts. At some sites the combined effect of raising the speed limit and increasing enforcement was to increase average speed. The scale and the evaluation methods used did not allow separation of the effects of publicity, enforcement, and changes in posted limits. The evaluation reports do not detail funding or resources devoted to the demonstrations, so judging cost-effectiveness is not possible. The conclusion of the Indiana evaluation (Tarko 2008, 1) was that "the joint impact of aggressive safe-speed campaign with police enforcement at selected sites on speed selection was minimal. Drivers drove at speeds they considered adequate for local conditions and the attempt to change their behavior through enforcement and campaigning was not easy." This result seems consistent with the demonstrations' modest scale with respect to road mileage, period of application, and intensity of enforcement and publicity. It would not be reasonable to extrapolate the results of a demonstration applied to short road segments over a period of months to predict the impact of applying the same speed management methods consistently over major portions of the road network in a region or state for a period of years.

Observations Concerning National Demonstrations

The results of the SESI and rational speed limits demonstration programs support the following observations about USDOT safety demonstrations and indicate how they might be made more valuable:

- In concept, the SESI program was a potentially valuable and appropriately designed demonstration. NHTSA recruited a large group of states to participate, defined a strategy that each state was to follow, provided some material support, and required participants to report results. The design of the rational speed limits demonstration program is more problematic, since it is unclear whether the scale of the activity was sufficient to serve as either a test or a demonstration of speed management methods. The goals of the speed demonstration program probably were overly ambitious for the resources available.
- Evaluation of program impacts was minimal in SESI. For the three case study states, survey results on public awareness of the programs and statewide annual alcohol-related fatalities are the only measures reported. No data were reported that would allow outcomes to be related to level of enforcement effort. As noted, NHTSA intended its report on SESI to serve as an implementation guide rather than an evaluation, but information on effort and expenditures required to attain a desired outcome would be necessary in planning implementation of an enforcement program. NHTSA has not published an evaluation or a summary of the results in all 15 participating states. Some of the ratio-

nal speed limits demonstration participants devoted greater care to evaluation, although USDOT has not disseminated the evaluations.
- USDOT's own resource constraints limit its capacity to conduct worthwhile large-scale demonstration of safety strategies. The experience of SESI suggests the following of a more productive demonstration:
  – USDOT would be able to offer participants more substantial support and in return could require more substantial and consistent state efforts and more rigorous reporting of efforts and outcomes. Challenge grants or more stringent matching requirements might increase federal leverage to stimulate higher levels of state funding commitment to these programs.
  – Quantitative evaluation would be conducted either directly by USDOT or by each state following specific and detailed USDOT standards. A demonstration is intended to publicize and teach effective methods and generally cannot be structured strictly as a scientific experiment; nonetheless, it must convincingly show that the methods yield worthwhile results.
  – The evaluation would include estimates of the cost-effectiveness of individual countermeasures.
  – USDOT would publish full results of the evaluation for all participating states and practical guides derived from the experience of the program.

Effective demonstration programs could be a valuable tool for reforming highway safety practice. To meet this promise, demonstrations will require adequate support and rigorous design and execution. Meaningful evaluation of demonstrations requires reliable historical baseline data on traffic characteristics, crash frequency and characteristics, road conditions, frequency of high-risk behaviors, and enforcement level of effort. In many jurisdictions, greater effort to establish this baseline will be a prerequisite to fully successful participation in demonstrations.

Strategic Highway Safety Plans

Preparation of an SHSP is a federal requirement first imposed by the 2005 federal surface transportation assistance act (Safe, Accountable, Flexible, Efficient Transportation Equity Act: A Legacy for Users Section 1401;

23 USC 148) as a condition of participation by a state in the federal highway safety improvement grant program. The state must prepare and carry out a strategic plan that includes a process for identifying highway safety problems and developing a program of projects or strategies to reduce them, and it must report annually to USDOT on the identified road hazards and the means and costs of mitigating them. The plan must establish an evaluation process to assess the results achieved by highway safety improvement projects. The law requires that the plan include "performance-based goals that . . . address traffic safety, including behavioral and infrastructure problems," although the law's specifications for the content of the plan refer mostly to identification and elimination of hazardous locations and elements on roads. The plan is to be prepared by the state department of transportation in consultation with the Governor's Highway Safety Representative, state and local enforcement officials, and other relevant state government agencies.

Each state is also required, as a condition for receipt of federal highway safety grant funds, to submit an annual highway safety plan to NHTSA describing the specific activities to be funded through the federal program and how they relate to the state's defined safety goals. States also submit annual reports to NHTSA describing the previous year's activities and progress toward goals (NHTSA n.d. b). These planning and reporting requirements have existed in some form since the federal safety program's inception in 1966.

The need for state strategic safety plans had been recognized earlier by AASHTO. The AASHTO SHSP, first published in 1997 and revised in 2005, sets broad goals for safety improvement, comprehensively identifies actions that each state should take with regard to each of 19 plan elements grouped in five areas (driver regulation, pedestrian and cyclist safety, vehicle safety, highway design, and emergency medical services), calls on each state to develop its own comprehensive safety plan (i.e., a plan addressing all five areas), and calls for increased federal aid for state safety programs (AASHTO 2005). To support its strategic plan, AASHTO sponsored development of detailed technical guidelines for countermeasures by NCHRP (AASHTO n.d.).

State implementations of the new SHSP requirement were reviewed in case studies of four states prepared in 2007 in NCHRP Project 17-18(016),

Creating a Traffic Safety Culture, and in a 2008 examination of six state plans conducted for FHWA (More and Munnich 2008). In addition, a report by an industry group summarized the priorities identified in the plans of 21 states (ATSSA 2007).

Content of the SHSPs

The purposes of the AASHTO guidance and of the federal SHSP requirement are (*a*) to encourage the states to take a multiyear perspective in program planning and in setting goals and (*b*) to coordinate all government activities affecting traffic safety, including vehicle and driver regulations, enforcement, highway design and operation, and emergency medical response. The older federally required annual highway safety plans addressed to NHTSA are narrower in scope; they address only programs funded with federal grants, in particular the NHTSA-administered highway safety grant programs and the hazard elimination program.

Before the 2005 federal requirement, some states (e.g., Washington, Oregon, and Wisconsin) had already prepared strategic safety plans in keeping with the AASHTO guidelines. After 2005, all states prepared SHSPs, typically modeled on the AASHTO SHSP, with additions to ensure that all the federally required elements are present. Most of the plans identify a list of, typically, five to six highest-priority program areas (e.g., reducing impaired driving and increasing seat belt use). The areas usually correspond to plan elements in the AASHTO document (ATSSA 2007; More and Munnich 2008, 7). The discussion of each priority program area in the plan often concludes with a list of relevant strategies (i.e., countermeasures), following the format of the AASHTO model plan. In some plans the strategies are concrete and specific, but in others they are stated generally. The strategies sometimes are described as "suggested" or "recommended," acknowledging that the authors of the plan cannot make a commitment that the strategies will be carried out (More and Munnich 2008, 4; PennDOT 2006, 8–16).

The states' annual highway safety plans addressed to NHTSA may refer to the priority areas identified in the SHSP and report on actions and progress toward SHSP goals. For example, Pennsylvania's 2009 Highway Safety Plan lists goals for the year related to each of the six focus areas in the state's strategic plan. For the focus area of reducing impaired driving, the 2009 goal is to make 500,000 motorist contacts through driving-under-the-influence enforcement activities (PennDOT 2008, 16).

In summarizing the SHSPs' contents, the FHWA-sponsored review concluded that "the six plans varied significantly in their overall completeness and depth. . . . Some plans prioritized the issues in each emphasis area. Others took a more general approach, which did little more than satisfy federal reporting requirements. . . . It is important to note however, that this was the first time some states had created a safety plan. As these plans are revised, it is likely they will become more complete and focused" (More and Munnich 2008, 7).

In 2009 FHWA released a draft SHSP implementation process model (FHWA 2009a). The document and its supporting material are intended as a guide to the states for developing and acting on their strategic safety plans. The guide is based on a review of the experience of six model states and was produced in collaboration with NHTSA and the Federal Motor Carrier Safety Administration. A 6-month, 10-state pilot test of the guide was conducted in 2009, and a revised version was to have been issued in 2010.

Observations Concerning the SHSP Requirement

The state offices preparing the SHSPs are severely limited in their ability to make multiyear commitments to sustain a strategy or to provide resources. The plans are prepared by the executive branch agencies responsible for the state's highways, with input from other state agencies and from local governments. However, a state plan cannot commit local governments to expend resources or to follow state direction in law enforcement and other activities relevant to safety. States can provide incentives for local cooperation, but they have limited resources for this purpose. In addition, safety program budgets are determined year to year by the legislature. The executive agency plan cannot commit the legislature to any level of funding or to any specific highway safety policy. The proponents of strategic planning expected the agencies writing the SHSPs to publish visionary and comprehensive statements of aspirations for highway safety over the next decade. However, the agencies, faced with the political reality of their limited authority, often produce plans that address concretely only the limited range of actions under their control.

The position of the U.S. state executive agencies contrasts with circumstances in most of the benchmark nations. Highway administration in most other high-income countries is more centralized than in the United States, and government ministers, at least in some cases, have been able to make multiyear commitments to a policy course and for provision of resources.

The SHSPs cannot provide for or ensure accountability because of the weak position of the state agencies preparing them and because of technical limits on state planning capacities. Plans do not present quantitative arguments projecting how much the proposed countermeasures, individually or collectively, will contribute toward attaining the quantitative safety goals. For example, many states list curbing aggressive driving (i.e., the complex of hazardous behaviors that includes speeding, illegal passing, tailgating, weaving, and ignoring signals) or speeding as among their priorities. However, few states have any systematic measures of aggressive driving (e.g., periodic speed surveys), and no state can project, on the basis of research evidence, the expected quantitative impact on aggressive driving or speeding (or on the resulting casualties) of the proposed countermeasures, at the level of effort that will be available.

Evidence is not available for determining how the states have changed their safety programs since the introduction of the strategic plans. To determine whether changes have occurred, systematic tracking of measures of level of effort and of intermediate outputs would be necessary. In addition, without such information, plans cannot analyze the level of effort or resources required to carry out the strategies they describe or how these requirements compare with available resources. A 2008 NHTSA report acknowledges that only one intermediate output measure, seat belt usage measured by roadside survey, is generally available for use in federal and state highway safety planning and management and that only limited enforcement level of effort measures (numbers of citations and arrests for certain violations) are available. NHTSA states that it intends to cooperate with the Governors Highway Safety Association in promoting speed monitoring as an additional intermediate output measure as well as in promoting other measures of enforcement effort (Hedlund 2008, i–ii).

Shortcomings in state planning parallel the description in the World Bank *Guidelines for the Conduct of Road Safety Management Capacity Reviews* of safety programs in countries where safety management capacity is limited and a strong lead safety agency is absent. The consequences of this lack, in the World Bank's observation, are that "coordination arrangements can be ineffective, supporting legislation fragmented, funding insufficient and poorly targeted, promotional efforts narrowly and sporadically directed to key road user groups, monitoring and evaluation systems ill-developed, and knowledge transfer limited. Interventions are fragmented and often do not reflect good practice. Little is known about the results they achieve" (Bliss and Breen 2009, 16). The World Bank guidelines include a checklist for evaluating the adequacy of lead agency functions and powers (Bliss and Breen 2009, 38) that states could apply in assessing their own safety organizational structure.

The constraints on the authority of the agencies preparing the SHSPs to make long-term commitments with regard to strategy or resources are an unavoidable aspect of U.S. government institutions. Despite these constraints, conditional commitments could be included in the plans. That is, the plans could contain statements from the safety agencies that if they are given certain specified resources, they will produce certain specified safety results. For such commitments to be credible, the states would need much stronger capabilities than they now have for monitoring and evaluating the costs and benefits of safety programs.

Uniform Guidelines for State Highway Safety Programs

The law that establishes the federal highway safety grant program requires that state highway safety programs, to be eligible for federal grants, be "in accordance with uniform guidelines promulgated by the Secretary [of Transportation]" (23 USC 402a). NHTSA has published 19 current guidelines, each outlining procedures for a particular safety program element. Among them are guidelines on motorcycle safety, driver education, licensing, judicial services, impaired driving, traffic records, emergency medical services, pedestrian and bicycle safety, traffic law enforcement, speed management, occupant protection, vehicle inspection, vehicle registration, legal codes, prosecutor training, debris cleanup, pupil transportation, accident investigation, and roadway safety. The program elements addressed by the guidelines correspond to activities for which the states may receive federal grants administered by NHTSA. The guidelines (originally called "uniform standards") have been a feature of the federal highway safety grant program since it was founded in the Highway Safety Act of 1966. NHTSA explains the purpose of the guidelines today as follows (NHTSA n.d. a):

> These guidelines offer direction to States in formulating their highway safety plans for highway safety efforts that are supported with section 402 and other grant funds. The guidelines provide a framework for developing a balanced highway safety program and serve as a tool with which States can assess the effectiveness of their own programs. NHTSA encourages States to use these guidelines and build upon them to optimize the effectiveness of highway safety programs conducted at the State and local levels.

The difficulties of developing and applying safety program standards in the federal context are indicated by an examination of the speed management guideline, revised in 2006 (NHTSA 2006). The guideline has seven sections: program management; problem identification; engineering countermeasures; communications program; enforcement countermeasures; legislation, regulation, and policy; and data and evaluation. The program that the guideline specifies reflects present understanding of the critical elements in successful traffic safety programs. It is consistent with internationally recognized best practices as described in the report of the OECD Speed Management Working Group (OECD and ECMT 2006b) and in the Global Road Safety Partnership (GRSP) speed management manual (GRSP 2008). It emphasizes the value of automated enforcement, as do the OECD and GRSP documents. However, whether states or local governments possess the technical or managerial capacity to conduct the program outlined in the guideline is questionable.

For most jurisdictions, following the guideline would require a radical change in management practices and a large increase in resources devoted to traffic safety. A state that wished to implement such a program would face significant obstacles. It would have no basis for estimating the budget required or identifying the personnel and other resources needed, no readily available source of technical support, and no basis for communicating to senior executives and the legislature what the impact of implementing such a program would be.

For example, the problem identification section of the guideline calls for rigorous and detailed speed monitoring and evaluation of the effect of changes in speed limits (NHTSA 2006, 2):

> Each State should provide leadership, training, and technical assistance to:
> - Monitor and report travel speed trends across the entire localized road network;
> - Identify local road segments where excessive and inappropriate vehicle speeds contribute to speeding-related crashes;
> - Monitor the effects on vehicle speeds and crash risk of setting appropriate speed limits; and
> - Coordinate, monitor, and evaluate the short- and long-term effect of State legislative and local changes that establish appropriate speed laws and posted speed limits on mobility and safety.

However, as the section on speeding countermeasures in Chapter 4 describes, systematic speed monitoring today is rare among state and local transportation agencies and (as noted in the section above on safety plans) seldom used for safety program planning.

States also would encounter difficulties in following the section of the guideline on communication (NHTSA 2006, 3), which stipulates the following:

> The State should aid established Speed Management Working Groups by providing the leadership, training, and technical assistance necessary to:
> - Develop and evaluate culturally relevant public awareness campaigns to educate drivers on the importance of obeying speed limits and the potential consequences of speeding;
> - Use market research to identify and clearly understand how, when, and where to reach high-risk drivers.

Most states have conducted media campaigns aimed at speeding or aggressive driving, and NHTSA offers technical advice on these campaigns (NHTSA 2009; NHTSA n.d. c). However, actual evaluations of safety impacts or cost-effectiveness of publicity campaigns are not available for guiding a state or local agency attempting to design such a marketing program (Hedlund et al. 2009, 3-21, 4-11, 4-13).

State and local agencies can find more extensive qualitative discussions of procedures in the NCHRP report *A Guide for Reducing Speeding-*

Related Crashes (Neuman et al. 2009), one of a series of guides developed to help state and local agencies implement the AASHTO SHSP. However, the NCHRP report offers few examples to demonstrate the feasibility of the methods proposed and no information about effectiveness. The report does not appear to be keyed to the NHTSA guideline; for example, it offers no advice for carrying out the speed monitoring and evaluation activities that NHTSA calls for. Additional guides are published by NHTSA, the International Association of Chiefs of Police, and others, but practical documentation of actual implementations that reduced crashes and casualties is lacking.

Quantitative Analysis Aids for Safety Planning

Safety planning and management require models analogous to those available to transportation administrators for air quality, pavement condition, and congestion evaluation. Needs include systems for screening of road networks, diagnosis of crash causes, and selection of cost-beneficial countermeasures. Formal safety planning and management tools recently developed, in part with federal government sponsorship and with sponsorship of the states through NCHRP, can support some of these capabilities if the states devote the necessary resources to their proper use. Among such tools are the Interactive Highway Safety Design Model, an expert system to evaluate the safety of highways in the planning and design stage, and SafetyAnalyst, an expert system to screen the road network for high-hazard locations and assess costs and benefits of countermeasures (Box 3-7).

These analysis aids can strengthen state safety planning by supporting assessment of how the state's capital program contributes to meeting safety objectives. States can use the aids in safety plans to set quantitative targets for their hazard elimination programs and for the safety performance of planned new construction and to help guide allocation of resources among roadway safety improvements and other safety programs.

The planning and analysis resources listed in Box 3-7 apply to highway design and traffic control. No analogous tools exist to aid decisions concerning behavioral interventions. However, since 2005, NHTSA has published and periodically revised *Countermeasures That Work* (Hedlund et al. 2009), a compendium of information on the effectiveness, current use, costs, and implementation time for most behavioral

BOX 3-7

Analysis Tools and Planning Resources for State Safety Programs

- AASHTO SHSP Implementation Guides (AASHTO n.d.): Nineteen volumes in the NCHRP Report 500 series identifying proven and unproven strategies, keyed to the AASHTO plan
- *Integrated Safety Management Process* (*NCHRP Report 501*) (Bahar et al. 2003)
  - Outlines procedure to optimize highway safety; emphasizes integration of relevant agencies
  - Measurable targets linked to federal requirements for state safety plans
  - Component of AASHTO safety planning initiative
- Interactive Highway Safety Design Model (FHWA n.d. b)
  - Expert system to evaluate highways in the planning and design stage
  - Predicts expected crash rates on tangents and curves according to cross section, median type, radius of curvature, and so forth
  - Determines whether design violates standards
  - Future module is for prediction of driver behavior (e.g., speed)
  - Developed by FHWA
  - Coordinated with development and organization of Safety-Analyst and the *Highway Safety Manual*
- SafetyAnalyst (FHWA n.d. c)
  - Applicable to existing roads
  - Expert system to
    1. Screen road network for locations with higher-than-expected (for facility type) crashes
    2. Determine crash patterns (e.g., rear-end)

3. Diagnose the driver errors leading to those crashes and propose related countermeasures
4. Assess costs and benefits of countermeasures given crash frequencies and expected effectiveness
– Intended to guide project selection and resource allocation
- *Highway Safety Manual* (AASHTO 2010)
  – Provides tools for evaluating safety consequences of road design and operational decisions
  – Includes the first U.S. compendium of accident modification factors [estimates of safety consequences of design choices (e.g., for cross section, radius of curvature, median type, shoulder type)] with a sound statistical basis
  – Is expected to elevate the importance of safety considerations in the project development process
- *Human Factors Guidelines for Road Systems* (Campbell et al. 2008)
  – Comprehensive set of guidelines in uniform, practical format for design of highway features (e.g., stopping sight distance, decision sight distance) based on driver requirements
  – Complement to *Highway Safety Manual* for completing detailed designs

countermeasures (including measures against impaired driving, speeding, and aggressive and distracted driving; promotion of seat belt use; regulation of younger and older drivers; and motorcycle, pedestrian, and bicycle safety), intended as a guide to safety administrators designing such programs.

Summary Observations on U.S. Nationally Organized Safety Initiatives

Evidence is lacking that the initiatives at the national level to reform traffic safety program management methods are sufficient to have had an impact on established practices. USDOT-sponsored demonstrations of new methods have been conducted with limited resources, and, at least in some instances, evaluations were inadequate to show that the methods demonstrated yielded results. Dissemination of lessons learned from the demonstrations sometimes appears to have been ineffectual. The primary purpose of demonstrations is not basic research on countermeasure effectiveness; however, if the goal is to induce states to adopt effective methods, convincing evidence of effectiveness will be an essential selling point.

The NHTSA Uniform Guidelines, originally envisioned as standards defining acceptable practice, are technically valid but presuppose technical and institutional capacities that state and local governments generally do not possess.

The impact of the SHSPs, a major national initiative aimed at changing the methods and procedures of traffic safety programs, is not yet evident. The state government agencies preparing the plans have limited control over most of the resources and policies that form the substance of traffic safety programs. Therefore, the plans do not embody commitments either to effort or to results.

Given this political reality, an alternative and potentially more valuable format for the SHSPs, rather than the lists of suggested or recommended actions that many now contain, would be to propose conditional commitments; that is, the agencies administering state safety programs would make commitments to produce specified safety results, provided they are given specified levels of resources. Resources include funding as well as legal authority; for example, funding for enforcement and publicity together with legal authority for sobriety checkpoints as components of a state's anti–drunk driving program.

REFERENCES

Abbreviations

AASHTO	American Association of State Highway and Transportation Officials
ATSSA	American Traffic Safety Services Association
CISR	Comité Interministériel de la Sécurité Routière
DfT	Department for Transport
ECMT	European Council of Ministers of Transport
FHWA	Federal Highway Administration
GRSP	Global Road Safety Partnership

NHTSA National Highway Traffic Safety Administration
OECD Organisation for Economic Co-operation and Development
ONISR Observatoire National Interministériel de Sécurité Routière
PACTS Parliamentary Advisory Council for Transport Safety
PennDOT Pennsylvania Department of Transportation

AASHTO. 2005. *AASHTO Strategic Highway Safety Plan.* Washington, D.C.

AASHTO. 2010. *Highway Safety Manual: 1st Edition.* Washington, D.C.

AASHTO. n.d. *Implementation Guides.* http://safety.transportation.org/guides.aspx.

ATSSA. 2007. *Strategic Highway Safety Plans: Compilation of State Safety Priorities.* March.

Australian Transport Council. 2008. *National Road Safety Action Plan 2009 and 2010.* Nov.

Bahar, G., M. Masliah, C. Mollett, and B. Persaud. 2003. *NCHRP Report 501: Integrated Safety Management Process.* Transportation Research Board of the National Academies, Washington, D.C.

Baxter, J., M. L. Halladay, and E. Alicandri. 2005. Safety Scans—A Successful Two-Way Street. *Public Roads,* Vol. 69, No. 1, July–Aug.

Bliss, T., and J. Breen. 2009. *Implementing the Recommendations of the World Report on Road Traffic Injury Prevention: Country Guidelines for the Conduct of Road Safety Management Capacity Reviews and the Specification of Lead Agency Reforms, Investment Strategies and Safe System Projects.* World Bank Global Road Safety Facility, Washington, D.C., June.

Breen, J., E. Howard, and T. Bliss. 2007. *An Independent Review of Road Safety in Sweden.* Dec. http://www22.vv.se/filer/52611/independent_review_of_road_safety_in%20_sweden.pdf.

Broughton, J., R. E. Allsop, D. A. Lyman, and C. M. McMahon. 2000. *The Numerical Context for Setting National Casualty Reduction Targets.* Transport Research Laboratory Ltd.

Broughton, J., and G. Buckle. 2008. *Monitoring Progress Towards the 2010 Casualty Reduction Target: 2006 Data.* Report 663. TRL Ltd., Oct. 8. http://www.trl.co.uk/online_store/reports_publications/trl_reports/cat_road_user_safety/report_Monitoring_progress_towards_the_2010_casualty_reduction_target_-_2006_data.htm.

Campbell, J. L., C. M. Richard, and J. L. Graham. 2008. *NCHRP Report 600A: Human Factors Guidelines for Road Systems: Collection A: Chapters 1, 2, 3, 4, 5, 10, 11, 13, 22, 23, 26.* Transportation Research Board of the National Academies, Washington, D.C.

Carnis, L. 2008. The French Automated Speed Enforcement Programme: A Deterrent System at Work. *Proc., Australasian Road Safety Research Policing Education Conference,* Adelaide, South Australia, Nov. 9–12, pp. 752–766. http://www.rsconference.com/pdf/RS080011.pdf.

Castle, J., D. Lynam, J. Martin, S. D. Lawson, and N. Klassen. 2007. *Star Rating Roads for Safety: UK Trials 2006–07.* IAM Motoring Trust, Dec.

Chapelon, J. 2004. *France: Recent Developments in the Field of Road Safety*. Observatoire National Interministériel de Sécurité Routière, Sept. 6.

CISR. 2006. Dossier de Presse. July 6.

D'Elia, A., S. Newstead, and M. Cameron. 2007. Overall Impact of Speed-Related Initiatives and Factors on Crash Outcomes. *51st Annual Proceedings: Association for the Advancement of Automotive Medicine: Annals of Advances in Automotive Medicine*, Vol. 51, pp. 465–484.

DfT. 2001. *Report on the Gloucester Safer City Project*.

DfT. 2007. *Second Review of the Government's Road Safety Strategy*. Feb. 26. http://www.dft.gov.uk/pgr/roadsafety/strategytargetsperformance/2ndreview/.

DfT. 2008a. *Annual Report 2008*. May.

DfT. 2008b. *Road Casualties Great Britain: 2007: Annual Report*. Sept. 25. http://www.dft.gov.uk/pgr/statistics/datatablespublications/accidents/casualtiesgbar/.

DfT. 2008c. *Road Safety Compliance Consultation*. Nov.

DfT. 2009a. *Road Statistics 2008: Traffic, Speeds and Congestion*. July.

DfT. 2009b. *Transport Statistics Bulletin: National Travel Survey: 2008*.

DfT. n.d. Seat Belts. http://www.dft.gov.uk/think/focusareas/invehiclesafety/seatbelts?page=Overview.

Documentation Française. 2006. La Sécurité Routière: Une Priorité Nationale. http://www.ladocumentationfrancaise.fr/dossiers/securite-routiere/index.shtml.

Elvik, R. 2005. *Has Progress in Road Safety Come to a Stop? A Discussion of Some Factors Influencing Long Term Trends in Road Safety*. Institute of Transport Economics, Oslo, Norway, Nov.

Fazzalaro, J. J. 2006. Connecticut Participation in "Rational Speed Limit Project." Connecticut Office of Legislative Research, Aug. 4.

Fell, J. C., E. A. Langston, J. H. Lacey, A. S. Tippetts, and R. Cotton. 2008. *Evaluation of Seven Publicized Enforcement Demonstration Programs to Reduce Impaired Driving: Georgia, Louisiana, Pennsylvania, Tennessee, Texas, Indiana, and Michigan*. National Highway Traffic Safety Administration, Feb.

FHWA. 2005. Rational Speed Setting and Enforcement Demonstrations. *Safety Programs Newsletter*, May–June.

FHWA. 2009a. *The Essential Eight: Fundamental Elements and Effective Steps for SHSP Implementation: Strategic Highway Safety Plan: Implementation Process Model: Draft*. May 11.

FHWA. 2009b. *Highway Statistics 2008*.

FHWA. 2009c. International Technology Scanning Program. Updated June 26. http://international.fhwa.dot.gov/scan/.

FHWA. n.d. a. Demonstration Projects on Setting and Enforcing Rational Speed Limits. http://safety.fhwa.dot.gov/speedmgt/eng_spd_lmts/.

FHWA. n.d. b. IHSDM Overview. http://www.tfhrc.gov/safety/ihsdm/ihsdm.htm.

FHWA. n.d. c. SafetyAnalyst Overview. http://www.safetyanalyst.org/index.htm.

Fiti, R., D. Perry, W. Giraud, and M. Ayres. 2008. *Statistical Bulletin: Motoring Offences and Breath Test Statistics: England and Wales 2006.* United Kingdom Ministry of Justice, April.

Fitzgerald, S. 2002. Managing the Police and Road Design Interface. Presented at Trafinz Conference, Dunedin, New Zealand, Sept. 9.

Freedman, M., D. De Leonardis, A. Polson, S. Levi, and E. Burkhardt. 2007. *Test of the Impact of Setting and Enforcing Rational Speed Limits in Gulfport, Mississippi.* National Highway Traffic Safety Administration, Oct.

Fuller, L. 2008. Statistics and World Studies. International Road Assessment Program. http://www.saferoaddesign.com/media/2204/france.pdf.

GRSP. 2008. *Speed Management: A Road Safety Manual for Decision-Makers and Practitioners.* Geneva. http://www.who.int/roadsafety/projects/manuals/speed_manual/speedmanual.pdf.

Guichet, B. 2005. Roundabouts in France: Safety and New Issues. Presented at National Roundabout Conference, Vail, Colo., May 24. http://www.teachamerica.com/Roundabouts/RA056A_ppt_Guichet.pdf.

Hedlund, J. 2008. *Traffic Safety Performance Measures for States and Federal Agencies.* National Highway Traffic Safety Administration, Aug.

Hedlund, J. H., B. Harsha, W. A. Leaf, A. H. Goodwin, W. L. Hall, J. C. Raborn, L. J. Thomas, and M. E. Tucker. 2009. *Countermeasures That Work: A Highway Safety Countermeasures Guide for State Highway Safety Offices: Fourth Edition 2009.* National Highway Traffic Safety Administration.

Jackson, P., and C. Hilditch. 2010. *A Review of Evidence Related to Drug Driving in the UK: A Report Submitted to the North Review Team.* Department for Transport, London, United Kingdom, June.

Johansson, R. 2007. Vision Zero—The Swedish Traffic Safety Policy. Road Safety Scotland Annual Seminar, Oct. 24. www.srsc.org.uk/Images/Roger%20Johansson_tcm4-455561.ppt.

Johnston, I. 2006. *Halving Roadway Fatalities: A Case Study from Victoria, Australia, 1989–2004.* Federal Highway Administration, April.

Knodler, M. A., Jr., D. Hurwitz, and H. A. Rothenberg. 2008. Evaluation of Rationally Implemented Speed Limits on Collector Roadways. Presented at 87th Annual Meeting of the Transportation Research Board, Washington, D.C.

MacDonald, D., C. P. Yew, R. Arnold, J. R. Baxter, R. K. Halvorson, H. Kassoff, K. Philmus, T. J. Price, D. R. Rose, and C. M. Walton. 2004. *Transportation Performance Measures in Australia, Canada, Japan, and New Zealand.* Federal Highway Administration, Dec.

Mackie, A., and P. Wells. 2003. *Gloucester Safer City: Final Report.* TRL Ltd.

More, A., and L. Munnich, Jr. 2008. *Rural Transportation Safety and the Strategic Highway Safety Plan: An Examination of Select State Programs and Practices.* Federal Highway Administration, Feb. http://conservancy.umn.edu/bitstream/5923/1/CTS08_02.pdf.

Neuman, T. R., K. L. Slack, K. K. Hardy, V. L. Bond, R. D. Foss, A. H. Goodwin, J. Sohn, D. J. Torbic, D. W. Harwood, I. B. Potts, R. Pfefer, C. Raborn, and N. D. Lerner. 2009. *NCHRP Report 500: Guidance for Implementation of the AASHTO Strategic Highway Safety Plan: Volume 23: A Guide for Reducing Speeding-Related Crashes.* Transportation Research Board of the National Academies, Washington, D.C.

Newstead, S., I. Bobovski, S. Hosking, and M. Cameron. 2004. *Evaluation of the Queensland Road Safety Initiatives Package.* Report 272. Monash University Accident Research Centre, Victoria, Australia, Dec.

Newstead, S. V., M. H. Cameron, and S. Narayan. 1998. *Further Modelling of Some Major Factors Influencing Road Trauma Trends in Victoria: 1990–96.* Monash University, Victoria, Australia, April.

New York State Governor's Traffic Safety Committee. 2008. *New York State Highway Safety Strategic Plan: FFY 2009.*

NHTSA. 2006. *Highway Safety Program Guideline No. 19: Speed Management.* Nov.

NHTSA. 2009. *Integrated National Communications Plan.* March. http://www.trafficsafetymarketing.gov/commplans.cfm.

NHTSA. n.d. a. Highway Safety Program Guidelines. http://204.68.195.250/nhtsa/whatsup/tea21/tea21programs/.

NHTSA. n.d. b. State Highway Safety Documents. http://www.nhtsa.dot.gov/nhtsa/whatsup/SAFETEAweb/index.htm.

NHTSA. n.d. c. Traffic Safety Marketing. http://www.trafficsafetymarketing.gov/index.cfm.

OECD. n.d. International Road Traffic Accident Database. http://www.swov.nl/cognos/cgi-bin/ppdscgi.exe?toc=%2FEnglish%2FIRTAD.

OECD and ECMT. 2006a. *Country Reports on Road Safety Performance: France.* Joint Transport Research Centre, July.

OECD and ECMT. 2006b. *Speed Management.* Joint Transport Research Centre.

OECD and International Transport Forum. 2008a. *Country Reports on Road Safety Performance: France.* July.

OECD and International Transport Forum. 2008b. *Country Reports on Road Safety Performance: Sweden.* July.

OECD and International Transport Forum. 2008c. *Country Reports on Road Safety Performance: United Kingdom (Great Britain).* July.

OECD and International Transport Forum. 2008d. *Towards Zero: Ambitious Road Safety Targets and the Safe System Approach: Summary Document.* Joint Transport Research

Centre. http://www.internationaltransportforum.org/jtrc/safety/targets/08Targets Summary.pdf.

OECD and International Transport Forum. 2010. Press Release: A Record Decade for Road Safety: International Transport Forum at the OECD Publishes Road Death Figures for 33 Countries. Sept. 15.

OECD and International Transport Forum. n.d. Country Reports on Road Safety Performance. http://www.internationaltransportforum.org/jtrc/safety/targets/Performance/performance.html.

ONISR. 2005. French Road Safety Policy. http://www.securiteroutiere.gouv.fr/IMG/pdf/FRSP.pdf.

ONISR. 2006a. Impact du Contrôle Sanction Automatisé sur la Sécurité Routière (2003–2005).

ONISR. 2006b. Observatoire des Vitesses: Second Quadrimestre 2006. Oct. 20. http://www.securiteroutiere.gouv.fr/IMG/pdf/observatoire_vitesse.pdf.

ONISR. 2008. *La Sécurité Routière en France: Bilan de l'Année 2007.*

ONISR. 2009a. Observatoire des Vitesses: Premier Quadrimestre 2009. July.

ONISR. 2009b. Observatoire National: Statistiques des Accidents. http://www2.securiteroutiere.gouv.fr/infos-ref/observatoire/index.html.

ONISR. 2009c. *La Sécurité Routière en France: Bilan de l'Année 2008.*

ONISR. 2010. *Bilan de la Sécurité Routière du 1er Semestre 2010 en Données Provisoires: Premiers Chiffres.* July.

PA Consulting Group and UCL. 2005. *The National Safety Camera Programme: Four-Year Evaluation Report.* Dec.

PACTS. 2008. Annual Review 07/08. Sept. 8. http://www.pacts.org.uk/briefings-and-articles.php?id=69.

Peden, M., R. Scurfield, D. Sleet, D. Mohan, A. A. Hyder, E. Jarawan, and C. Mathers (eds.). 2004. *World Report on Road Traffic Injury Prevention.* World Health Organization.

PennDOT. 2006. *Comprehensive Strategic Highway Safety Improvement Plan.* Oct.

PennDOT. 2008. *Highway Safety Plan: Federal Fiscal Year 2009.*

PennDOT. n.d. *Highway Safety Annual Report: FY 2008.*

Raynal, F. 2003. Road Safety: The French Change Direction. *Label France,* No. 52, 4th quarter. http://www.diplomatie.gouv.fr/en/france_159/label-france_2554/presentation_8452.html.

Scrase, R. 2008. Circle of Influence: How France Has Used Roundabouts to Cut Casualties. International Road Assessment Program. http://www.saferoaddesign.com/media/2204/france.pdf.

Son, H., M. Fontaine, and B. Park. 2007. Field Evaluation of Rational Speed Limits. Presented at 86th Annual Meeting of the Transportation Research Board, Washington, D.C.

State Government of South Australia. 2008. *South Australian Road Safety Action Plan 2008–2010.* July.

State Government of Victoria. 2001. *Arrive Alive! Victoria's Road Safety Strategy, 2002–2007.* Nov. http://www.arrivealive.vic.gov.au/index.html.

State Government of Victoria. 2008. *Victoria's Road Safety Strategy: Arrive Alive 2008–2017.*

Syner, J., B. Jackson, L. Dankers, B. Naff, S. Hancock, and J. Siegler. 2008. *Strategic Evaluation States Initiative—Case Studies of Alaska, Georgia, and West Virginia.* National Highway Traffic Safety Administration, April.

Tarko, A. P. 2008. Can Enforcement and Education Affect Speed on County Roads? Presented at 87th Annual Meeting of the Transportation Research Board, Washington, D.C.

Wundersitz, L. N., K. Hiranandani, and M. R. J. Baldock. 2009. *Annual Performance Indicators of Enforced Driver Behaviours in South Australia, 2007.* Centre for Automotive Safety Research, University of Adelaide, Australia, Aug.

4

Case Studies of Safety Interventions

Chapter 3 described how successful traffic safety programs in other countries function effectively at three levels: the technical implementation of specific countermeasures, agency-level management and planning of the safety program, and maintenance of political and public support. Political leadership has been essential to successful safety initiatives in other countries, at the U.S. federal level, and in the U.S. states. Sustained, high-level political support provides resources, accountability, and buffering from opponents of rigorous interventions. Communication between political leaders and the professional and research communities also has been vital in ensuring that political initiatives lead to effective safety interventions.

The experience of safety programs in the United States and abroad also shows that leadership and competence of senior public-sector executives are critical. Managers must define safety program objectives and strategies, budget and allocate resources, coordinate programs across agencies, evaluate the effectiveness of interventions and progress toward program objectives, and communicate expert advice to elected officials.

To learn about the sources of leadership and management commitment, the committee examined case studies of the development and implementation of particular countermeasures in the United States. The cases focus on single categories of safety problems and countermeasures for the sake of simplicity, but it is recognized that traffic safety strategy must be comprehensive, integrating driver behavior regulation, road engineering, vehicle safety, and medical services.

The objective of the case studies was to examine whether progress is being made in the United States against the selected categories of traffic hazards, to identify the sources of progress and obstacles to progress with regard to those hazards, and to compare the U.S. experience with experiences in other countries. If U.S. progress has been slower than abroad in any of the cases, the difference may be that other countries' intervention techniques, or their management of interventions, are more effective than methods used in the United States. Alternatively, differences may reflect changes in risk factors such as travel patterns.

The case studies do not constitute a comprehensive catalog or review of effectiveness of countermeasures. As Chapter 1 explained, the committee did not survey all categories of safety practice. Among the categories not examined in the cases are countermeasures aimed at distracted driving, aggressive driving, and drug-impaired driving; truck safety programs; driver training; vehicle safety rating; vehicle design improvements; graduated drivers' licensing; and emergency medical response. The omitted categories include some areas of U.S. success and leadership (e.g., graduated licensing) as well as some (e.g., vehicle improvements) that probably account for important shares of recent traffic safety improvement in the benchmark countries. Some of the omitted categories can make important contributions in the future. For example, safety agencies worldwide have recognized the great potential of in-vehicle information technology applications for reducing crash risk (Farmer 2008). Technologies being tested can effectively and instantaneously warn drivers of external collision risks and of their own high-risk driving behavior (e.g., unsafe speed) and can intervene in vehicle control in high-risk situations.

The five intervention cases selected were alcohol-impaired driving prevention, speed control, seat belt laws, motorcycle helmet laws, and practices with regard to roadway hazard elimination and safe road design. These five kinds of safety interventions present contrasting management, compliance, and legislative challenges. Seat belt laws and helmet laws are primarily state legislative issues; the laws are effective and relatively easy to enforce once enacted. Impaired driving prevention and speed control are ongoing management responsibilities of state and local law enforcement and highway agencies; the legislature is responsible for laws concerning limits, penalties, and enforcement techniques and for providing agency resources. Highway network screening (identification of high-hazard locations) has been largely a federally motivated activity, with federal grants partially paying for state capital improvements to correct high-hazard locations and for state data systems to identify locations; the legislature's responsibility has been to provide resources for the program. In general, helmet laws are highly visible issues politically, impaired driving and speed control receive legislative attention when regulations are revised or automated enforcement is proposed, and highway network screening receives attention only when a particular hazard attracts local interest.

For each of the case study topics, the sections below describe the following:

- The value of the safety intervention: the magnitude of the safety problem addressed and the potential effectiveness of the intervention in reducing risk. It is important to know whether safety management and political leadership are steering safety practices in a productive direction.
- Trends in crashes and fatalities that are related to the risks addressed and trends in government attention and resources devoted to the problem.
- Benchmark nation comparisons: comparison of U.S. trends and practices with those of other countries with successful safety programs.
- Illustrative histories of particular U.S. state or federal regulations and safety initiatives. Ideally, the histories would reveal the nature of the political forces that motivated actions of legislatures on safety laws, safety budgets, and oversight of safety programs; the relationship between public opinion and political leadership; and the importance of management leadership and skills within government agencies as sources of improved safety practices.
- Conclusions on how political and public support and management commitment have been obtained.

Although management practices and allocation of resources differ among the benchmark countries, a suite of countermeasures recognized as accepted practice and addressing the full range of risks is in general use in all the high-income countries. Application methods have been codified and scientific evaluations of many have been carried out (e.g., Hedlund et al. 2009; Dinh-Zarr et al. 2001; Shults et al. 2001; TRB 2003–2009).

ALCOHOL-IMPAIRED DRIVING PREVENTION

The sections below describe trends in measures of alcohol-impaired driving in the United States and in selected benchmark countries, interventions that are applied in the benchmark countries and in the United States to curtail alcohol-impaired driving, and the U.S. federal government role in impaired-driving prevention. The final section contains concluding observations.

Trends in Alcohol-Related Fatalities

The best evidence of the success of national campaigns against alcohol-impaired driving would be a decline in the percentage of drivers on the road with a blood alcohol content (BAC) level above some threshold. However, data for a sample of all drivers are rarely available in the United States. Instead, data on BAC levels of persons involved in crashes usually are used to indicate the magnitude of the drunk driving problem and the success of interventions. For example, the National Highway Traffic Safety Administration (NHTSA) tabulates numbers of alcohol-related fatal crashes, defined as fatal crashes in which at least one driver or one involved pedestrian had a BAC exceeding 0.01 percent. A decline in the annual number of alcohol-related crashes is weak evidence of success of impaired-driving prevention efforts if the total of all crashes is declining at a similar rate. When such a trend is observed, it is possible that other factors (e.g., more general highway safety measures, speed reductions caused by increased congestion) are reducing the frequency of all kinds of crashes and that anti–drunk driving activities are having little effect. However, a faster rate of decline in the number of alcohol-related crashes than in all crashes is better evidence of the success of anti–drunk driving interventions. (On "related factors" in fatal crash statistics, see Box 4-1.)

Another difficulty in measuring the impact of BAC programs is that only about 40 percent of U.S. drivers involved in fatal crashes receive BAC tests. Drivers who receive tests are unlikely to be representative of all drivers in fatal crashes. NHTSA estimates the total frequency of alcohol-related fatal crashes from the reported BAC data (Subramanian 2002), but the reliability of the estimates is difficult to judge. Comparisons

BOX 4-1

"Related Factors" in Fatalities

The NHTSA Fatality Analysis Reporting System (FARS) traffic fatality database includes information on circumstances of crashes that are believed to be related to crash risk or to the expected severity of the crash. The numbers of fatalities in 2007 determined by NHTSA to be speeding-related and alcohol-related and the number of deaths of light-vehicle occupants who were not using restraints (seat belts or safety seats) were as follows:

Type of Fatality	Number
Speeding-related fatalities	13,040
Fatalities in crashes in which a driver had BAC ≥ 0.01 percent	15,387
Car or light-truck occupants killed who were not wearing restraints	14,390

More than one of these factors were present in some fatal crashes. Total fatalities in 2007 were 41,259.

NHTSA's bases for these classifications are as follows:

- Speeding-related: A driver involved in the crash is charged with a speeding-related offense or a police officer indicates that racing, driving too fast for conditions, or exceeding the posted speed limit was a contributing factor in the crash (NHTSA 2007d). As the section on speed in this chapter describes, the great variation among the states in the fraction of fatal crashes coded as speed-related suggests that this classification is not consistently coded in the FARS data.
- Restraint use: Use is determined by police reports. Of the 29,000 passenger car and light-truck occupant deaths in 2007 in FARS, 7 percent are reported as "restraint use unknown,"

(continued on next page)

> BOX 4-1 *(continued)*
> **"Related Factors" in Fatalities**
>
> 42 percent as "restraint used," and 49 percent as "restraint not used" (NHTSA 2008a, 40).
>
> - Alcohol-related: Before 2008, NHTSA's annual FARS summary (e.g., NHTSA 2007b, 32) reported "total fatalities in alcohol-related crashes," defined as the number of deaths in crashes in which a driver or involved nonoccupant (e.g., a pedestrian) had a BAC ≥ 0.01 percent. Starting with the FARS 2007 summary report, the term "alcohol-related crashes" is no longer used, and NHTSA tabulates only crashes in which a driver had BAC ≥ 0.01 percent (NHTSA 2008a, 7, 32). For fatal crashes in which alcohol test results are unknown, NHTSA estimates the distribution of driver BAC levels.
>
> The related-factors data may have use in setting priorities for enforcement of driver behavior regulations but must be interpreted with caution. Characterizing the alcohol and speeding data as tabulations of crash causes would be inaccurate, since there is little basis for estimating what fraction of alcohol- or speeding-involved fatalities would not have occurred if these related factors had not been present. Conversely, some crashes not coded as "speed-related" probably would have been avoided or mitigated if the vehicles involved had been traveling at lower speeds.

among countries are complicated further by differences in definitions of an alcohol-related crash and in methods of data collection.

Finally, crash records in the United States and other countries indicate the presence of an impaired driver or pedestrian, but not whether the impairment was a cause of the crash. Some fraction of the alcohol-related fatal crashes would have occurred even if none of the involved persons had been impaired.

TABLE 4-1 Trends in Alcohol-Related Crashes and Pedestrian Fatalities, 1982–2008

	1982	1995	2005	2008
Fatalities in alcohol-related crashes[a]				
Number	24,200	16,000	16,100	13,900
Number as a percentage of all traffic fatalities	55	38	37	37
Percentage of pedestrians killed who had BAC > 0	49	41	39	42

[a] Before 2008, NHTSA defined an alcohol-related crash as one in which any involved driver or pedestrian had a BAC > 0. NHTSA tabulations no longer use this term. The values shown in the table for fatalities in alcohol-related crashes as a percentage of all fatalities are the fraction of all fatalities that occurred in crashes in which any driver had a BAC > 0.
SOURCE: NHTSA 2009c, Tables 13, 20.

U.S. Trends

NHTSA estimates show progress in reducing the share of traffic fatalities that are alcohol-related from the early 1980s until the mid-1990s. Since that time, progress appears almost to have ceased (Table 4-1).

Roadside surveys of alcohol impairment conducted by NHTSA in 1973, 1997, and 2007 and by the Insurance Institute for Highway Safety (IIHS) in 1986 indicate continuous decline in the frequency of impaired driving throughout this period (Table 4-2). In these surveys, a random sample of drivers is stopped and asked to submit to an alcohol test voluntarily. The response rate in the 2007 survey was high, and the analysis included imputation of the impairment rate among nonrespondents on the basis of responses to supplementary survey questions. Eighty-six percent of drivers stopped provided a breath sample; BACs for 87 percent of those who refused could be estimated from a passive alcohol sensor reading (Compton and Berning 2009).

The decline in the fraction of all fatalities determined to be alcohol-related is consistent with the pattern of enforcement effort in this period.

TABLE 4-2 Percentage of All Drivers with BAC ≥ 0.8 g/L

	1973	1986	1997	2007
Weekend nighttime drivers	7.5	5.4	4.3	2.2
Drivers younger than legal drinking age	5.5	3.0	1.3	0.9

SOURCE: Compton and Berning 2009, Figures 1 and 5.

Arrests for alcohol-impaired driving increased by 300 percent from 400,000 in 1970 to 1.6 million (1 arrest per 100 licensed drivers) in 1983, the period of rapid reduction in the fraction of crashes that are alcohol-related, and has since declined (Figure 4-1).

Since 1995, the decline in the percentage of pedestrians killed in traffic accidents who had positive BAC has been nearly as great as the decline in the percentage of all traffic fatalities that are alcohol-related. Because

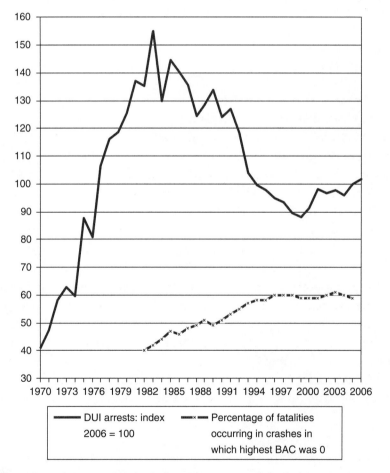

FIGURE 4-1 Driving-under-the-influence arrests and alcohol-involved fatalities, 1970–2007. (SOURCE: Pastore and Maguire n.d., Tables 4.27.2007, 3.103.2006.)

most intervention efforts are aimed at drivers, the similarity of the trends in driver and pedestrian alcohol involvement suggests that factors other than the interventions may be driving the trends.

The percentage of traffic fatalities that are alcohol-related is close to the national average in most states, but some states are outliers. In NHTSA estimates for 2008, 45 percent or more of all fatalities were in crashes in which a driver had a BAC $\geq$ 0.01 percent in 6 states (Hawaii, Montana, North Dakota, Rhode Island, South Carolina, and Wyoming). The highest shares were 50 percent in North Dakota and South Carolina. The lowest shares were 20 percent in Utah and 21 percent in Vermont (NHTSA 2009c, Table 117).

International Comparisons

Most of the benchmark countries track alcohol-related crashes by using measures similar to those of the United States. Trends are summarized below for four countries noted for strong anti–drunk driving controls. In general, experiences in the United States and internationally appear similar: slowing progress over the past decade in reducing the fraction of all crashes that are alcohol-related.

In Great Britain the proportion of all fatally injured drivers who had BAC over the 0.08 percent (0.8 g/L) legal limit declined from the early 1970s through the mid-1990s but since has crept upward:

	1975	*1995*	*2005*
Percentage of all fatally injured drivers with BAC > 0.8 g/L	35	21	24
Fatalities in accidents involving illegal alcohol levels	1,500	540	550

In 2006, police administered 602,000 roadside screening breath tests in England and Wales. Authorities speculate that the cause of the recent lack of progress is a reduction in the frequency of tests. However, the number of tests in 2006 was greater than in any year before 1994 and the number of convictions resulting from the tests is unchanged from the 1990s (DfT 2008, 27–31; DfT 2007, 27–31; Sweedler et al. 2004).

Since at least 1975, Germany has steadily reduced the proportions of all traffic injury crashes and of all traffic fatalities that are alcohol-related, defined as crashes in which at least one involved person had a BAC exceeding 0.3 g/L (data in all years include East Germany):

	1975	1995	2005
Alcohol-related injury accidents			
Number	52,000	37,000	22,000
As percentage of all injury accidents	14	10	6
Alcohol-related fatalities			
Number	3,500	1,700	600
As percentage of all fatalities	20	18	11

Gains are still being made, although the trend appears nearly to have flattened after 2000, after a spike in the early 1990s followed by a steep decline in the late 1990s (Schoenebeck 2007; Sweedler et al. 2004). Recent traffic safety trends have been affected by the reunification of East and West Germany. The former Eastern bloc countries experienced rapid growth in automobile travel and have higher injury and fatality rates, but more rapid rates of improvement, than the West.

In Australia, the fraction of all fatally injured drivers and motorcycle riders with BAC exceeding the 0.05 percent (0.5 g/L) legal limit fell from 44 percent in 1981 to 30 in 1992, but then fluctuated between 26 and 30 percent through 1998. The fraction of all fatalities that were alcohol-related fell from 43 percent in 1988 to 35 percent in 1992, then fluctuated between 35 and 38 percent from 1992 to 2001. More recent data are not available (IIHS 2005; Haworth and Johnston 2004; Sweedler 2007).

In Sweden, the fraction of fatally injured drivers who had BAC exceeding 0.02 percent rose from 19 percent (43 out of 230 drivers killed) in 1998 to 27 percent (50 out of 187) in 2004, then declined to 24 percent (48 out of 200) in 2007 (Swedish Road Administration 2009, 32). In 1992 the legal BAC limit was changed from 0.05 percent to 0.02 percent. Enforcement, including random breath testing on a large scale, was intense for several years after 1992. Enforcement efforts have been reduced somewhat since their peak in the 1990s. Also, per capita alcohol consumption was increasing between 1996 and 2002 (Sweedler et al. 2004; Sweedler 2007). Swedish Road Administration officials interpret the recent increase in the percentage of drivers in fatal crashes who are alcohol-impaired as partly the consequence of the reduction in the total number of fatal crashes, while the frequency of impaired driving has remained constant (Breen et al. 2007, 30).

Interventions

Deaths and injuries caused by alcohol-impaired driving are one manifestation of the complex social and public health problem of alcohol abuse. Consequently, a range of interventions is needed, and strategies combine measures that attack the broader public health problem with more narrowly targeted traffic safety measures. A NHTSA report has categorized the available countermeasures as follows (Hedlund et al. 2007, 1-2-1-4):

- Deterrence: action to enact, publicize, and enforce laws against alcohol-impaired driving:
    - Laws: administrative license revocation at time of BAC test failure, test refusal penalties, stronger sanctions for higher-BAC drivers, laws against open containers, young driver restrictions
    - Enforcement techniques: sobriety checkpoints, saturation patrols, integrated enforcement (e.g., combined seat belt and alcohol campaigns), preliminary and passive breath test devices
    - Adjudication: court sanctions (license revocation, fines, jail, community service), elimination of diversion programs and plea bargains that expunge alcohol-related offenses from offenders' records, special driving-while-intoxicated (DWI) courts, citizen monitoring of court handling of impaired-driving cases
    - Offender monitoring: monitoring of sentence completion, alcohol interlocks
- Prevention: actions to reduce drinking and to prevent drinkers from driving
    - Responsible beverage service (training of beverage servers)
    - Alternative transportation provision
    - Designated drivers
    - Alcohol screening and brief intervention in general medical practice
    - Underage drinking and other alcohol sales enforcement
- Communications: establishment of positive social norms with regard to drinking and driving
    - Mass-media campaigns
    - School and youth education programs

- Treatment to reduce alcohol dependency among drivers, including court assignment to treatment
- General traffic safety measures that protect impaired drivers as well as others, for example, enforcement of seat belt laws

Interventions in the Benchmark Countries
The interventions used in the benchmark countries that are believed to have the greatest effectiveness are high-frequency roadside alcohol testing, low BAC limits, intensive follow-up on offenders through the judicial system, and the coupling of social marketing techniques with enforcement. Ignition interlocks that prevent an alcohol-impaired person from operating a motor vehicle are coming into use in several countries.

Laws, enforcement methods, and intensity of enforcement against impaired driving in France, Australia, Sweden, and the United Kingdom are summarized in Chapter 3. Random alcohol test checkpoints (that is, enforcement in which all drivers stopped at a roadside checkpoint are tested, not only those for whom the enforcement officer has grounds to suspect impairment) are used in France, Australia, and Sweden and in most European countries except the United Kingdom, but they are illegal in the United States as a violation of the Fourth Amendment's protection against unreasonable searches. As described in Chapter 3, rates of alcohol testing in many countries are high enough that a driver can expect to be tested at least once every few years [for example, 280 tests per 1,000 drivers annually in France (Table 3-1)] and appear much higher than U.S. test rates, although few U.S. data on enforcement effort are available.

In nearly all of Europe except the United Kingdom and Ireland, and in Australia, the per se BAC limit is 0.05 percent or lower. The limit is 0.08 in the United States, Canada, and the United Kingdom.

U.S. Intervention Priorities
For transportation officials responsible for proposing or carrying out an impaired-driving prevention program, selecting from among the possible countermeasures to design a strategy depends on a balancing of effectiveness, cost, and political feasibility. Research has evaluated the effectiveness of many of the countermeasures listed above (Hedlund

et al. 2009), and several national groups have identified combinations of actions that they believe should receive the highest priority. The priority lists indicate expert opinion about the most needed actions and generally reflect the findings of the body of scientific evaluation research. The lists suggest that a consensus exists on the need for certain measures.

NHTSA, on the basis of the scope of federal government responsibilities and capabilities, has identified four strategies for special promotion through its technical assistance and coordination activities (NHTSA 2007a):

- High-visibility enforcement,
- Support for prosecutors and DWI courts,
- Medical screening and brief intervention for alcohol abuse problems, and
- Enactment of primary seat belt laws.

NHTSA's activities with regard to impaired driving are described in the section below on federal responsibilities.

NHTSA's high-priority strategies are consistent with the recommended actions to reduce alcohol-impaired driving of the Task Force on Community Preventive Services, a nongovernmental expert panel convened by the Centers for Disease Control and Prevention that publishes public health policy recommendations founded on rigorous reviews of research on effectiveness. Addressed to state and local governments and community organizations, the task force's recommendations for measures that are not already generally applied are as follows (Task Force on Community Preventive Services n.d.):

- Sobriety checkpoints: A sobriety checkpoint is a site where police systematically stop drivers, look for signs of impairment, and administer a breath test when there is reason to suspect impairment.
- Intervention training programs for servers of alcoholic beverages: These programs teach servers ways to prevent intoxication among their patrons (for example, by delaying or denying service).
- Mass-media campaigns: The evidence for effectiveness applies mainly to media campaigns that use pretested messages; attain high exposure through paid advertising; and complement local-level, high-visibility enforcement.

- School-based instructional programs aimed at discouraging students from riding with drinking drivers.
- Multicomponent intervention with community mobilization: This strategy involves recruiting participation of community coalitions or task forces in the design and execution of interventions such as those listed above.
- Ignition interlocks: An alcohol ignition interlock is a device installed in a vehicle that prevents a driver with BAC above a preset level from starting the engine. Use of an interlock may be required by the court as a condition of probation for an impaired-driving offender.

The task force also recommends retention of three laws that are already in force in all states: the 0.08 percent BAC limit, lower legal BAC limits for young or inexperienced drivers, and the minimum legal drinking age of 21 years. The task force's research review found that these three laws are effective in reducing motor vehicle occupant injuries.

Finally, the National Transportation Safety Board has published a list of recommended actions to reduce fatalities and injuries involving "the hard core drinking driver," a category defined to include repeat offenders and high-BAC offenders. The recommendations include special penalties for high-BAC offenders, lower BAC limits for repeat offenders, administrative license revocation, sobriety checkpoints, vehicle sanctions including impoundment and interlocks, alternatives to confinement involving strict supervision, restriction of plea bargaining, and elimination of diversion programs (NTSB 2000).

Reviews of evaluation studies have concluded that random sobriety checkpoints and checkpoints conducted under U.S. rules [which allow police to stop all vehicles (or vehicles selected according to some rule, such as every third vehicle) at a preannounced location and time period, observe their drivers, and administer sobriety tests to those that show signs of intoxication] were both effective in reducing alcohol-related fatal crashes. Furthermore, U.S. methods, applied with sufficient intensity and efficiently managed, can equal the effectiveness of random testing enforcement (Shults et al. 2001, 76; Elder et al. 2002).

Research evidence also indicates that lowering the U.S. BAC limit from 0.08 percent to the 0.05 percent limit prevailing elsewhere would be an effective safety measure. A comprehensive review of research studies concluded that lowering the BAC limit from 0.10 to 0.08 in the United States reduced alcohol-related crashes and casualties. The review concluded that lowering the limit from 0.08 to 0.05 in other countries reduced alcohol-related fatalities and that this effect cannot be accounted for solely by changes in publicity or enforcement that were introduced in some countries simultaneously with the lowering of the BAC limit. Research has found that crash risk is substantially higher for drivers with BAC of 0.05 than for drivers with 0.00 BAC and that lowering the limit to 0.05 can reduce the incidence of impaired driving at much higher BAC levels (i.e., at BAC over 0.15 percent). The authors conclude that the introduction of more stringent laws serves as a general deterrent to drinking and driving (Fell and Voas 2006).

Implementation and Obstacles

The federal requirements described in the following section have contributed to a progressive strengthening of state laws with regard to the legal drinking age, BAC limits, and other alcohol control measures. IIHS rates the adequacy of the laws of all the states concerning alcohol-impaired driving. In the 2009 survey, 19 states earned an overall "good" rating for their laws and one state was rated as "poor." The remainder received "fair" or "marginal" ratings. In comparison, 16 states were rated good and one poor in 2006, and in the 2000 survey eight were good and five poor. A good rating means the state has a 0.08 percent BAC limit, has an administrative license revocation law and a "zero tolerance" law (imposing a stricter impaired-driving standard on new drivers) that IIHS judges to be effective, and allows sobriety checkpoints. A poor rating means that no more than one of these laws is adequate (IIHS 2009a; IIHS 2006; IIHS 2000).

State legislative actions on impaired driving are monitored by the National Conference of State Legislatures (NCSL). In the 2009 review, NCSL reported that 229 impaired-driving bills were introduced in legislatures in 2009 and that 25 states enacted laws relating to impaired driving (Savage et al. 2010). Contents of legislative activity reported by NCSL included the following:

- High-BAC countermeasures: By 2009, 43 states and the District of Columbia had laws providing stronger sanctions for high-BAC offenses

(offenses in which the driver has BAC above a threshold ranging from 0.15 to 0.20 percent). Two states enacted high-BAC laws in 2009.
- Ignition interlocks: As of November 2009, nine states required ignition interlock devices on the vehicles of all convicted drunk drivers, including two states that passed such laws in 2009. [The total rose to 12 states in 2010 (GHSA n.d. a).] Thirty-two states considered some form of ignition interlock legislation during the year.

Much less information is available on the level of effort the states devote to implementation of countermeasures than on the laws in place in each state. The NHTSA report that presented the categorization of countermeasures summarized above (Hedlund et al. 2007) also attempted to judge the extent of use of each countermeasure, with ratings ranging from "high use" to "low use." Among the effective measures with low or unknown use are DWI courts (low), citizen monitoring of court performance in impaired-driving cases (low), and passive breath sensors (unknown). Sobriety checkpoints are rated "medium use" on the basis of the number of states that allow checkpoints; however, it is noted that few states make regular use of checkpoints and that a 2003 survey found only 11 states that conduct checkpoints on a weekly basis (Hedlund et al. 2007, 1-15). In 10 states (Idaho, Iowa, Michigan, Minnesota, Oregon, Rhode Island, Texas, Washington, Wisconsin, and Wyoming), sobriety checkpoints are not permitted under state law, and two states (Alaska and Montana) never use checkpoints as a matter of policy (MADD n.d.).

Federal Government Engagement

Authority for regulation of traffic and of alcohol rests with the states and local governments. Therefore, federal responsibility for drunk driving prevention is limited. However, federal laws and programs have significantly influenced state practices. Federal involvement has taken three forms: mandates requiring the states to enact certain restrictions as a condition for receiving federal funding; incentive grants to fund state safety programs that meet federal standards; and NHTSA programs that aim to provide leadership, coordination, and technical support for state alcohol safety initiatives.

Mandates

The 1998 federal surface transportation aid legislation (the Transportation Equity Act for the 21st Century) penalized any state that did not enact a repeat intoxicated-driver law (providing stronger penalties for repeat offenders) and an open container law (forbidding possession of an open alcohol container in a vehicle) satisfying federal criteria. States without such laws lose up to 3 percent of their federal highway construction aid funding. The lost construction funding is transferred to the state's federal highway safety funding and may be used only for drunk driving prevention programs or road hazard elimination. In 2000, Congress enacted a provision requiring each state to enact a 0.08 percent BAC limit or lose up to 8 percent of its federal aid construction funds (GHSA n.d. b; Thiel 2003).

Forty-three states complied with the federal repeat offender law mandate and 43 with the open container law mandate by 2010; many of these state laws were enacted after imposition of the federal requirements. All states now have a 0.08 percent BAC limit law. Before 1998, 0.10 percent was the limit in most states and only 16 states had 0.08 percent BAC laws (GHSA n.d. a; Thiel 2003). Reducing the limit nationwide to 0.08 has reduced the gap between regulations in the United States and most of the other high-income countries.

The 1998 and 2000 laws follow the precedent of 1984 federal legislation that required all states to enact a minimum legal drinking age of 21 years or lose a portion of federal highway aid. By 1987, all states were in compliance (Task Force on Community Preventive Services 2005, 350).

Incentive Grants

Federal grants specifically to promote and fund programs aimed at drunk driving have been provided to the states since at least the 1980s. The most recent federal surface transportation aid legislation [the Safe, Accountable, Flexible, Efficient Transportation Equity Act: A Legacy for Users (SAFETEA-LU)] authorized an average of $129 million annually over 2006–2009 in the Alcohol-Impaired Driving Countermeasures Incentive Grants Program, for distribution by NHTSA by a formula (depending on state population and road miles) among all states that meet certain qualifications. This amount was more than three times the authorization in the previous federal-aid program ($220 million over 6 years). States could qualify in 2009 if they operated at least five of the following eight programs:

- A high-visibility impaired-driving enforcement program,
- An outreach program to educate prosecutors and judges on repeat offender prosecution,
- A program to increase the fraction of drivers involved in fatal crashes that are tested for BAC,
- A law that imposes stronger penalties on drivers with BAC exceeding 0.15 percent,
- A rehabilitation program or oversight by a special DWI court for repeat offenders,
- An underage-drinking prevention program,
- An administrative license suspension or revocation law for offenders, and
- Provision for applying the fines paid by offenders to fund local government impaired-driving prevention.

States may also qualify if they have relatively low alcohol-related fatality rates, and a separate grant program is available to the 10 states with the highest alcohol-related fatality rates in a year (NHTSA n.d.; Savage et al. 2007).

SAFETEA-LU also authorizes grants in several traffic safety categories with more general eligibility criteria, which the states may use to fund drunk driving prevention. These include the State and Community Highway Safety Grants, Information System Improvement Grants, and High Visibility Enforcement Grants, which are authorized, in total, at about $290 million annually (NHTSA n.d.).

Guidance and Coordination
NHTSA spends about $40 million annually in technical assistance and demonstration activities promoting alcohol and drug countermeasures; vehicle occupant protection; traffic law enforcement; emergency medical care systems; traffic records; and safety of motorcyclists, bicyclists, pedestrians, pupils, and younger and older drivers (USDOT 2007). As noted above, NHTSA promotes four strategies through its technical

assistance and leadership activities: high-visibility enforcement, support for prosecutors and DWI courts, medical screening and brief intervention for alcohol abuse problems, and enactment of primary seat belt laws (NHTSA 2007a).

High-visibility enforcement initiatives are enforcement crackdowns, either of short duration or sustained, aimed particularly at enforcing drunk driving and seat belt laws and coinciding with media publicity. NHTSA's role has been to organize multijurisdictional, high-visibility enforcement efforts to take advantage of the economies of scale and enhanced impact of regional and national crackdowns. The slogan of the current campaign is "Drunk Driving. Over the Limit. Under Arrest." Ten thousand police agencies nationwide have committed to coordinating enforcement crackdowns through this program, and NHTSA is assisting with media publicity and technical aid. NHTSA reports that evaluation of an earlier phase of the high-visibility enforcement initiative showed that it produced a sustained reduction in alcohol-related fatalities (NHTSA 2007a, 4).

NHTSA promotes special training for prosecutors handling impaired-driving cases and encourages establishment of special state DWI courts to hear cases and monitor compliance with sentences, in order to improve the effectiveness of adjudication of impaired-driving cases. The initiative is needed because lack of capacity in the court system to prosecute offenders successfully and to oversee sanctions has undermined enforcement and encouraged recidivism. NHTSA's involvement has been to provide grant funding of state Traffic Safety Resource Prosecutor positions and technical assistance and training for prosecutors and DWI courts.

Screening and brief intervention can be performed by doctors during emergency room visits or checkups to identify patients with alcohol use problems and to encourage treatment or other action. NHTSA reports that evidence shows that the technique reduces impaired driving among problem drinkers (NHTSA 2007a, 7). NHTSA's involvement has been in working with other federal agencies and medical organizations to promote screening and brief intervention as routine medical practices.

NHTSA includes enactment of primary seat belt laws among its four crucial anti–drunk driving strategies because fatally injured drunk drivers are far less likely to have been wearing seat belts than fatally injured drivers with zero BAC. Stronger enforcement of seat belt laws would therefore be expected to reduce alcohol-related motor vehicle deaths. NHTSA research demonstrating the benefits of seat belts and of primary seat belt laws and its information programs that publicize these benefits aid efforts to enact state primary seat belt laws.

Concluding Observations

After at least 15 years of progress, in the past decade almost no reduction has been achieved in the annual numbers of fatalities in alcohol-related crashes in the United States. Several of the benchmark countries, including Great Britain, Australia, and Sweden, have experienced similar slowdowns or reversals of progress in reducing alcohol-related traffic fatalities. In some countries these developments correlate with slackening of enforcement efforts or increases in alcohol consumption; however, the causes are not well understood, and other factors, for example demographic trends, may be important. Data on the extent and patterns of impaired driving in the United States are incomplete and of uncertain reliability. Improved data could help in understanding the causes of the recent slowdown in progress and in design of more effective programs.

Several countermeasures that have proved effective and are regularly used in some jurisdictions in the United States remain little used in much of the country. Examples are sobriety checkpoints, close monitoring of offenders, and ignition interlocks. Federal involvement in prevention of alcohol-impaired driving has had mixed success. Federal mandates have caused many states to strengthen anti–drunk driving laws, but NHTSA technical assistance and coordination programs operate with limited resources. The impact of federal grants for state alcohol programs is unknown.

Although differences in measurement methods complicate comparisons, Germany, Great Britain, Sweden, and Australia all appear to have attained lower rates of alcohol-involved traffic fatalities, per vehicle kilometer of travel and as a fraction of all fatalities, than the United States. Getting progress started again in the United States apparently will require more widespread and systematic application of the proven countermeasures and greater coordination of strategy among law enforcement agencies, the court system, and public health programs aimed at alcohol abuse. The federal government may have a role in providing leadership for such efforts. All of these actions will require increases in funding.

In countries that have introduced sustained, high-frequency programs of random sobriety testing, including Australia, Finland, and France, reductions of 13 to 36 percent in the frequency of alcohol-involved fatal injury crashes have been achieved. Evaluations of intensive campaigns of selective testing at sobriety checkpoints in U.S. jurisdictions (following procedures now legal in most states) have reported reductions of 20 to 26 percent in alcohol fatal injury crashes (Shults et al. 2001, 76; Fell et al. 2004, 226). In the United States in 2008, 12,000 persons were killed in crashes involving a driver who was alcohol-impaired (NHTSA 2009c, 113). Therefore, widespread implementation of sustained, high-frequency sobriety testing programs in the United States could be expected to save 1,500 to 3,000 lives annually.

SPEED CONTROL

The first four sections below describe the relationship between speed control and crash and casualty risk, summarize U.S. trends in speed and speed enforcement, compare U.S. speed trends and enforcement practices with those of the benchmark countries, and describe examples of recent U.S. speed control initiatives. Summary observations are presented in the final section.

Value of Speed Control in Reducing Crash Risks

The Governors Highway Safety Association (GHSA), summarizing a survey of the states on speeding enforcement, reports that "states are becoming increasingly concerned that gains made in the areas of safety restraint usage and impaired driving have been offset by increased fatalities and injuries due to higher speeds" (GHSA 2005, 5). In contrast, in several of the countries that are making the greatest progress in highway safety, speed control is one of the interventions receiving the greatest attention and resources. If speed control is weakening in the United States, this trend may explain part of the safety performance gap between the United States and other countries.

A 2006 report of the Organisation for Economic Co-operation and Development (OECD), the product of an international expert panel, expresses the high priority that many safety professionals place on speed control (OECD and ECMT 2006, 3):

> Speeding . . . is the number one road safety problem in many countries, often contributing to as much as one third of fatal accidents and speed is an aggravating factor in the severity of all accidents. . . .
> Research indicates that co-ordinated actions taken by the responsible authorities can bring about an immediate and durable response to the problem of speeding. Indeed, reducing speeding can reduce rapidly the number of fatalities and injuries and is a guaranteed way to make real progress towards the ambitious road safety targets set by OECD/ECMT countries. . . .
> Speed management . . . should be a central element of any road safety strategy.

The two subsections below summarize current understanding of the effect of speed on crash and injury risk and the effect of regulation and enforcement on speed.

Effect of Speed on Crash and Injury Risk

Despite the assurance of the OECD statement above, researchers have found that sorting out the effects of speed and speed controls on overall crash and injury risk is a difficult task. For example, one U.S. research review concluded: "Speed has a demonstrated negative effect on safety in that it increases the severity of accidents. While it is suspected that speed may also contribute toward the incidence of accidents, there are so many other factors that are also affected by speed, and which simultaneously affect safety, that it is difficult to distinguish the effect of speed on the occurrence of an accident" (Wilmot and Khanal 1999, 329). Similarly, a Transportation Research Board (TRB) committee that reviewed speed management practices found that "drivers' speed choices impose risks that affect both the probability and severity of crashes. Speed is directly related to injury severity in a crash. . . . [T]he strength of the relationship between speed and crash severity alone is sufficient reason for managing speed. . . . Speed is also linked to the probability of being in a crash, although the evidence is not as compelling because crashes are complex events that seldom can be attributed to a single factor" (TRB 1998, 4).

In the United States, the safety effects of speed control became especially controversial during the term of the 55-mph National Maximum

Speed Limit (NMSL) (in effect, with modifications, from 1974 to 1995). One prominent study concluded that, in states that raised the speed limit on rural Interstates, as Congress permitted in 1987, statewide fatalities were reduced by 3 to 5 percent. The authors attributed the reduction to attraction of traffic from less safe roads to the Interstates and the freeing of police to patrol the more dangerous roads rather than the Interstates (Lave and Elias 1994). The TRB speed limit committee concluded that, after the 1987 change in the law, "in the immediately following years, most states that raised limits observed increases" in speeds and speed dispersion on roads where limits were raised and that "[t]hese speed changes were generally associated with statistically significant increases in fatalities and fatal crashes on the affected highways" (TRB 1998, 5). That committee's review of studies of the effects of the 1995 repeal of the NMSL showed the same results; however, the committee acknowledged that systemwide safety effects could be negative but had not been adequately studied.

Notwithstanding the past controversies over the effect of speed on risk, present speed control programs are based on the assumption that average speed is directly related to injury crash frequency on a road and, therefore, that reducing average speed by enforcement will reduce injuries and deaths. A review of estimates of the speed–crash relationship concluded that the best description of the relationship, as a rule of thumb, is that "a 1 percent increase in speed results approximately in 2 percent change in injury crash rate, 3% change in severe crash rate, and 4% change in fatal crash rate" and that "an increase in average speed was found to increase the risk of a crash more on minor than on major roads" (Aarts and van Schagen 2006, 223, 220).

Effectiveness of Speed Regulation and Enforcement

The accepted view of conventional practice with regard to speed limits and speed control is that "generally, motorists do not adhere to speed limits but instead choose speeds they perceive as acceptably safe. . . . The impact of law enforcement on compliance with speed limits is, generally, limited and transitory" (Wilmot and Khanal 1999, 315, 320). Similarly, an essay on speed management published by the AAA Foundation for Traffic Safety concludes that "current methods for controlling speed are virtually powerless in the face of this [U.S.] speeding culture" (Harsha and Hedlund 2007, 1).

However, experience (e.g., in France and Australia, as described in Chapter 3) has demonstrated that the combination of appropriately determined limits, persistent and well-managed enforcement with adequate resources, and public outreach can effectively control speeds. The necessary elements of such a program, according to the OECD speed management report, are as follows (OECD and ECMT 2006, 3):

- Targeted education and information to the public and policy makers.
- Assessments of appropriate speed and a review of existing speed limits. . . .
- Infrastructure improvements which are aimed at achieving safe, 'self explaining' roads [i.e., roads with features like intersection roundabouts that naturally induce drivers to operate their vehicles in a safer manner]. . . .
- Sufficient levels of traditional police enforcement and automatic speed control, encompassing all road users. . . .

The recommendations of the TRB speed limit committee are consistent with the OECD recommendations. The committee advised the following (TRB 1998, 8–13):

- Establishment of limits that are reasonable for the road and that are enforceable (i.e., setting limits with primary reference to actual speeds; a well-accepted guideline is that the limit should equal the actual 85th percentile speed on the road, with adjustments for special conditions affecting speed risk);
- Sustained long-term commitment to conventional police enforcement, use of automated enforcement, and judicious use of traffic calming; and
- Use of public information campaigns.

A final set of recommendations for speed control programs in the United States is presented in the essay from the AAA Foundation cited above. The authors argue that two strategic elements will be necessary in a successful nationwide program to reduce speeding: first, political leadership at the federal, state, and local levels, starting with congressional action, to establish speed control as a high-level safety priority; and second, a staged approach to speed control campaigns that starts with campaigns to eliminate speeding in specific locations and situations where public support already exists and where evidence indicates that speeding is a specially significant risk factor. Such initial efforts will increase public awareness and support for expanding speed control (Harsha and Hedlund 2007).

Cost-Effectiveness of Speed Control
The speed control programs in France, Australia, Sweden, and the United Kingdom described in Chapter 3 all rely heavily on automated enforcement (i.e., detection and identification of speeding vehicles by means of automated cameras and speed-measuring devices installed in the roadway). In the United Kingdom (as noted in Chapter 3), 90 percent of all speed offenses cited are identified by the camera system. Chapter 3 also described the dramatic reduction in speeding reported in France (a two-thirds reduction in vehicles traveling 10 km/h or more over the limit from 2000 to 2008) since expansion of automated enforcement and the substantial systemwide safety benefits that French and Australian evaluations attribute to speed control, as well as the smaller benefits estimated in Sweden and the United Kingdom.

In the United States, automated enforcement is rare and politically difficult to impose. Conventional U.S. speed enforcement tactics are labor-intensive and expensive. Such a large disparity in the cost of application between the United States and the benchmark countries probably does not apply to any of the other countermeasures that are prominent in the benchmark countries' safety programs. Therefore, despite the international research evidence that speed control is an effective safety measure, it is necessary to consider whether U.S. speed control methods are cost-effective. Within a state safety program, speed control would be cost-effective if the resources required (including program funds and police and other agency personnel time) to produce safety benefits could not be used to produce greater benefits in any alternative application. In a broader context, assessment of the cost-effectiveness of speed control would take into account the time cost to travelers of slower travel speeds, as well as the costs to safety agencies.

The most intensive speed enforcement tactic commonly used in the United States is the high-visibility enforcement campaign, often targeting other forms of aggressive driving (e.g., illegal passing, tailgating, and weaving) as well as speeding. NHTSA's review of countermeasure effectiveness, *Countermeasures That Work,* defines the tactic as follows: "In the high-visibility enforcement model, law enforcement targets selected high-crash or high-violation geographical areas using either expanded regular patrols or designated aggressive driving patrols.... to convince the public that speeding and aggressive driving actions are likely to be detected and that offenders will be arrested and punished.... Enforcement is publicized widely" (Hedlund et al. 2009, 3-13).

The speed management volume of the American Association of State Highway and Transportation Officials (AASHTO) strategic planning safety guide (*NCHRP Report 500*) states that "consistent speed enforcement can be effective in deterring drivers from speeding" (Neuman et al. 2009, V-30). However, the research cited there does not quantify the relationship between enforcement and speed and does not address cost-effectiveness. *Countermeasures That Work* concludes that "taken together, the evaluation evidence suggests that high-visibility, aggressive driving enforcement campaigns have promise but success is far from guaranteed.... As with alcohol-impaired driving and seat belt use enforcement campaigns, the main costs are for law enforcement time and for publicity." Research support cited is from NHTSA demonstration projects, which were inconclusive on the whole. The review rates costs as "high" (Hedlund et al. 2009, 3-13–3-14).

The NHTSA speed management demonstrations described in Chapter 3 mostly attained small reductions in speed, which presumably were transient; however, the scale of the demonstrations was such that they may not be a fair indication of the effectiveness of high-visibility enforcement. The demonstration evaluations did not provide cost information and therefore give no indication of cost-effectiveness. The Minnesota speed management demonstration, described later in this section, appears to be the best U.S. evidence that speed management using conventional enforcement techniques can produce worthwhile safety results for an extended period over major portions of a road system at a practical cost.

Reliable assessment of the cost-effectiveness of speed control or of other countermeasures is not possible in the United States today because most enforcement and safety agencies do not systematically maintain data on level of enforcement effort or on intermediate outputs (i.e., speed trends correlated with enforcement effort). The NHTSA speed management uniform guideline (described in Chapter 3) recommends collection and use of these data to evaluate speed management programs.

Trends in Speed, Speed-Related Crashes, and Speed Enforcement

The subsections below summarize available information on trends in speed and speeding, speed-related crashes, and speed control enforcement effort to determine whether there is any evidence at the national level that speed management is becoming more intense or more effective.

Speeds and Speeding

Programs to compile summary data on speed trends are an indication of management attention and interest. The speed management programs in other countries described in Chapter 3 rely on close monitoring of speeds to measure performance, to direct resources, and to communicate the effectiveness of the program to political officials and the public. Speed trends also provide a test of the GHSA report's conclusion cited above that speed is a worsening safety problem and that gains from successful safety interventions have been offset.

The Federal Highway Administration (FHWA) published data from the states on average speeds and speed distributions for various road classes from the 1940s until 1993 (Figures 4-2 and 4-3). After the repeal of the NMSL and the associated state speed data reporting requirements, FHWA ceased compiling the data; consequently, no current aggregate national summary of speed trends exists. The reliability of the state-reported data, particularly in the later years of the NMSL, is suspect. The FHWA data show gradually increasing speeds and frequency of speeding from the 1970s through the early 1990s.

A 2006 survey of the states conducted by NHTSA found only six states that published statewide speed surveys on the Internet and 30 that reported that they systematically monitor speeds (OECD and ECMT 2006, 255). Figures 4-4 and 4-5 show speed trends in Minnesota for 1995–2002 and in Washington for 2000–2010, respectively. In Minnesota, 85th percentile speeds increased by 4 to 5 mph on freeways and other rural divided highways in the period shown. Speed limits were increased by 5 mph on rural and urban freeways and by 10 mph on other rural divided highways in 1997. Speeds on road classes where the limits were not changed showed no

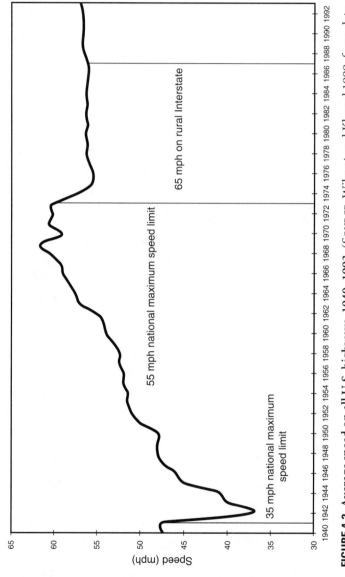

FIGURE 4-2 Average speed on all U.S. highways, 1940–1993. (SOURCE: Wilmot and Khanal 1999, from data published in FHWA's *Highway Statistics* series; copyright, Taylor and Francis; used with permission.)

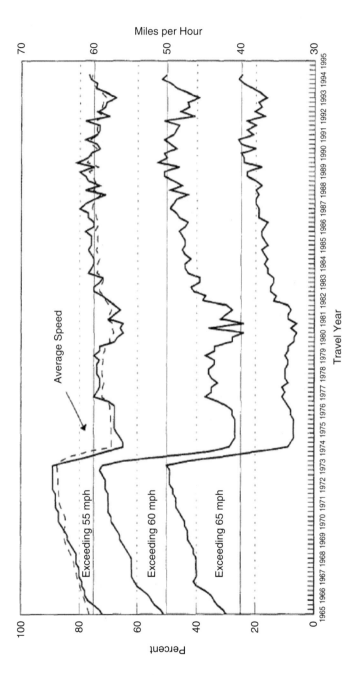

The data from 1965 to 1979 represent free-moving traffic on level, straight, uncongested sections of the rural Interstate system. Beginning with fiscal year 1980, the data show all vehicle travel on the rural Interstate system. Between 1965 and 1975, speed trend information was collected by several state highway agencies normally during the summer months and submitted in annual speed trend reports. Since October 1975, all states have monitored speeds at locations on several highway systems, including the Interstate system, as part of the 55 miles-per-hour (mph) speed limit monitoring program. Since April 1987, most of the rural Interstate system had been exempted from the 55 mph speed limit pursuant to Public Law 100-17, Section 174, dated April 2, 1987. The reported speed is for those highways which are still signed for 55 mph. The data are reported to the Federal Highway Administration on a quarterly basis.

FIGURE 4-3 Speed trends on rural Interstate highways, 1965–1995.

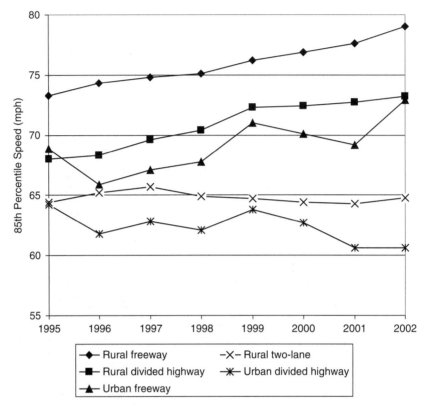

FIGURE 4-4 Speed trends on Minnesota roadways, 1995–2002. [Source: Minnesota Department of Transportation (http://www.dot.state.mn.us/speed/index.html).]

trend. In Washington, average speeds on Interstates and other arterials and the fraction of vehicles on Interstates exceeding the limit show no clear trend over the 2000–2010 period, although speeding on non-Interstate arterials appears to be increasing.

The fragmentary data available do not demonstrate that speed is a growing problem. However, traffic flow studies show that on roads with heavy traffic, for a given road class and traffic volume, drivers travel faster today on average than they did in past decades. That is, drivers slow down less on a crowded road than they formerly did (TRB 2003, 55). This change in driver behavior may be affecting the relationship between speed and

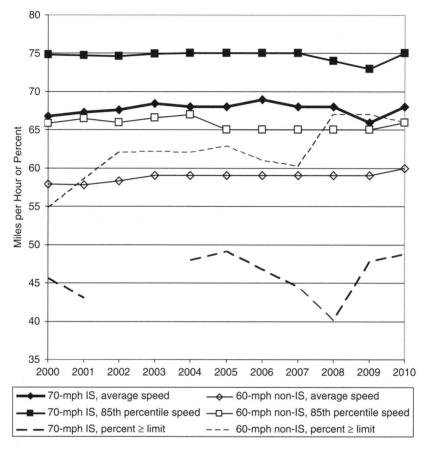

FIGURE 4-5 Speed trends, 2000–2010, Washington State. KEY: 70-mph IS = Interstate highway with 70-mph speed limit; 60-mph non-IS = non-Interstate arterial with 60-mph speed limit. Data are for January to March of each year. (SOURCE: Washington State Department of Transportation quarterly speed reports.)

crash and casualty risk. Shorter following distances may increase risk, but declining speed variance would tend to reduce risk.

Crashes and Fatalities Attributed to Speed

NHTSA publishes data on the numbers of fatalities and fatal crashes that are speeding related (Box 4-1). A speeding-related crash is defined

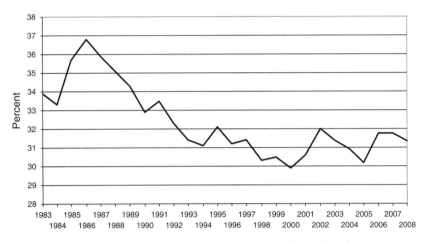

FIGURE 4-6 Percentage of annual fatalities that are speeding related, 1983–2008.
(SOURCES: NHTSA 2005a; NHTSA 2007b; NHTSA 2007e; NHTSA 2008a; NHTSA 2009c.)

as one in which "the driver was charged with a speeding-related offense or . . . an officer indicated that racing, driving too fast for conditions, or exceeding the posted speed limit was a contributing factor in the crash" (NHTSA 2007d, 1). (Before 2002, NHTSA used a different definition.) NHTSA-reported speeding-related fatalities were 31 percent of total fatalities in 2008; the fraction declined from the 1980s through the mid-1990s and since has fluctuated (Figure 4-6).

This percentage often is presented as an indicator of the magnitude of the speeding problem's contribution to highway fatality risk (e.g., NHTSA 2007d) and might be taken as an index of the success of speed management practices (e.g., to test the GHSA statement that speed is a growing risk factor). However, the significance of the statistic is not evident. The prevalence of crashes meeting NHTSA's definition of "speeding-related" cannot by itself reveal the numbers of fatalities that could be avoided if speeding were reduced because, in the NHTSA definition, every crash that involves a vehicle that is speeding is "speeding-related." Also, the large and seemingly patternless variations among states in the speeding-related share of fatalities that NHTSA reports [from over 45 percent in five states (Alaska, Pennsylvania, Hawaii, Alabama, Missouri) to under 12 percent in three (New Jersey, Arkansas, Iowa) in 2008 (see Figure 4-7)]

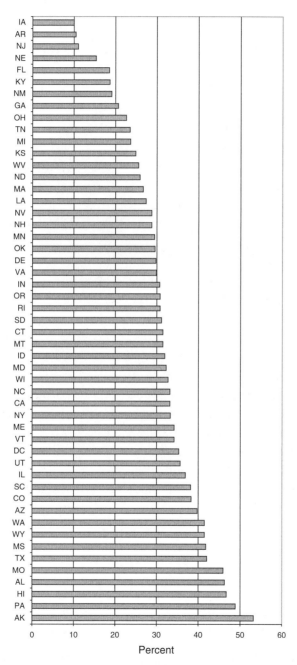

FIGURE 4-7 Percentage of fatalities that are speeding related, by state, 2008.

suggest that some factor such as variability in police crash-reporting procedures may be distorting the measure. The downward trend in the measure may reflect the raising of speed limits during the 1980s and 1990s. Measuring how speed affects crash risk requires exposure data (i.e., data on average speed and the speed distribution for all vehicles on the road), which generally are not available in the United States.

In comparison with the NHTSA statistic that 30 percent of fatalities are speeding-related, an estimate based on crash investigations found speeding to be a "causal factor" in 19 percent of a sample of crashes in 1996–1997 (Hendricks et al. 2001). It has been reported, however, that a common view among law enforcement officers is that speeding is involved in almost all serious crashes (Harsha and Hedlund 2007, 259).

Enforcement Effort

Spending for highway law enforcement and safety programs has been fairly stable in recent decades and has been rising in the past 10 years (Figure 4-8), per vehicle mile of highway travel and as a share of total noncapital highway spending, according to the FHWA national highway finance summaries. [FHWA defines this spending category as follows: "Highway law enforcement and safety expenditures are: traffic supervision activities of State highway patrols; highway safety programs including driver education and training, motorcycle safety; vehicle inspection programs; and enforcement of vehicle size and weight limitations. General police expenses associated with drug interdiction, criminal investigation, and security activities are excluded" (FHWA 2006, IV-7).] In a survey conducted for the 1998 TRB speed limit study, most states reported that from 20 to 50 percent of total state police officer time spent on traffic enforcement is devoted to speed enforcement (TRB 1998, 146–147).

Comparisons with Benchmark Countries

The 2005 GHSA state survey on speed management asked about speed limits, availability of speed and speed-related crash data, and enforcement and other speed control efforts. The following are among the findings:

- Few states were able to cite a state-level program focusing on speed control (Washington and Arizona were exceptions). Most responded

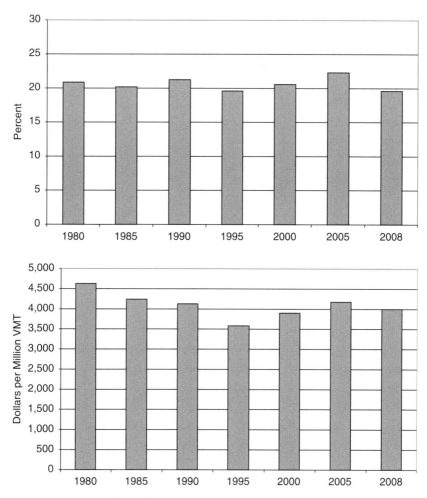

FIGURE 4-8 (*top*) Highway law enforcement and safety expenditures, U.S. total, as percentage of total noncapital expenditures, 1980–2008; (*bottom*) constant-dollar enforcement and safety expenditures (2000 dollars), U.S. total, per million vehicle miles traveled, 1980–2008. NOTE: Price index is gross domestic product implicit price deflator from Bureau of Economic Analysis. (SOURCES: FHWA 1997, Tables HF-210, VM-201; FHWA 2001, Tables HF-10, VM-1; FHWA 2006, Tables HF-10, VM-1; FHWA 2010, Tables HF-10, VM-1.)

that speed control was one of several risks addressed in state Selective Traffic Enforcement Programs (STEPs). A STEP is a high-visibility, short-duration intensive enforcement and public awareness campaign targeting specific high-risk behaviors in a specific area. The technique has been most commonly applied in promoting seat belt use but has not commonly been used against speeding or aggressive driving (Nerup et al. 2006, v; Nichols et al. 2007, 1; Hedlund et al. 2007, 3–8).

- Most states were not able to isolate federal highway safety grant funds received that were allocated specifically to speed control.
- Thirty-one states reported maintaining speeding-related citation or conviction data in a statewide database, although some include only state police–issued citations.
- In response to a question asking about the impact of speeding or aggressive driving programs in the past 2 years, states that responded reported trends in statewide speeding-related crashes or fatalities or in total highway fatalities. No state reported results of a scientific evaluation of speed control programs.

These responses lend support to the conclusion of the AAA Foundation essay cited above that speed control has not attained high priority in safety programs.

Speeding is common in most high-income countries, according to a 2006 OECD survey (OECD and ECMT 2006, 256–259). The fraction of drivers exceeding the limit on undivided major highways in several countries is reported as follows:

Country and Limit	Percentage
Austria, 100 km/h	47
Canada, 100 km/h	15 to 76, depending on province
Ireland, 60 mph	30
Korea, 85 km/h	85
Netherlands, 100 km/h	20
Poland, 100 km/h	42
Portugal, 90 km/h	65
Sweden, 110 km/h or lower	59
United Kingdom, 60 mph	10
United States, 65 or 55 mph (three states)	52 to 77

The United Kingdom, the Netherlands, and British Columbia claim substantial compliance with speed limits on this road class; however, the high rates of speeding that are typical of the United States are observed in several other countries.

The speed management programs in France, Australia, Sweden, and the United Kingdom, described in Chapter 3, have produced speed reductions that can be linked with reductions in crashes and fatalities. These programs are of long duration, with enforcement and information campaigns extending over a period of years; they are applied over extensive portions of the national or state road systems; and they rely on automated enforcement. There appears to be no U.S. speed management program of comparable scale.

In France, as part of the nationwide traffic safety initiative launched in 2002, an extensive automated enforcement system was installed. Speeding citations increased 22 percent from 2000 to 2003 and then doubled from 2003 to 2004, the result of the automated enforcement system. The total of license point penalties assessed increased 44 percent in 2004 compared with 2003, and license suspensions increased 87 percent, largely the result of speed enforcement (OECD and International Transport Forum 2006; ONISR 2005). Speed data show the results of stepped-up enforcement. The percentage of light vehicles in free-flowing traffic exceeding the speed limit by more than 10 km/h has declined each year, from 36 percent in 2001 to 16 percent in 2006 and 12 percent in 2008 (ONISR 2006; ONISR 2009b). The national safety statistical agency has estimated that 75 percent of the total reduction in casualties (fatalities plus injuries) from 2002 through 2005 can be attributed to speed reductions over the period (CISR 2006, 6). Annual fatalities declined 31 percent from 2002 to 2005. As noted in Chapter 3, this estimate is not derived from direct observation of the effect of reduced speeds on crashes on French roads during the period of increased enforcement.

In the state of Victoria, Australia, in 2000–2004, new laws lowered the urban speed limit, greatly increased the density of the speed camera system first set up 10 years earlier, and increased penalties for speeding. Anti–drunk driving enforcement was strengthened at the same time (Johnston 2006, 10–11). Implementing the new 50-km/h speed limit in urban areas is a major component of the strategy. Average speeds on all types of roads were observed to decline. Fatalities have declined, and the patterns of decline reportedly indicate that speed reduction has been a major contributor, although the relationship has not been quantitatively demonstrated (OECD and ECMT 2006, 11).

As Chapter 3 described, road officials in Sweden and the United Kingdom attribute more modest safety benefits to current speed control programs than do the French and Australian authorities. One source of this difference may be that speed compliance was better in Sweden and the United Kingdom before inauguration of the automated systems, but the available information is not sufficient to account for the difference definitively.

Examples of U.S. Speed Control Programs

The first subsection below describes the federal government's involvement in speed control through the NMSL of 1974–1995. The second presents examples of present state and local speed management programs.

National Maximum Speed Limit

The 1974–1995 NMSL is a well-documented example of speed management as a political issue. The NMSL was undertaken with high-level political leadership and enjoyed initial public acceptance, yet it quickly lost support as benefits dwindled and costs became apparent, and eventually it failed. Implementation of the NMSL departed in several respects from the speed management practices recommended in the OECD, TRB, and AAA Foundation reports cited above: limits were not set with reference to actual speeds, and local risk factors and enforcement practices were dictated by federal compliance requirements rather than by safety considerations.

The NMSL was initiated as a fuel conservation measure in response to the oil embargo of 1973. The president first appealed to the states to lower their limits in a national address in November 1973, and in January 1974 Congress enacted the requirement that states lower speed limits to 55 mph as a condition for receipt of federal highway funds. Originally a 1-year emergency measure, the NMSL was made permanent in 1975. Congress had been aware of possible safety benefits at the time of the original enactment, and an immediate apparent safety impact strengthened support for continuing the measure. Highway fatalities dropped 16 percent, from 54,000 in 1973 to 45,000 in 1974. (Vehicle miles traveled declined by 2.5 percent in 1974 as a result of recession and the oil embargo. Crashes and crash rates typically decline during recessions more rapidly than the long-term trend.)

After the energy crisis subsided, efforts began in Congress to repeal or relax the limit. Western states especially saw the limit as unnecessarily burdensome. In 1987 states were allowed to raise the limit to 65 mph on rural Interstates, and in 1995 the NMSL was abolished (as a provision in the legislation that also removed federal penalties for failure to enact a state motorcycle helmet use law). Safety advocacy groups, for example, Public Citizen and IIHS, vigorously opposed repeal. Opponents of the NMSL pointed out the costs in time and convenience, the ambiguous data on safety benefits, and the misallocation of police enforcement efforts resulting from the federal requirement that states certify enforcement, and they argued that the states have the responsibility and the competence to manage their own road systems (Yowell 2005; Bashem and Mengert 1974; Kemper and Byington 1977; U.S. Department of Justice 1989).

State and Local Speed Management Campaigns

Three examples of speed management campaigns undertaken by local and state governments are described below. Each is a pilot program, that is, a test or a demonstration of techniques rather than a permanent program with a long-term charge and objectives. These pilots may be typical of recent speed control initiatives. Other state and local initiatives that involve data collection and evaluation may be in place as well, although NHTSA's guidebook *Countermeasures That Work* observes that pedestrian safety programs similar to Heed the Speed and high-visibility speed and aggressive driving enforcement campaigns both are rarely used strategies (Hedlund et al. 2009, 3-13).

Minnesota Speed Management Program The Minnesota Departments of Transportation and Public Safety conducted an evaluation of a trial of a speed management program in operation from September 2005 until August 2006 (Harder and Bloomfield 2007). The program had four elements:

- Speed limits were raised from 55 to 60 mph on 850 miles of two-lane rural roads and urban expressways, which were selected on the basis of a design review.
- State and local police increased speed enforcement on selected segments of the roads with increased speed limits and on selected segments of the state's network of 1,870 miles of freeways and divided highways with limits of 65 or 70 mph. Stepped-up enforcement was organized in a series of 6- to 8-week waves, with periods of normal enforcement intervening.
- An extensive publicity campaign was organized.
- Evaluation was conducted by means of speed monitoring, before-and-after comparisons of the frequency of serious crashes, and opinion surveys.

The cost of the 1-year trial was $3 million, of which $2.5 million was the cost of the increase in police enforcement hours. Additional enforcement of 22,000 person-hours (beyond normal levels) was applied (Harder and Bloomfield 2007, 5, 40, 41).

The evaluation was motivated in part by proposals in the legislature to raise speed limits in the state. The department of transportation opposed general increases but supported selective increases on 55-mph roads with appropriate design.

The evaluation showed that during the trial, average speeds were reduced on all categories of roads in the test, including roads on which the speed limit was raised and roads outside and within the zones of enhanced enforcement. The reduction was between 0.2 and 1.8 mph, depending on the road category and enforcement level. The frequency of speeding was substantially reduced. The frequency of serious crashes declined for all categories of road in the test compared with the average frequency during the same months in the preceding 5 years.

The evaluation report recommends that the elements of the speed management program, including the evaluation, be continued and that funding be provided for the costs (mainly for increased enforcement).

Phoenix "Heed the Speed" Program A pilot study was initiated in Phoenix and Peoria, Arizona, in 2002 to test and demonstrate methods of speed control in urban residential streets as a means of reducing crash risks and especially pedestrian injuries. Campaigns of 3 to 6 months were conducted in three neighborhoods, with a variety of countermeasures tested in various combinations, including traffic calming, pavement markings, intensive police enforcement, and several forms of publicity. The evaluation was designed and carried out by NHTSA with the participation of the local governments. Evaluation was by means of speed measurements and resident surveys. The pilot was judged a success because it demonstrated that neighborhoodwide speed reductions could be obtained. Average speed reductions of between 0.5 and 3.5 mph and reductions in the number of vehicles exceeding the speed limit by more than 7 mph of between 14 and 70 percent were observed, depending on the road (Blomberg and Cleven 2006). The pilot built on earlier pedestrian safety programs in Phoenix, and the techniques have seen further application in at least one Phoenix neighborhood (Gordon 2007).

Scottsdale Loop 101 Speed Camera Demonstration and Arizona Photo Enforcement Program The city of Scottsdale, Arizona, in cooperation with the state, carried out a demonstration and evaluation of automated speed enforcement on a section of Arizona Highway 101 in 2006 and 2007. The city describes the project as the first U.S. test of photo enforcement on a freeway (City of Scottsdale n.d.).

The demonstration used six fixed speed camera installations on the 8-mile portion of the highway within the city limits. The cameras were activated from February to October 2006 and from February to June 2007. Activation was accompanied by publicity. The evaluation concluded that camera enforcement reduced average speeds by about 9 mph, reduced the proportion of vehicles traveling 11 mph or more over the speed limit by 90 percent, and reduced the number of injury crashes by 28 to 48 percent. The estimated impact on user costs—travel time and crash costs—was positive. Travel time was reduced despite lower average speed because delay caused by crashes was avoided (Washington et al. 2007, 1–12). Impacts on agency traffic enforcement costs were not examined.

The evaluation report proposes procedures to be followed in the design, evaluation, and deployment of speed cameras on freeways in the state (Washington et al. 2007, 131–134). After the demonstration, the city transferred the freeway enforcement program to the state. With a new state law as authorization, the Arizona Department of Public Safety expanded the photo enforcement network to include 36 fixed camera installations on freeways in the Phoenix and Scottsdale areas and 36 mobile photo enforcement units (Arizona Department of Public Safety n.d.). In 2010, after a change in administration in the state government, the department decided to discontinue the speed camera program. Automatic enforcement encountered political opposition, and at the time the program was discontinued opponents were organizing a ballot initiative to ban their use in the state (Newton 2010).

Concluding Observations

There are grounds for concern that speed management has been underemphasized in federal and state safety programs in comparison, for example, with the prominent and generally effective efforts devoted to drunk driving, seat belts, and vehicle crashworthiness and occupant protection. Some state officials believe that this underemphasis is one reason why U.S. crash and fatality rates show only small improvement compared with the progress in other countries in recent years.

The lack of speed trend and related data in the United States and the lack of scientific evaluations of enforcement efforts are evidence that speed management has not received the highest priority. Intensive speed enforcement programs used elsewhere depend on data to determine whether goals are being met and to allocate enforcement resources. Rapid publication and dissemination of performance information are vital for communication with the public and political leaders and for accountability of the transportation and enforcement agencies.

There appears to be no U.S. speed management program in operation today that is comparable in scale, visibility, and high-level political commitment with the most ambitious speed management programs in other countries. Such programs are of long duration, with enforcement and information campaigns extending over a period of years; they are applied over extensive portions of the national or state road systems; and they

TABLE 4-3 Speed Management in Benchmark Countries Compared with the United States

	France, United Kingdom, and Australia	United States[a]
Management and planning	Focused program with goals, strategy, and budget	Routine, low-level activity; reactive management; no long-term plan
	Timely monitoring and publication of relevant speed and crash data	No speed data; no meaningful crash data
	Long-term, multiyear, or permanent perspective	Episodic attention; occasional enforcement crackdowns
Technical implementation of countermeasures	Major portions of national or state road network targeted	Haphazard or spot enforcement
	Automated plus traditional enforcement	Automated enforcement not authorized or rarely used
	Penalties designed as part of the integrated program	Little attention to effectiveness of penalties
Political and public support	Active support and leadership of elected officials; management held accountable for results	Politically invisible except when speed limits altered or automated enforcement proposed

[a] Not necessarily all states.

rely on automated enforcement (Table 4-3). The gap between U.S. practice and that in at least some other jurisdictions ought to raise the following questions for public officials responsible for the road system: Could the United States substantially reduce traffic injuries and fatalities by better speed management? If so, what kind of effort would be required, what are the best models of initiatives in the United States or elsewhere, and what are the obstacles to carrying out such programs? Other countries that introduced automated speed enforcement had to overcome public opposition on grounds similar to the objections that have been raised in the United States. U.S. safety program managers considering adoption of the methods of these countries can use the international experience to anticipate difficulties and to learn possible ways to address public concerns (Delaney et al. 2005).

The Minnesota speed management trial described above attained average speed reductions on the order of 1 mph on rural roads and urban expressways and substantial reduction in the frequency of speeding by the use of available personnel (diverted to speed enforcement from other duties) and standard techniques. The review of research on the relationship between speed and crash risk cited above (Aarts and van Schagen 2006) concluded that a 1 percent reduction in average free-flow speed on a road system will yield a 4 percent reduction in crash fatalities; thus, a 1-mph reduction would reduce crashes by 6 percent. Application of this relationship, with the assumption that the Minnesota speed reduction results could be attained on half of all U.S. roads, leads to an order-of-magnitude estimate of a reduction in fatalities of 3 percent, or 1,100 lives annually.

SEAT BELTS

Regulations requiring vehicles to be equipped with seat belts and requiring occupants to use belts have been among the most beneficial safety interventions of the past three decades in the United States and all the benchmark nations. The sections below describe the effectiveness of seat belts in reducing traffic fatalities and of government actions promoting belt use, describe trends in use and in interventions in the United States, and compare U.S. experience and practices with those of benchmark countries. As a case study, this section describes only seat belt use and regulation; other kinds of occupant restraints, such as child safety seats and air bags, also have important safety benefits.

Effectiveness of Seat Belts and Belt Use Promotion Measures

NHTSA has estimated that lap–shoulder belts are 45 percent effective in preventing fatal injury to front seat passenger car occupants in crashes and 60 percent effective for front seat light-truck occupants. That is, out of 100 hundred front seat car occupants not wearing belts who were killed in a crash, 45 would have been saved had they been wearing belts. Such estimates are derived by analysis of crashes of vehicles with two front seat occupants, one or both of whom were killed in the crash. For example, the chances of survival of two unbelted front seat occupants are about equal in a crash, but in crashes in which the driver is belted and the passenger is unbelted, the driver's risk of death is less than half that of the passenger. The NHTSA estimate corrects for overreporting of belt use by crash survivors (Kahane 2000). Other countries have observed generally similar effectiveness (e.g., ONISR 2008, 158). Use of seat belts also mitigates nonfatal injuries; that is, in a crash in which an unbelted occupant probably would have suffered a severe injury, a belted occupant has an increased chance of escaping with a minor or moderate injury.

NHTSA estimates indicate that each percentage point increase in belt use from the present level would prevent about 280 deaths annually (NHTSA 2008a, 207). Thus, according to this estimate, if belt use were increased from the 2009 level of 84 percent (for front seat passenger vehicle occupants) to 90 percent, U.S. fatalities would be reduced by 4.5 percent.

In addition, the effectiveness of interventions to increase seat belt use is well established. Enactment of a primary seat belt law in place of a secondary law has been estimated to increase belt use by 14 percentage points on average and to reduce occupant fatalities by 8 percent (Hedlund et al. 2009, 2-11). A primary enforcement law is a state law authorizing police to stop a vehicle and issue a citation solely on the grounds of failure to use a seat belt. Secondary laws are laws that allow police to issue a citation for failure to use a belt only after the vehicle has been stopped for some other violation. In 2009, 26 states and the District of Columbia had primary enforcement seat belt laws (NHTSA 2009e).

NHTSA has analyzed interstate differences in seat belt use rates to identify interventions and other factors correlated with high rates. Seat belt use rates vary greatly among the states. Rates for front seat occupants in 2008 were 95 percent or higher in five states (California, Hawaii, Michigan, Oregon, and Washington) and below 75 percent in nine states (Arkansas, Kentucky, Massachusetts, Mississippi, New Hampshire, Rhode Island, South Dakota, Wisconsin, and Wyoming) (NHTSA 2009d). The NHTSA analysis (Hedlund et al. 2008; NHTSA 2008c), based on 2005 use rates, found that existence of a primary seat belt use law and high enforcement effort (as measured by the rate of belt citations per capita issued in each state during the annual NHTSA-sponsored "Click It or Ticket" enforcement campaign) were correlated with high belt use rates. Among demographic and geographic differences examined, high population density was strongly correlated with high belt use. Other external factors analyzed in the study did not appear to be major determinants of the overall usage pattern, although the predominance of West Coast states among those with the highest rates suggests that some cultural factors may affect usage.

Another NHTSA evaluation indicates that publicity campaigns linked to enforcement in the annual Click It or Ticket campaign increase belt use. Among the states participating in the 2002 campaign, the change in belt use increased consistently with increasing extent of state-paid advertising (Hedlund et al. 2009, 2-23). However, NHTSA's analysis of factors correlated with higher state seat belt use rates found that states with low belt use tend to devote a larger fraction of their resources during Click It or Ticket campaigns to publicity, as opposed to police enforcement, than do states with high use rates (NHTSA 2008c).

Significantly increasing seat belt use rates in the states that already have primary laws and serious enforcement will require increasing use among the population groups with consistently low rates historically. Such groups include men, younger drivers, rural drivers, pickup truck drivers, and possibly minorities (Hedlund et al. 2009, 2-24). High-visibility campaigns have been shown to increase use among these groups, but not necessarily to close the gap between these groups and the median. NHTSA has sponsored a series of demonstrations of techniques to reach the low-belt-use populations, which are conducted in conjunction with the annual Click It or Ticket campaign. The techniques tested included publicity and education activities targeted to particular geographic areas or demographic groups and adjustments to enforcement methods. Evaluations of these demonstrations report increases in belt use among the targeted populations after the campaign, but it is not clear whether the increases are greater than would have occurred through a standard state Click It or Ticket campaign without the supplemental targeted activities (Blomberg et al. 2008; Blomberg et al. 2009; Hedlund et al. 2009, 2-25).

Trends in Seat Belt Use and Belt Laws

By 2009, belt use had reached 84 percent for passenger vehicle front seat occupants in the United States, an increase of 16 percentage points since 1999. The rate was 88 percent in states with primary seat belt laws and 77 percent in other states. As seat belt use rates have increased in the United States, the percentage of persons killed in crashes who were not wearing a belt at the time of the crash has decreased (Figure 4-9). Belt use

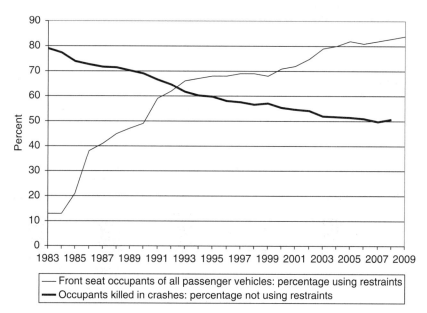

FIGURE 4-9 Percentage wearing seat belts, all passenger vehicle front seat occupants; and percentage not wearing seat belts, all passenger car and light truck occupants killed in crashes, United States, 1983–2009.
(SOURCES: Hedlund et al. 2009, 2-1; NHTSA 2009c, Table 22; NHTSA 2009b.)

among persons killed in crashes is much lower than among all vehicle occupants. In 2007, 50 percent of all passenger vehicle occupants killed in crashes and 42 percent of front seat occupants killed were not wearing belts. In comparison, an average of 18 percent of front seat occupants of all vehicles on the road at any given time in 2007 were not wearing belts (NHTSA 2008a, 119; NHTSA 2008b; NHTSA 2009f).

Federal law has required new cars sold in the United States to be equipped with seat belts since 1968 (Traffic Safety Center 2002). In 1984, New York became the first state to enact a law requiring vehicle occupants to use belts. Through 1989, 33 states and the District of Columbia had enacted seat belt laws, and by 1995 all states except New Hampshire had laws. Progress in enacting primary belt laws has been more gradual, but continuous. Thirty-one states and the District of Columbia had primary laws as of October 2010, an increase from 17 states with primary laws in 1999 (Figures 4-10 and 4-11).

178 Achieving Traffic Safety Goals in the United States

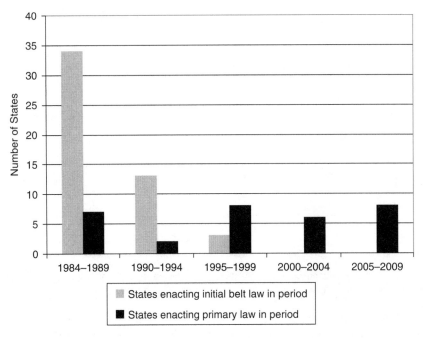

FIGURE 4-10 Enactment of state seat belt laws, United States, 1984–2009. (Source: IIHS 2009b.) Note: In 2010 through September, one new primary seat belt law (in Kansas) went into effect.

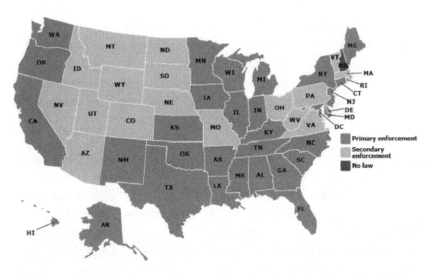

FIGURE 4-11 State seat belt use laws as of October 2010. (Source: IIHS 2010; used with permission.)

Comparisons with Benchmark Countries

The laws of nearly every high-income country require use of seat belts (OECD and ECMT 2006, 25). The fraction of front seat occupants who use seat belts is lower in the United States than in Western Europe, Australia, or Canada but higher than in Japan (OECD and ECMT 2006, 25). Seat belt use rates by passenger vehicle occupants in some of the benchmark countries and in the United States in 2007 are compared in Table 4-4.

Use of seat belts by rear seat occupants of passenger vehicles was required by law as of 2006 in all OECD countries except Japan, Korea, Georgia, Mexico, and the United States (OECD and International Transport Forum 2006, 25). Laws in 25 states and the District of Columbia require rear seat belt use (IIHS 2010). The U.S. rear seat belt use rate appears to be more comparable with those in other high-income countries than the front seat belt use rate.

The history of seat belt use in the United States shows the consequence of decentralized safety regulation. Usage grew during the 1980s and early 1990s until all states had seat belt laws. The use rate has continued to grow, but more slowly, in the past 15 years as the number of states with primary laws has increased (Figure 4-12).

In the United Kingdom, a national law requiring front seat occupant seat belt use went into effect in 1983, and belt use immediately jumped

TABLE 4-4 Seat Belt Use Rates in Passenger Vehicles, 2007

	Drivers		Front Seat Occupants, All Roads	Adult Rear Seat Occupants, All Roads
	Expressways (Autoroutes)	Urban Areas		
Germany	98	93		
France	99	98	98	83
Netherlands		93		
Sweden[a]			94	74
Great Britain		92	94	69
United States	84[b]	89[b]	82	76

NOTE: Rates are percentages.
[a] Rates are for 2006.
[b] Drivers and front seat passengers.
SOURCES: ONISR 2009a; ONISR 2008, 157; Breen et al. 2007, 55; DfT 2007; NHTSA 2008b; NHTSA 2009f.

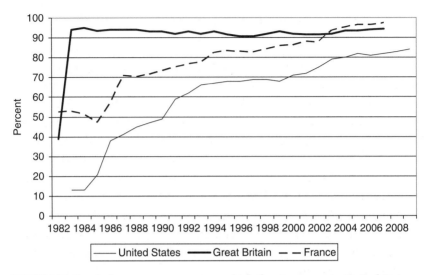

FIGURE 4-12 Seat belt use rates, passenger vehicle front occupants, United States, Great Britain, and France, 1982–2009. (SOURCES: Hedlund et al. 2009, 2-1; NHTSA 2009e; ONISR 2008, 157; DfT 2007.)

from 37 to 95 percent. A slight decline occurred after the initial spike, but rates have returned to the 95 percent level (Figure 4-12). Seat belt use by adult rear seat occupants was required in 1991.

France approached belt use laws more gradually: a front seat occupant seat belt law was enacted in 1973, applicable only on rural roads and in vehicles first registered in 1970 or later. A 1975 law required belts on urban expressways and all urban roads at night, and a 1979 law required belt use by front occupants on all urban roads at all times. In 1989, belt use in light trucks was required, and in 1990 rear seat belt use was required in vehicles so equipped. In 1994, a point penalty toward license suspension for failure to wear a belt was introduced (ONISR 2008, 247–250). The 1979 urban use law brought belt use above 50 percent, and usage has increased nearly continuously since that time (Figure 4-12). The high-intensity nationwide traffic safety enforcement and publicity campaign initiated in 2002 (described in Chapter 3) probably helped raise seat belt use above the 90 percent level.

Differences in historical belt use rates among the United States, the United Kingdom, and France do not appear to be part of the explanation of slower improvement in safety in the United States in recent decades. The substantial absolute increase in the seat belt use rate probably explains a large share of U.S. safety progress over the past 20 years. In the United Kingdom and France, increasing belt use probably has accounted for a smaller share of total improvement in the period because use rates were initially higher than in the United States.

The effort devoted to seat belt law enforcement in the United Kingdom and France today is light in terms of frequency of citations. The low frequency of citations is consistent with the high belt usage rates in these countries; that is, violations of the law are uncommon. Citations for failure to wear seat belts in 2007 in France were 3 percent of all moving violations, and the rate of citations was 10 per 1,000 registered drivers (Table 3-1); in Great Britain in 2006, they were 5 percent of all moving violations and the rate of citations was 7 per 1,000 drivers (Table 3-2). The seat belt citation rate in Sweden in 2006 was 9 per 1,000 drivers (Breen et al. 2007, 32, 55). For comparison, in New York State in 2007, citations for failure to wear seat belts were 11 percent of all traffic safety law violations ticketed, and the rate of citations was 41 per 1,000 drivers (New York State Governor's Traffic Safety Committee 2008, 22). New York's seat belt use rate in 2007 was 83.5 percent, slightly above the national average.

Some of the benchmark countries are giving increased attention to increasing belt use by rear seat occupants and commercial vehicle occupants.

Summary Observations

The cases of seat belts and of motorcycle helmets (discussed in the next section) provide clear illustrations of how public and political attitudes can restrain risk-reducing measures despite the availability of effective and well-managed countermeasure programs in many states. The effectiveness of seat belts in reducing casualties and of specific interventions (primary laws and high-visibility enforcement) in increasing usage are well established by research and by the experience of many states. The interventions are not complex or expensive compared with the efforts required for speed control or impaired-driving control. Nonetheless, some jurisdictions have chosen not to apply these measures.

The benchmark countries have attained higher rates of seat belt usage than the United States through uniform national imposition and enforcement of seat belt laws. Consequently, increasing belt use is not as high a priority for most of these countries as it is in the United States.

MOTORCYCLE HELMET LAWS

This section follows the same general outline as the preceding section on speed control: the first subsection below describes the effectiveness of helmet laws in reducing injury risk; the second presents trends in motorcycle fatalities, helmet use, and helmet regulations; the third contains international comparisons; the fourth presents some illustrative histories of changes in federal and state helmet laws; and the final subsection contains conclusions.

Effects of Helmet Use and Helmet Laws on Injury Risk

NHTSA estimates that motorcycle helmets are 37 percent effective in preventing motorcycle occupant fatalities; that is, of the 2,146 unhelmeted motorcycle occupants killed in crashes in 2008, 37 percent, or 794, would have survived if they had been wearing helmets. NHTSA derived the estimate from an analysis of fatal crashes of motorcycles with two occupants during 1993–2002. For example, in crashes where neither the rider (i.e., the driver) nor the passenger was helmeted and in crashes where both were helmeted, the passenger was about 10 percent less likely to be killed than the rider. However, in crashes where the passenger wore a helmet and the rider did not, the passenger was 60 percent less likely than the rider to be killed (NHTSA 2004; NHTSA 2007c).

Other data support NHTSA's conclusion about the effectiveness of motorcycle helmets. An analysis of injuries to motorcycle occupants in crashes found that unhelmeted occupants were three times more likely to suffer brain injuries than helmeted occupants (NHTSA 2005b). Studies of the effects of repeal of helmet laws in Colorado, Kentucky, and Louisiana showed changes in fatality frequency correlating with changes in helmet use after repeal (NHTSA 2004, 4). Some published studies have reported contrary findings, but the preponderance of research indicates that wearing a helmet reduces the risk of injury and death

(Neiman 2007, 14–17). Opponents of helmet laws have argued that helmets restrict sight and hearing and therefore may increase the risk of a crash, offsetting the benefit of lower injury risk in the event of a crash. NHTSA has sponsored a test-track study that concluded that effects of helmets on hearing and sight are inconsequential (McKnight and McKnight 1994).

Helmet laws have been shown to be highly effective in ensuring helmet use, in large part because a violation of the law is always evident. A 1991 General Accounting Office review summarized nine studies that reported compliance rates of 92 to 100 percent with universal helmet laws (i.e., laws requiring all motorcycle occupants to wear a helmet), helmet use rates of 42 to 59 percent in states with no law or a law with limited applicability, and low compliance with state laws requiring use by minors only (GAO 1991, 4). A June 2009 NHTSA roadside survey found that the rate of use of helmets complying with federal standards was 86 percent in states with universal helmet laws and 55 percent in other states (NHTSA 2009a). NHTSA studies have also reported that repeal of a helmet law in a state leads to a reduction in use and that enactment of a law increases use (NHTSA 1998; Ulmer and Preusser 2003).

Trends: Motorcycle Crashes, Helmet Regulation, and Helmet Use

Annual motorcycle occupant fatalities increased by 138 percent from 2,227 in 1995 to 5,290 in 2008. Motorcycle occupant fatalities rose from 5 percent of all U.S. traffic fatalities in 1995 to 14 percent in 2008. The occupant fatality rate per registered motorcycle increased 23 percent, and the rate per mile of motorcycle travel increased 67 percent in this period (Figure 4-13) (NHTSA 2009c, 18, 28; NHTSA 2010). (Part of the discrepancy between the increases in the two rates may be the result of problems in measuring motorcycle mileage.) Annual motorcycle occupant fatalities declined 16 percent in 2009, to 4,462, the first annual decline in 12 years. The decline may have been a consequence of the economic recession. The motorcycle occupant fatality rate per vehicle mile was 34 times greater than the rate for passenger car occupants in 2004 (NHTSA 2007c). The causes for the rapid rise in motorcycle fatality rates are not understood, although NHTSA reports that the market share

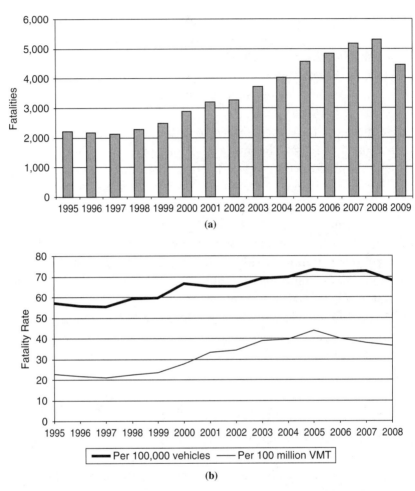

FIGURE 4-13 (*a*) Annual motorcycle occupant fatalities, 1995–2009 and (*b*) motorcycle occupant fatality rates, United States, 1995–2008. (SOURCES: NHTSA 2009c, 18, 28; NHTSA 2010.)

of motorcycles with larger engine sizes has increased. Helmet use among fatally injured motorcycle occupants has remained constant in the past decade (Shankar and Varghese 2006).

In 2010, 20 states had laws requiring all motorcycle occupants to use helmets, a decline from a peak of 47 states with such laws in 1975 (Figure 4-14). Fifty-six percent of all motorcycle registrations in 2000 were in states without a universal helmet use law (Ulmer and Preusser 2003).

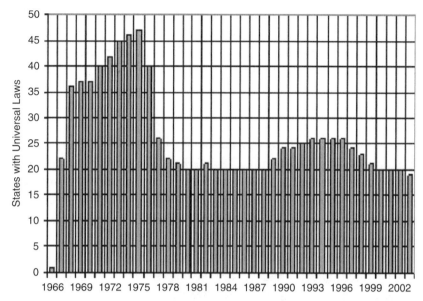

FIGURE 4-14 Number of states with universal motorcycle helmet use laws, 1966–2003. (SOURCE: Ulmer and Northrup 2005.) NOTE: Since 2003, one state (Louisiana in 2004) has enacted a universal helmet law.

Most states have laws requiring minors to wear helmets, and a few require helmets only for minors and newly licensed riders. A few states have required riders not wearing helmets to have medical insurance (Ulmer and Preusser 2003; Hedlund et al. 2007).

NHTSA's periodic roadside helmet use surveys found the following trend in use (Glassenbrenner and Ye 2006; NHTSA 2009a):

Survey Date	Percentage of Occupants with Helmets
October 1994	63
October 1996	64
October 1998	67
October 2000	71
June 2002	58
June 2004	58
June 2005	48
June 2006	51
June 2007	58
June 2008	63
June 2009	67

The apparent trend in the annual survey results probably is affected by a seasonal difference between use rates in June and October. Therefore, the actual long-term trend is not clear, although helmet use rates rose consistently from 2005 through 2009.

Comparisons with Benchmark Nations

By some measures, motorcycle crashes appear as an even more serious health problem in Europe than in the United States. In 14 European Union countries in 2004, 5,500 motorcycle and moped riders and passengers were killed. This was 20 percent of all road accident fatalities, twice the U.S. motorcycle share of fatalities. Annual motorcycle and moped fatalities declined by 6 percent in the decade 1995–2004 (ERSO 2007).

Motorcycle and moped fatality rates per registered vehicle are similar in the United States (65 fatalities per 100,000 vehicles in 2002, 68 in 2008), in France (60 in 2002), and in the United Kingdom (59 in 2002), but they are reportedly much lower in Italy (14 in 1998) and in Spain (19 in 2002) (SafetyNet 2005). The source of the divergence of rates among European countries is not evident but may relate to differences in the mix of motorcycles and mopeds.

IIHS reports that laws requiring motorcyclists to wear helmets are in effect in nearly every European country, Canada, Australia, New Zealand, and Japan (IIHS 2007), although the scope of laws in these countries is not reported and compliance in some regions may be relatively low.

At least one European country has acted recently to strengthen its helmet rules. In Italy, a 2000 law required helmet use for all motorcycle, motorbike, and moped occupants. The previous law, in effect since 1986, required helmets for all motorcycle riders but only for moped riders under age 18. Italy has twice as many mopeds in use as motorcycles. An evaluation of the impact of the law after 1 year reported high rates of compliance and a 66 percent reduction in hospital admissions for traumatic head injuries to motorcycle and moped occupants in one region of Italy (Servadei et al. 2003).

European countries recognize the need for additional motorcycle safety initiatives, including infrastructure design and vehicle design measures. Research has identified hazards in rural road conditions that are particularly significant for motorcycles (ACEM 2009b). Also, the European Union has considered adoption of a standard for advanced braking systems for motorcycles (ACEM 2009a). The European motorcycle manufacturing industry sponsors a safety research and promotion program (ACEM 2006). The industry organization has begun promoting the use of protective clothing and asserts that data from a motorcycle crash investigation study sponsored jointly by industry and government demonstrate the effectiveness of protective clothing (e.g., specially designed boots, gloves, and jackets) in reducing the severity of motorcycle crash injuries (ACEM 2010).

Examples of Changes in Helmet Laws

Federal Helmet Use Laws

Enactment and repeal of state helmet laws has been largely a consequence of changes in federal highway safety program requirements. Two safety acts enacted in 1966 created the predecessor organizations to NHTSA and authorized the Secretary of Transportation to issue Highway Safety Program Standards. States would be required to comply with the standards or lose a portion of federal-aid highway funds. The first standards, issued in 1967, included a requirement for a universal helmet use law. By 1975, 47 states had enacted such a law. In 1975, for the first time, three states (California, Illinois, and Utah) were threatened with penalties for failure to enact helmet laws, but Congress intervened by repealing the penalties. By 1980 the number of states with universal helmet laws had fallen to 20.

A few additional states enacted laws in the early 1990s. In 1992, Congress reinstated milder penalties for states without universal helmet laws (part of the federal-aid highway funds for states without helmet laws were to be transferred to the states' highway safety programs) and provided incentive grants rewarding states that enacted and enforced both helmet laws and safety belt laws. This program appears to have had little effect on state legislation. Congress eliminated the new penalties in 1995 (Ulmer and Preusser 2003; Hedlund 2007; LaHeist 1998; Hedlund et al. 2007). Nearly all the state universal helmet laws in effect today were originally enacted to comply with the federal requirement.

The history of federal helmet laws is similar in some respects to that of the NMSL. The federal government forcefully intervened in a regulatory matter that had formerly been exclusively determined by the states; state practices initially were greatly changed, but a reaction, in part on philosophical states-rights grounds, led to a rollback of federal involvement. The 1995 National Highway System Designation Act eliminated the federal penalty for states without helmet laws as well as the NMSL. Both provisions were part of a package of program reforms aimed at reducing federal control over state highway programs.

State Helmet Laws
Most of the repeals of state helmet laws occurred in the 1970s (Figure 4-14) after the elimination of federal sanctions. However, several states have changed their laws more recently. Since 1990, Arkansas (1997), Florida (2000), Kentucky (1998), Louisiana (1999), Pennsylvania (2003), and Texas (1997) have repealed universal helmet use requirements, and California (1992), Connecticut (1990), Louisiana (2004), Maryland (1992), and Washington (1990) have enacted such requirements. Louisiana has enacted a universal helmet use law three times: in 1968 (repealed in 1976), 1982 (repealed in 1999), and 2004. Texas enacted a law in 1967, repealed it in 1977, reinstated it in 1989, and repealed it again in 1997 (NHTSA 2007b, 184–185).

NHTSA has published evaluations of the recent helmet law repeals in Florida, Kentucky, Louisiana, Arkansas, and Texas (Ulmer and Northrup 2005; Ulmer and Preusser 2003; Preusser et al. 2000). The evaluations compare motorcycle injury and fatality trends in the subject states with national trends before and after the state law changes. For example, in Kentucky (repeal in 1998), motorcycle occupant fatalities per registered motorcycle increased 39 percent from 1996–1997 to 1999–2000, compared with 14 percent for the entire United States; in Louisiana (repeal in 1999), fatalities per registered motorcycle increased 74 percent from 1997–1998 to 2000, compared with 16 percent in the United States. Injury rates increased in both states and declined in the United States.

The NHTSA state studies do not describe the political debate that led to the changes in state laws, but NHTSA has summarized the common arguments of opponents of motorcycle helmet laws in these debates (NHTSA 1998):

- Helmet laws violate individual rights: because motorcycle riders suffer the primary consequences of crashes, they should have the right to decide whether the benefits of helmets outweigh their disadvantages.
- Helmets cause neck injuries and impair hearing and sight, increasing the likelihood of crashes.
- Statistical studies do not definitively show safety benefits from helmet laws because they do not properly take into account nonfatal crashes or changes in motorcycle ownership and use.
- Laws requiring only minors or new riders to wear helmets are effective and sufficient.

NHTSA-conducted surveys have concluded that 80 percent of U.S. adults and 50 percent of adult motorcycle riders support helmet use laws (NHTSA 2005b).

A 2004 *Wall Street Journal* article described motorcyclist organizing and lobbying efforts leading to repeal of the Pennsylvania universal helmet use law in 2003. The state chapter of the bikers' organization Alliance of Bikers Aimed Toward Education (ABATE) organized an effective grassroots campaign that included hiring a full-time lobbyist to promote legislation and organizing constituent visits to legislators. ABATE established a relationship with the governor through participation in a hospital charity and gained his endorsement. Legislators reported receiving contacts from numerous bikers in the weeks before the vote and from few opponents of repeal (Lundegaard 2004). In Pennsylvania and other states, ABATE chapters have set up political action committees, BikePACs, to contribute to election campaigns of politicians supporting their legislative agenda. ABATE chapters endorse political candidates and publish voters' guides and legislative issues guides. Motorcyclist political organizations have been active in some states since the early 1970s, when they were formed in response to the first federal motorcycle and helmet regulations (ABATE of California n.d.; Jones and Bayer 2007).

In Louisiana, the governor, a motorcyclist, led the legislative initiative that resulted in repeal of the state's helmet law in 1999. The succeeding governor actively supported reinstatement of the law in 2004. Evidence of increased motorcycle fatalities after repeal and of the cost to the state for medical care was reported to have influenced legislators' votes on reinstating the helmet requirement (Stone 2004).

Concluding Observations

- Well-organized grassroots advocacy on legislative issues is effective in the United States, especially for issues that most affect a well-defined group and do not attract strong interest in the general population. On an issue like motorcycle helmets, the lobbying of mainstream safety groups may inevitably be less politically effective than that of the single-issue groups opposing them. The importance of advocacy groups may be a significant difference between the United States and many other countries in the forming of safety policy.
- Motorcycle helmet laws are a more purely legislative issue than most other forms of safety interventions; that is, historically, enacting laws has been sufficient to produce results. In contrast, in other areas of highway safety, such as speed control and hazard elimination, effective execution of programs poses great management challenges and is at least as critical for success as the legal framework.
- The history of federal motorcycle helmet regulation is similar to that of the federal speed limit laws. In both cases, the penalty of loss of federal highway construction funds was used to induce conformity of state laws to federal standards. Both lost support and were repealed on account of the states' interest in limiting federal control over their transportation programs.
- High-level political leadership in the legislature or by the governor was essential in enactment of the only recent universal helmet use law (Louisiana) and in opposing initiatives to overturn laws in other states (e.g., in the case of the Michigan governor's veto of a 2006 repeal bill).
- Information about the safety consequences and costs to the state of helmet law repeal has influenced legislators when it has been presented in a timely and forceful manner. Coordinated, proactive information campaigns from the executive agencies when repeal bills have been introduced have discouraged repeals in some states.
- Motorcycle safety programs employing training, education, licensing, and enforcement are conducted in states with no universal helmet use

law. Such activities receive the support of motorcyclists. Research has failed to demonstrate that rider training can reduce motorcycle crashes (IIHS 2007), although training programs are endorsed by NHTSA as one component of its Motorcycle Safety Program (NHTSA 2003). NHTSA's *Countermeasures That Work* (Hedlund et al. 2009, 5-4–5-22) describes three categories of interventions to prevent motorcycle casualties in addition to helmets: measures targeting alcohol-impaired motorcycle use, operator licensing and training, and communications to promote use of protective and conspicuous clothing and motorist awareness of motorcyclists. According to the review, evaluations of motorcyclist training have found only minimal effectiveness and no evaluations of the other interventions have been carried out, although some of them are commonly used and the authors view some as potentially effective (e.g., alcohol enforcement targeting cyclists and improvements in conspicuity). Motorcycle operation by persons without the required license or endorsement is common and may be an underemphasized risk factor. Emphasis on these kinds of safety efforts would be consistent with the recommendation of the FHWA report *Halving Roadway Fatalities* that the necessary elements of a successful program are identifying the greatest safety problems, selecting interventions that are demonstrated to be effective, and then systemically implementing those that can gain political and public support (Johnston 2006, 16).

HIGHWAY NETWORK SCREENING AND SAFE ROAD DESIGN

In contrast to speed management and motorcycle helmet laws, which seek to reduce high-risk driver behavior, highway network screening aims to make the infrastructure inherently safer for the average driver. Every U.S. state highway agency has a program to identify locations on the road system with a relatively high frequency of crashes and to apply treatments to reduce the excess risk at these locations. Such a program requires a data system that records the location and characteristics of each crash and the characteristics of each road segment on the system, an analysis method for identifying and prioritizing the high-hazard locations, and a repertoire of treatments that can be used in designing a correction for each of the highest-priority locations. Treatments may include alignment adjustments, widening of shoulders, removal of roadside obstacles, improvement of signing and pavement markings, intersection improvements, installation of barriers, and increases in traffic law enforcement (although these programs traditionally emphasize minor capital and traffic control improvements and may not always coordinate with enforcement agencies).

For new roads and projects to reconstruct or rehabilitate roads, design standards promulgated by FHWA (applicable to projects funded with federal aid) and design guides published by AASHTO offer rules with regard to alignment, cross section [lane, shoulder, and median widths and superelevation (banking) on curves], the roadside environment, and other features intended to provide an acceptable level of safety. The AASHTO *Highway Safety Manual* and its supporting design tools (See Box 3-7 in Chapter 3) are expected to provide a sounder basis than traditional design standards for assessing the safety of designs for new roads and road improvements.

The first section below discusses the relationship of roadway characteristics to safety. The second describes U.S. hazard elimination practices, and the third describes related activities in other countries. The final section presents summary observations.

Relationship of Road Characteristics to Crash and Injury Risk

A 1987 TRB committee, in a study that recommended design practices for highway resurfacing, restoration, and rehabilitation (RRR) projects, explained the relationship between highway characteristics and crash risk as follows (TRB 1987, 78):

> Highway features affect safety by:
>
> - Influencing the ability of the driver to maintain vehicle control and identify hazards. Significant features include lane width, alignment, sight distance, superelevation (i.e., banking on curves), and pavement surface characteristics;
> - Influencing the number and types of opportunities that exist for conflicts between vehicles. Significant features include access control, intersection design, number of lanes, and medians;

- Affecting the consequences of an out-of-control vehicle leaving the travel lanes. Significant features include shoulder width and type, edge drop, roadside conditions, side slopes, and guardrail; and
- Affecting the behavior and attentiveness of the driver, particularly, the choice of travel speed. Driver behavior is affected by virtually all elements of the roadway environment.

Driver behavior is affected by lane width and alignment, the appearance to the driver of the roadside environment, the design of signs and markings intended to inform the driver, and many other design features of the roadway environment (Smiley 2008).

A connection between safety and road characteristics is evident in data on fatality rates per mile of travel for different road classes. On rural Interstates in 2007, the rate was 0.6 fatalities per 100 million vehicle kilometers of travel; on other rural arterials, 1.4; and on rural minor roads (collector and local road classes), 1.8, three times higher than the rural Interstate rate and five times higher than the urban Interstate rate (FHWA n.d. a) (see Figure 2-13 in Chapter 2). The design of Interstates eliminates or greatly reduces the risk of head-on collisions, collisions with fixed objects, and intersection crashes (Evans 2004, 102–105). In urban areas the difference is less (0.6 fatalities per 100 million vehicle miles on Interstates, 1.1 on urban local and collector roads), presumably in part because many local urban roads are low speed.

Crash circumstances also indicate the connection between safety and road design. For example, NHTSA reports that 22 percent of all fatal crashes in 2008 occurred at intersections or were intersection-related and that 42 percent of all fatal crashes were single-vehicle run-off-road crashes (NHTSA 2010, 51–52).

The TRB RRR committee observed that despite decades of research to measure the effects of road design features on safety, highway agencies still had limited ability to predict the safety benefits resulting from a roadway improvement (TRB 1987, 78). This conclusion still appears valid. Measurement is difficult because of the multiple factors that affect crash risk; because of chronic deficiencies in data; and because some critical factors, including vehicle characteristics and driving habits, change over time. To design and prioritize projects to treat high-hazard locations, states use the best available information to develop tables of crash reduction factors, which are estimates of the likely safety gain from individual road improvements. For example, research commissioned by the TRB RRR committee estimated that on a two-lane rural road with a 5-foot-wide roadside clear zone, widening the clear zone to 20 feet would reduce the number of single-vehicle, head-on, and sideswipe crashes by 35 percent on average (TRB 1987, 85–86).

FHWA has estimated that the cumulative impact of the Hazard Elimination Program and the grade crossing program was to prevent 58,000 deaths and 1.1 million nonfatal injuries between 1974 and 1995. FHWA has also estimated that each $100 million spent in targeted highway safety capital improvements results in 14.5 fewer fatalities per year (FHWA 1996). A more recent analysis found a nationwide benefit–cost ratio of 11 for all Hazard Elimination Program projects and 8 for highway–rail grade crossing projects conducted from 1995 to 2000 (Li et al. 2004). To the extent that these estimates were based on the states' projections of project benefits rather than on evaluations after projects were completed, their reliability is unknown. It would be useful to know whether any states have retrospectively evaluated the results of their improvements at high-hazard locations to determine the extent to which expected crash reductions were attained.

In contrast to these estimates, the studies described in Chapter 2 that have used statistical methods to explain differences in crash rates among the states or among countries have not found a strong correlation between safety and infrastructure spending or condition. For example, the study of effects of road investment and other factors on U.S. state road casualty frequency concluded that "changes in highway infrastructure that occurred between 1984 and 1997 have not reduced traffic fatalities and injuries and have even had the effect of increasing total fatalities and injuries. . . . [T]he fact that adding new and higher design standard lane miles leads to increased fatalities and injuries suggests that new 'improved' design standards are not achieving safety benefits" (Noland 2003, 610). As explained in Chapter 2, the author's interpretation of the statistical results is problematic because the study excludes vehicle miles of travel as an explanatory variable. In addition, because this study used data on overall upgrading of highway system standards and not on spot improvement projects, its results are not directly relevant to highway network screening programs. Nonetheless, its results challenge standard assumptions in highway design.

A research program sponsored by the U.S. Department of Transportation and by the states through AASHTO has increased understanding of the safety effects of highway design and traffic control features and has developed new knowledge and organized existing knowledge into tools for application in project development (see Box 3-7 in Chapter 3). The *Highway Safety Manual* published by AASHTO in 2010 is a first step in providing a methodology that quantifies the expected safety effects of proposed highway improvement projects and allows highway designers to compare the expected safety performance of design alternatives. Software tools to implement the *Highway Safety Manual* procedures include the SafetyAnalyst and the Interactive Highway Safety Design Model. To achieve safety improvement, the *Highway Safety Manual* procedures and the available software tools will need to be institutionalized in the safety management process and the project development process.

U.S. Practices

The two subsections below describe a representative state highway network screening program and the main federal grant program for state and local highway hazard elimination projects. Funding for hazard elimination in most states is mainly from grants from the federal-aid highway program specifically provided for the purpose [formerly the Hazard Elimination and Highway–Rail Grade Crossings Programs, now the Highway Safety Improvement Program (HSIP) defined in the 2005 federal surface transportation act (SAFETEA-LU)]. Projects eligible for federal funding assistance are defined as follows [23 U.S.C. Section 148(a)]:

> In general.—The term "highway safety improvement project" means a project described in the State strategic highway safety plan that (i) corrects or improves a hazardous road location or feature; or (ii) addresses a highway safety problem.

The act also lists categories of eligible projects. The state strategic highway safety plans that the act requires are described in Chapter 3.

Example of a State Highway Network Screening Program

The following outline of Oregon's Highway Safety Program (ODOT 2007) is presented to illustrate the procedures in a representative state program to identify and correct high-hazard locations.

The Oregon Department of Transportation (ODOT) currently spends approximately $28 million annually on its Highway Safety Program. Funding includes $14 million from the federal HSIP and an equal amount from state funds and other federal funds. The state probably is unusual in doubling its federal HSIP grant; the minimum required state matching share is 10 percent. For comparison, the ODOT highway budget is approximately $1 billion annually.

The Highway Safety Program funds mainly small infrastructure improvement projects at high-hazard locations. For example, eligible improvements include alignment adjustments, signal installation, guardrails, barriers, illumination, pavement markings, signs, roadside fixed-object removal, and traffic-calming features. With a few exceptions, noninfrastructure treatments such as increased enforcement are funded through other programs. Projects may be on any public road in the state owned by state or local government.

Each of ODOT's five regions receives a funding allocation, and projects are developed and nominated by the regions. The department conducts statewide analyses to identify high-hazard locations. The Safety Priority Index System (SPIS) evaluates the state highway system in 0.1-mile segments to identify problem locations on the basis of crash frequency, severity, and rate. Each region is given a list of the sites in its territory to which the SPIS has assigned a priority in the top 5 percent of all sites statewide. The regions then evaluate these sites for possible corrective action. A separate analysis [the Safety Investment Program (SIP)] ranks 5-mile segments of the state highway system according to the frequency of fatal and serious injury crashes in a 3-year period.

Local governments may also nominate projects to their regional office for inclusion in the Highway Safety Program. Each region assembles a package of project requests, limited by its funding allocation and prioritized according to criteria specified by ODOT (including SPIS ranking, SIP ranking, and benefit–cost ratio). The Oregon Transportation Commission makes the final decision on which safety projects are included in the Statewide Transportation Improvement Program.

A noteworthy component of Oregon safety activities is the state's safety corridor program, which constitutes a more comprehensive and systematic approach to reducing the risk of travel on a particular road than the traditional, infrastructure-oriented hazard elimination program. The state publishes an annual Safety Corridor Plan that identifies corridors on state highways that have been given high priority for crash reduction. The plan also reports on progress in meeting crash reduction objectives in each corridor. Corridor treatments are designed that combine enforcement, education (including publicity campaigns and school programs), engineering (traffic control devices and capital improvements to the roads in the corridor), and emergency medical services (EMS) improvements. Coordination is required with local governments on enforcement and EMS and with the state's capital programming process where capital improvements are called for. Other states also conduct corridor safety programs. For example, the California program, which has treated 123 corridors since 1993, depends on cooperation of the highway patrol, the state highway agency, local police, and local EMS.

Federal HSIP

The federal HSIP established in SAFETEA-LU (Section 1401) is the current version of a grant program that has been in operation since at least 1975. The law authorizes $1.2 billion annually for 2006–2009 for projects to correct high-hazard locations on any public road. Funds are allocated by formula to the states. Within the program, the law sets aside $220 million annually for rail–highway grade crossing projects and $90 million annually for improvements on high-risk rural roads.

A new provision requires each state to coordinate its hazard elimination program with the state's federally required Strategic Highway Safety Plan. The intent of the strategic plan is to identify critical highway safety problems and opportunities. The plan must be based on accurate and timely safety data; be developed in consultation with local governments and private stakeholders; specify performance-based goals; and incorporate strategies involving infrastructure improvement, driver behavior regulation, education, and emergency services. State data systems supporting the plan must be capable of identifying high-hazard locations and evaluating countermeasures. The state's HSIP is to be developed within the framework of the strategic plan, presumably to ensure that interested parties are consulted in forming the program and that the full range of countermeasures is considered (FHWA 2005).

Practices in the Benchmark Countries

The four benchmark country safety programs described in Chapter 4, and probably the programs of all the high-income countries, include a traditional hazard elimination component. In addition, all countries have design standards for new construction and reconstruction that are intended to provide for safety. However, a shift in design emphasis appears to be emerging in some of the benchmark countries' road programs that departs from conventional practice in three ways. First, designs are more firmly based on the results of research on the relationship of design to crash and casualty risk (for example, an appreciation of the influence of geometric design on driver behavior, especially selection of speed). Second, risk reduction is given higher priority and earlier attention in the design of projects and in project programming. Finally, designs show a willingness to trade a degree of traveler convenience for the sake of safety. The new approach entails greater road agency accountability for the safety consequences of road designs—the designer is expected to quantify the expected crash frequency on the new or improved road and to justify the design level of risk as acceptable. Activities such as the road safety audit and the road assessment programs described below reinforce accountability. This design philosophy is an ideal articulated in national safety plans that has yet to be fully realized in practice; nonetheless, it is influencing practice in some countries.

Several of the benchmark countries highlight road design as central to their long-term safety strategies. Examples are the following:

- In Sweden, the Vision Zero policy described in Chapter 3 emphasizes road design. Roads are to be built or reconstructed with features that ensure low casualty risk, and risk reduction opportunity is a factor in project selection. Safety design features include roundabouts replacing intersections, barriers separating opposing lanes, and the 2+1 lane design.

- In Australia, the most recent Australian Transport Council Action Plan, described in Chapter 3, endorses a "safe system" framework, which has been adopted in several of the Australian state safety plans. The framework embodies a systems perspective, that is, a design philosophy that seeks to optimize the performance of the road system as a whole, with consideration of the characteristics of vehicles, roads, and users. The safety plans acknowledge that, now that Australia has made large safety improvements through intensified enforcement, greater focus on safe infrastructure design will be necessary to sustain improvement in the future.
- In the Netherlands, the strategy of the "sustainable safety" policy has similarities with the Swedish Vision Zero strategy. It adopts the systems perspective and emphasizes road design as a means of regulating driver behavior. The road system is classified by function, and design features identified as appropriate to each function are being introduced, for example, traffic-calming features in built-up areas and alignment and lane width adjustments on two-lane roads that signal appropriate speeds to drivers. This design technique is referred to as the self-explaining road (Kraay 2002, 2–3, 6–7).

Because these strategies involve road reconstruction, they can only be brought to fruition gradually over time. In addition, fully implementing them will require the analytical ability to design a road to meet a quantitative crash risk standard (i.e., a specified expected crash risk on a road, given stated assumptions about traffic characteristics). This ability is not yet fully in place in the United States or other countries, although, as described above, some of the necessary analytical tools have been under development in the United States.

Road Assessment Programs
A new evaluation practice, the Road Assessment Program (RAP), in operation in Europe and Australia and under development in the United States, is bringing greater attention to the problem of upgrading the inherent safety of road infrastructure. RAPs assemble and publicize crash data and other safety information for individual road segments. The programs publish maps that indicate the relative safety of each of the roads in

a jurisdiction. Leadership in creating and managing the programs has come from the national automobile clubs in those countries, in cooperation with governmental agencies. In the United States, the AAA Foundation is organizing pilot implementations of usRAP in cooperation with eight states (Iowa, Michigan, Florida, New Jersey, Illinois, Kentucky, New Mexico, and Utah) (usRAP 2008; Harwood et al. 2010).

The creation of RAP was inspired by the success of the European New Car Assessment Program (NCAP), which was organized in the mid-1990s as a joint effort of automobile clubs, governments, and the European Commission to conduct new-car crash tests and publish the results as consumer information. The NCAP is believed to have influenced vehicle designs strongly as manufacturers competitively seek higher ratings for their new models. In Europe, the RAP maps attract considerable public attention, which exerts pressure on road agencies to act on the high-crash locations.

RAP is a potentially significant experiment in highway safety action. A nongovernmental initiative, it aims to increase public demand for safety and to make public officials more accountable for safety performance of highways by revealing and publicizing hazards. The road protection scores and star ratings produced by the RAP assessments (Harwood et al. 2010, 113–150) are useful as intermediate output measures of state hazard elimination programs.

Road Safety Audits

A second evaluation practice in use in the benchmark nations and in some U.S. states, road safety audits, is increasing awareness of the potential for reducing casualty risk through changes in road design and is reinforcing public accountability of road agency managers. A road safety audit is a formal, independent examination of the safety of the design of a road construction or reconstruction project. A similar procedure, called a road safety audit review in the United States, has been developed for roads already in use. Road safety audits originated in the United Kingdom, where they have been compulsory since 1991 for major projects, and are practiced in Canada, Australia, New Zealand, Germany, and some U.S. states (Wilson and Lipinski 2004, 1–4, 21–25; ETSC 2005).

FHWA identifies critical differences between a road safety audit and conventional methods of checking the safety of a road design (FHWA n.d. b). The audit

- Is performed by a team independent of the project;
- Is performed by a multidisciplinary team (for example, expertise of team members may include traffic engineering, road design, traffic enforcement, roadway maintenance, and crash investigation);
- Considers interactions of motor vehicles, bicycles, and pedestrians;
- Considers especially human factors issues in the design, that is, the demands the road environment places on the driver's attention, reactions, and judgment;
- Generates a formal audit report; and
- Requires a formal response to the audit from the parties responsible for the audit.

The requirements for independence of the audit and for a formal report and response reinforce accountability of the agency conducting the project. The interdisciplinary approach ensures that features affecting risk that road designers have not been technically prepared to recognize in the past are not overlooked.

Summary Observations

Although hazard elimination programs are prominent in the safety strategies of most state transportation programs, the overall performance of these programs is difficult to assess. A systematic comparative evaluation to determine how much the programs contribute to safety improvement and to identify the attributes of the most effective programs would be worthwhile. In-depth examinations of hazard elimination programs in a sample of states (possibly supplemented with international comparisons) would seek to answer the following questions:

- Do the state hazard elimination programs produce appreciable reductions in crashes at reasonable cost? Especially, are there state programs that are much more effective than the average, or practices in other countries that are more effective than U.S. programs? Overall evaluations

of the effectiveness of these programs have been rare and have used imperfect methodologies.
- Do states successfully manage the interagency coordination that an effective hazard elimination program requires? The parties that may be involved include several offices within the highway agency (which administers the federal HSIP funds), the state agency responsible for administering NHTSA highway safety grants (which may fund enforcement, data systems, public information programs, or EMS improvements), state and local police, local governments, and interested private groups. Participation of all of these parties may be needed to identify the highest-priority locations and to carry out the most effective remedies.
- Does the highway network screening process have any influence on the overall state highway capital and maintenance programs? For example, when the state plans and designs its major highway capacity projects or its pavement resurfacing program, does information about high-hazard locations influence priorities and project designs? Or, alternatively, is the screening used solely to direct the spending of earmarked safety funds?
- Does highway network screening influence the priorities and practices of agencies outside the state department of transportation—state police, local police, local roads programs, and metropolitan planning organizations?
- Have state hazard elimination programs achieved an appropriate balance between spot safety improvements (i.e., improvements to short segments or individual intersections) and corridor-based safety improvements (i.e., broadly based improvement packages for extended road sections with the highest identified risk levels)?
- How can the impact of the hazard elimination program and related safety analysis and planning activities be evaluated, either on a project-by-project basis or cumulatively over a period of years for an entire state?
- If evidence from the states with the best programs or from other countries shows that hazard eliminations could make a much greater contribution to reducing traffic injuries, what strategy can be used to reform the lagging programs and increase the resources available to

them? The restructured HSIP of SAFETEA-LU was intended to raise the stature of the program by increasing funding and by linking it to comprehensive state highway safety plans. Has the new federal structure enhanced the performance of the state programs?

REFERENCES

Abbreviations

ABATE	Alliance of Bikers Aimed Toward Education
ACEM	Association des Constructeurs Européens des Motocycles
DfT	Department for Transport
ECMT	European Council of Ministers of Transport
ERSO	European Road Safety Observatory
ETSC	European Transport Safety Council
FHWA	Federal Highway Administration
GAO	General Accounting Office
GHSA	Governors Highway Safety Association
IIHS	Insurance Institute for Highway Safety
MADD	Mothers Against Drunk Driving
NHTSA	National Highway Traffic Safety Administration
NTSB	National Transportation Safety Board
ODOT	Oregon Department of Transportation
OECD	Organisation for Economic Co-operation and Development
ONISR	Observatoire National Interministériel de Sécurité Routière
TRB	Transportation Research Board
USDOT	U.S. Department of Transportation

Aarts, L., and I. van Schagen. 2006. Driving Speed and the Risk of Road Crashes: A Review. *Accident Analysis and Prevention,* Vol. 38, No. 2, pp. 215–224.

ABATE of California. n.d. History of ABATE. http://www.abate.org/aboutus/history/.

ACEM. 2006. Safety Innovations by Industry: Indicative Overview. http://www.acem.eu/media/d_Annex3IndicativeoverviewofSafetyInnovations_61541.pdf.

ACEM. 2009a. Contribution to the Public Consultation on a Proposal for a Framework Regulation of the European Parliament and of the Council on Type-Approval of Two- and Three-Wheel Motor Vehicles. Feb. 23.

ACEM. 2009b. *News from the Motorcycle Industry in Europe.* No. 18, Feb. www.acem.eu.

ACEM. 2010. *Protective Equipment for Riders.* March.

Arizona Department of Public Safety. n.d. Photo Enforcement Program. http://www.azdps.gov/Services/Photo_Enforcement/.

Bashem, W. M., and P. H. Mengert. 1974. The Effects of the Energy Crisis on Rural Roads in Maine. *Public Roads*, Dec., pp. 100–105.

Blomberg, R. D., and A. M. Cleven. 2006. *Pilot Test of Heed the Speed, a Program to Reduce Speeds in Residential Neighborhoods*. National Highway Traffic Safety Administration, Aug.

Blomberg, R. D., F. D. Thomas III, and A. M. Cleven. 2008. *Increasing Seat Belt Use Through State-Level Demonstration Projects: A Compendium of Initial Findings*. National Highway Traffic Safety Administration, Aug.

Blomberg, R. D., F. D. Thomas III, and A. M. Cleven. 2009. *Innovative Seat Belt Demonstration Programs in Kentucky, Mississippi, North Dakota, and Wyoming*. National Highway Traffic Safety Administration, March.

Breen, J., E. Howard, and T. Bliss. 2007. *An Independent Review of Road Safety in Sweden*. Dec.

CISR. 2006. Dossier de Presse. July 6.

City of Scottsdale. n.d. Photo Enforcement Program. http://www.scottsdaleaz.gov/photoradar.asp.

Compton, R., and A. Berning. 2009. *Traffic Safety Facts Research Note: Results of the 2007 National Roadside Survey of Alcohol and Drug Use by Drivers*. National Highway Traffic Safety Administration, July.

Delaney, A., H. Ward, M. Cameron, and A. F. Williams. 2005. Controversies and Speed Cameras: Lessons Learnt Internationally. *Journal of Public Health Policy*, Vol. 26, pp. 404–415.

DfT. 2007. *Road Casualties Great Britain 2006*. Sept.

DfT. 2008. *Road Casualties Great Britain 2007*. Sept.

Dinh-Zarr, T. B., D. A. Sleet, R. A. Shults, S. Zaza, R. W. Elder, J. L. Nichols, R. S. Thompson, and D. M. Sosin. 2001. Reviews of Evidence Regarding Interventions to Increase the Use of Safety Belts. *American Journal of Preventive Medicine*, Vol. 21, No. 4, Supplement 1, Nov., pp. 48–65.

Elder, R. W., R. A. Shults, D. A. Sleet, J. L. Nichols, S. Zaza, and R. Thompson. 2002. Effectiveness of Sobriety Checkpoints for Reducing Alcohol-Involved Crashes. *Traffic Injury Prevention*, Vol. 3, No. 4, pp. 266–274.

ERSO. 2007. *Traffic Safety Basic Facts 2006: Motorcycles and Mopeds*. European Commission, Jan.

ETSC. 2005. Road Safety Audit. ETSC Fact Sheet No. 5, July.

Evans, L. 2004. *Traffic Safety*. Science Serving Society, Bloomfield Hills, Mich.

Farmer, C. F. 2008. *Crash Avoidance Potential of Five Vehicle Technologies*. Insurance Institute for Highway Safety, Arlington, Va., June.

Fell, J. C., J. H. Lacey, and R. B. Voas. 2004. Sobriety Checkpoints: Evidence of Effectiveness Is Strong, but Use Is Limited. *Traffic Injury Prevention*, Vol. 5, No. 3, Sept., pp. 220–227.

Fell, J. C., and R. B. Voas. 2006. The Effectiveness of Reducing Illegal Blood Alcohol Concentration (BAC) Limits for Driving: Evidence for Lowering the Limit to .05 BAC. *Journal of Safety Research*, Vol. 37, pp. 233–243.

FHWA. 1996. *1996 Annual Report on Highway Safety Improvement Programs.*

FHWA. 1997. *Highway Statistics Summary to 1995.* July.

FHWA. 2001. *Highway Statistics 2000.*

FHWA. 2005. *Highway Safety Improvement Program: Questions and Answers.* Sept. 14.

FHWA. 2006. *Highway Statistics 2005.*

FHWA. 2010. *Highway Statistics 2008.*

FHWA. n.d. a. Fatality Rate by Road Function Class Table. http://safety.fhwa.dot.gov/speedmgt/data_facts/.

FHWA. n.d. b. Road Safety Audits (RSA). http://safety.fhwa.dot.gov/rsa/.

GAO. 1991. *Highway Safety: Motorcycle Helmet Laws Save Lives and Reduce Costs to Society.* July.

GHSA. 2005. *Survey of the States: Speeding.*

GHSA. n.d. a. Drunk Driving Laws. www.ghsa.org/stateinfo/laws/impaired_laws.html.

GHSA. n.d. b. State Highway Safety Grant Programs. www.ghsa.org/html/stateinfo/grants/index.html.

Glassenbrenner, D., and J. Ye. 2006. *Motorcycle Helmet Use in 2006—Overall Results.* National Highway Traffic Safety Administration, Nov.

Gordon, P. 2007. Mayor Gordon Says Heed the Speed. Press release, March 29. www.philgordon.org.

Harder, K. A., and J. R. Bloomfield. 2007. *Evaluating the Effectiveness of the Minnesota Speed Management Program.* Minnesota Department of Transportation, St. Paul, May.

Harsha, B., and J. Hedlund. 2007. Changing America's Culture of Speed on the Roads. In *Improving Traffic Safety Culture in the United States: The Journey Forward*, AAA Foundation for Traffic Safety, Washington, D.C., April.

Harwood, D. W., D. K. Gilmore, and K. M. Bauer. 2010. *U.S. Road Assessment Program—Phase III: Final Report.* AAA Foundation for Traffic Safety, Washington, D.C., May.

Haworth, N. L., and I. R. Johnston. 2004. Why Isn't the Involvement of Alcohol in Road Crashes in Australia Lower? Abstract. Presented at 17th International Conference on Alcohol, Drugs, and Traffic Safety, Glasgow, United Kingdom.

Hedlund, J. 2007. Traffic Safety in the United States—Timeline of Notable Events: Draft. March 3. http://www.lifesaversconference.org/webfiles2007/Hedlund1.doc.

Hedlund, J., S. H. Gilbert, K. Ledingham, and D. Preusser. 2008. *How States Achieve High Seat Belt Use Rates*. National Highway Traffic Safety Administration, Aug.

Hedlund, J. H., B. Harsha, and W. A. Leaf. 2007. *Countermeasures That Work: A Highway Safety Countermeasures Guide for State Highway Safety Offices*. National Highway Traffic Safety Administration.

Hedlund, J. H., B. Harsha, W. A. Leaf, A. H. Goodwin, W. L. Hall, J. C. Raborn, L. J. Thomas, and M. E. Tucker. 2009. *Countermeasures That Work: A Highway Safety Countermeasures Guide for State Highway Safety Offices: Fourth Edition*. National Highway Traffic Safety Administration.

Hendricks, D. L., J. C. Fell, and M. Freedman. 2001. *The Relative Frequency of Unsafe Driving Acts in Serious Traffic Crashes: Summary Technical Report*. National Highway Traffic Safety Administration, Jan.

IIHS. 2000. How State Laws Measure Up. *Status Report*, Vol. 35, No. 10, Dec. 20, pp. 1–7.

IIHS. 2005. *Status Report*, Vol. 40, No. 4, April 2.

IIHS. 2006. How State Laws Measure Up: As of March 2006.

IIHS. 2007. Q&A: Motorcycle Helmet Use Laws as of June 2007. http://www.iihs.org/research/qanda/helmet_use.html#10.

IIHS. 2009a. How State Laws Measure Up. Dec. http://www.iihs.org/laws/measureup.aspx.

IIHS. 2009b. Safety Belt Use Laws: October 2009.

IIHS. 2010. Safety Belt Use Laws: October 2010. http://www.iihs.org/laws/SafetyBelt Use.aspx.

Johnston, I. 2006. *Halving Roadway Fatalities: A Case Study from Victoria, Australia, 1989–2004*. Federal Highway Administration, April.

Jones, M. M., and R. Bayer. 2007. Paternalism and Its Discontents: Motorcycle Helmet Laws, Libertarian Values, and Public Health. *American Journal of Public Health*, Vol. 97, No. 2, Feb., pp. 208–217.

Kahane, C. J. 2000. *Fatality Reduction by Safety Belts for Front-Seat Occupants of Cars and Light Trucks: Updated and Expanded Estimates Based on 1986–99 FARS Data*. National Highway Traffic Safety Administration, Dec.

Kemper, W. J., and S. R. Byington. 1977. Safety Aspects of the National 55 MPH Speed Limit. *Public Roads*, Sept., pp. 58–67.

Kraay, J. H. 2002. The Netherlands Traffic and Transport Plan: Road Safety with Special Focus on Speed Behavior. Presented at International Cooperation on Theories and Concepts in Traffic Safety Workshop, Nagoya, Japan. www.ictct.org.

LaHeist, W. G. 1998. *Highway Traffic Assessment: A Summary of Findings in Ten States*. National Highway Traffic Safety Administration, June.

Lave, C., and P. Elias. 1994. Did the 65 mph Speed Limit Save Lives? *Accident Analysis and Prevention*, Vol. 26, No. 1, Feb., pp. 49–62.

Li, X., L. Yu, and V. Garg. 2004. Evaluation of the Overall Effectiveness of Highway Safety Improvement Projects at the National Level. In *Applications of Advanced Technologies in Transportation Engineering* (K. C. Sinha, T. F. Fwa, R. L. Cheu, and D.-H. Lee, eds.), American Society of Civil Engineers, Reston, Va.

Lundegaard, K. 2004. Risky Riders: Touting Freedom, Bikers Take Aim at Helmet Laws. *Wall Street Journal,* Nov. 30, p. A1.

MADD. n.d. Sobriety Checkpoint FAQs. http://www.madd.org/Drunk-Driving/Drunk-Driving/Campaign-to-Eliminate-Drunk-Driving/Law-Enforcement/Sobriety-Check point-FAQs.aspx.

McKnight, J., and A. S. McKnight. 1994. *The Effects of Motorcycle Helmets upon Seeing and Hearing.* National Highway Traffic Safety Administration, Feb.

Neiman, M. 2007. Motorcycle Helmet Laws: The Facts, What Can Be Done to Jump-Start Helmet Use, and Ways to Cap the Damages. http://works.bepress.com/melissa_neiman/1/.

Nerup, P., P. Salzberg, J. VanDyk, L. Porter, R. Blomberg, F. D. Thomas, and L. Cosgrove. 2006. *Ticketing Aggressive Cars and Trucks in Washington State: High Visibility Enforcement Applied to Share the Road Safely.* National Highway Traffic Safety Administration, May.

Neuman, T. R., K. L. Slack, K. K. Hardy, V. L. Bond, R. D. Foss, A. H. Goodwin, J. Sohn, D. J. Torbic, D. W. Harwood, I. B. Potts, R. Pfefer, C. Raborn, and N. D. Lerner. 2009. *NCHRP Report 500: Guidance for Implementation of the AASHTO Strategic Highway Safety Plan: Volume 23: A Guide for Reducing Speeding-Related Crashes.* Transportation Research Board of the National Academies, Washington, D.C.

New York State Governor's Traffic Safety Committee. 2008. *New York State Highway Safety Strategic Plan: FFY 2009.*

Newton, C. 2010. Arizona to Eliminate Speed-Enforcement Cameras on Freeways. *Arizona Republic,* May 6. http://www.azcentral.com/news/articles/2010/05/06/20100506 arizona-to-eliminate-speed-cameras.html.

NHTSA. 1998. *Without Motorcycle Helmets We All Pay the Price.* Aug.

NHTSA. 2003. *Motorcycle Safety Program.* Jan.

NHTSA. 2004. *Motorcycle Effectiveness Revisited.* March.

NHTSA. 2005a. *Analysis of Speeding-Related Fatal Motor Vehicle Traffic Crashes.* June.

NHTSA. 2005b. *Motorcycle Helmet Use Laws.* March.

NHTSA. 2007a. *The Nation's Top Strategies to Stop Impaired Driving.* Feb.

NHTSA. 2007b. *Traffic Safety Facts 2005.*

NHTSA. 2007c. *Traffic Safety Facts: 2005 Data: Motorcycles.*

NHTSA. 2007d. *Traffic Safety Facts: 2005 Data: Speeding.*

NHTSA. 2007e. *Traffic Safety Facts 2006.*

NHTSA. 2008a. *Traffic Safety Facts 2007.*

NHTSA. 2008b. *Traffic Safety Facts Research Note: Seat Belt Use in 2008—Overall Results.* Sept.

NHTSA. 2008c. *Traffic Safety Facts Traffic Tech—Technology Transfer Series: How States Achieve High Seat Belt Use Rates.* Aug.

NHTSA. 2009a. *Motorcycle Helmet Use in 2009—Overall Results.* Dec.

NHTSA. 2009b. *Seat Belt Use in 2009—Overall Results.* Sept.

NHTSA. 2009c. *Traffic Safety Facts 2008.*

NHTSA. 2009d. *Traffic Safety Facts Crash-Stats: Seat Belt Use in 2008—Use Rates in the States and Territories.* April.

NHTSA. 2009e. *Traffic Safety Facts Research Note: Seat Belt Use in 2009—Overall Results.* Sept.

NHTSA. 2009f. *Traffic Safety Facts Research Note: Seat Belt Use in Rear Seats in 2008.* May.

NHTSA. 2010. *Highlights of 2009 Motor Vehicle Crashes.* Aug.

NHTSA. n.d. SAFETEA-LU Fact Sheets. http://www.atssa.com/galleries/default-file/NHTSA%20FACT%20SHEETS.pdf.

Nichols, J. L., K. A. Ledingham, and D. F. Preusser. 2007. *Effectiveness of the May 2005 Rural Demonstration Program and the Click It or Ticket Mobilization in the Great Lakes Region: First Year Results.* National Highway Traffic Safety Administration, April.

Noland, R. B. 2003. Traffic Fatalities and Injuries: The Effect of Changes in Infrastructure and Other Trends. *Accident Analysis and Prevention,* Vol. 35, No. 4, July, pp. 599–611.

NTSB. 2000. *Safety Report: Actions to Reduce Fatalities, Injuries, and Crashes Involving the Hard Core Drinking Driver.* June 27.

ODOT. 2007. *Highway Safety Program Guide.* Feb.

OECD and ECMT. 2006. *Speed Management: Summary Document.* Joint Transport Research Centre.

OECD and International Transport Forum. 2006. *Country Reports on Road Safety Performance.* July.

ONISR. 2005. *French Road Safety Policy.*

ONISR. 2006. Observatoire des Vitesses: Second Quadrimestre 2006. Oct. 20. http://www.securiteroutiere.gouv.fr/IMG/pdf/observatoire_vitesse.pdf.

ONISR. 2008. *La Sécurité Routière en France: Bilan de l'Année 2007.* Dec.

ONISR. 2009a. *La Sécurité Routière en France: Bilan de l'Année 2008.* http://www2.securiteroutiere.gouv.fr/infos-ref/observatoire/accidentologie/le-bilan-de-l.html.

ONISR. 2009b. Observatoire des Vitesses: Premier Quadrimestre 2009. July.

Pastore, A. L., and K. Maguire (eds.). n.d. *Sourcebook of Criminal Justice Statistics Online.* http://www.albany.edu/sourcebook/.

Preusser, D. F., J. H. Hedlund, and R. G. Ulmer. 2000. *Evaluation of Motorcycle Helmet Law Repeal in Arkansas and Texas.* National Highway Traffic Safety Administration, Sept.

SafetyNet. 2005. *Traffic Safety Basic Facts 2004: Motorcycles and Mopeds.* European Commission.

Savage, M., M. Sundeen, and J. Majeur. 2007. *Traffic Safety and Public Health: State Legislative Action 2006.* Transportation Series, No. 31, National Conference of State Legislatures, Denver, Colo., March.

Savage, M., A. Teigen, and N. Farber. 2010. *Traffic Safety and Public Health: State Legislative Action 2009.* Transportation Series, No. 34, National Conference of State Legislatures, Denver, Colo., Feb.

Schoenebeck, S. 2007. Alcohol Related Road Accidents in Germany—Status Till 2005. *Proc., International Council on Alcohol, Drugs and Traffic Safety.* http://www.icadts2007.org/scientific/proceedings/index.html.

Servadei, F., C. Begliomini, E. Gardini, M. Giustini, F. Taggi, and J. Kraus. 2003. Effect of Italy's Motorcycle Helmet Law on Traumatic Brain Injuries. *Injury Prevention,* Vol. 9, No. 3, pp. 257–260.

Shankar, U., and C. Varghese. 2006. *Recent Trends in Fatal Motorcycle Crashes: An Update.* National Highway Traffic Safety Administration, June.

Shults, R. A., R. W. Elder, D. A. Sleet, J. L. Nichols, M. O. Alao, V. G. Carande-Kulis, S. Zaza, D. M. Sosin, and R. S. Thompson. 2001. Reviews of Evidence Regarding Interventions to Reduce Alcohol-Impaired Driving. *American Journal of Preventive Medicine,* Vol. 21, No. 4, Supplement 1, Nov., pp. 66–88.

Smiley, A. 2008. Driver Behavior: A Moving Target. *TR News,* No. 254, Jan.–Feb., pp. 19–24.

Stone, J. L. 2004. Statement of Judith Lee Stone, President, Advocates for Highway and Auto Safety: Special Commendation to Louisiana Legislature and Governor Blanco for Reinstatement of Lifesaving All-Rider Helmet Law. Advocates for Highway and Auto Safety, June 18.

Subramanian, R. 2002. *Transitioning to Multiple Imputation—A New Method to Impute Missing Blood Alcohol Concentration (BAC) Values in FARS.* National Highway Traffic Safety Administration, Jan.

Swedish Road Administration. 2009. *Årsredovisning 2008* [Annual Report 2008].

Sweedler, B. M. 2007. Worldwide Trends in Alcohol and Drug Impaired Driving. *Proc., International Council on Alcohol, Drugs and Traffic Safety.* http://www.icadts2007.org/scientific/proceedings/index.html.

Sweedler, B. M., M. B. Biecheler, H. Laurell, G. Kroj, M. Lerner, M. P. M. Mathijssen, D. Mayhew, and R. J. Tunbridge. 2004. Worldwide Trends in Alcohol and Drug Impaired Driving. *Traffic Injury and Prevention,* Vol. 5, No. 3, Sept., pp. 175–184.

Task Force on Community Preventive Services. 2005. *Guide to Community Preventive Services.* Oxford University Press, New York.

Task Force on Community Preventive Services. n.d. Motor Vehicle Occupant Injury. http://www.thecommunityguide.org/mvoi/default.htm.

Thiel, C. 2003. The Federal 0.08 BAC Requirement and the Potential Loss of Highway Funding. *State Notes,* Michigan Senate Fiscal Agency, May–June.

Traffic Safety Center, University of California at Berkeley. 2002. Getting People to Buckle Up. *Traffic Safety Center Online Newsletter,* Vol. 1, No. 2, Dec.

TRB. 1987. *Special Report 214: Designing Safer Roads: Practices for Resurfacing, Restoration, and Rehabilitation.* National Research Council, Washington, D.C.

TRB. 1998. *Special Report 254: Managing Speed: Review of Current Practice for Setting and Enforcing Speed Limits.* National Research Council, Washington, D.C.

TRB. 2003. *Special Report 271: Freight Capacity for the 21st Century.* National Academies, Washington, D.C.

TRB. 2003–2009. *NCHRP Report 500: Guidance for Implementation of the AASHTO Strategic Highway Safety Plan, Volumes 1–23.* National Academies, Washington, D.C.

Ulmer, R. G., and V. S. Northrup. 2005. *Evaluation of the Repeal of the All-Rider Motorcycle Helmet Law in Florida.* National Highway Traffic Safety Administration, Aug.

Ulmer, R. G., and D. F. Preusser. 2003. *Evaluation of the Repeal of Motorcycle Helmet Laws in Kentucky and Louisiana.* Oct.

U.S. Department of Justice. 1989. Brief for the Respondents in Opposition; State of Nevada, Petitioner, v. Samuel K. Skinner, Secretary of Transportation, et al., in the Supreme Court of the United States.

USDOT. 2007. Fiscal Year 2008 Budget in Brief: National Highway Traffic Safety Administration. www.dot.gov/bib2008/bibpart07nhtsa.htm.

usRAP. 2008. *Phase III Plans.* http://www.aaafoundation.org/pdf/usRAPphaseIIIplans.pdf.

Washington, S., K. Shin, and I. van Schalkwyk. 2007. *Evaluation of the City of Scottsdale Loop 101 Photo Enforcement Demonstration Program.* Arizona Department of Transportation, Nov.

Wilmot, C. G., and M. Khanal. 1999. Effect of Speed Limits on Speed and Safety: A Review. *Transport Reviews,* Vol. 19, No. 4, Oct., pp. 315–399.

Wilson, E. M., and M. E. Lipinski. 2004. *NCHRP Synthesis of Highway Practice 336: Road Safety Audits.* Transportation Research Board of the National Academies, Washington, D.C.

Yowell, R. O. 2005. The Evolution and Devolution of Speed Limit Law and the Effect on Fatality Rates. *Review of Policy Research,* Vol. 22, No. 4, pp. 501–518.

5

Conclusions and Recommendations

The study charge asks the committee to examine the experience of other nations in reducing traffic deaths and the strategies these nations use to build public and political support for traffic safety interventions. The committee's conclusions and recommendations in four areas are presented below: overall lessons from the benchmark nations, safety program management, countermeasures, and sources of political and public support. The conclusions identify the accomplishments of the benchmark nations, sources of success, and differences between U.S. and international practices. The recommendations, addressed to elected officials and to government safety professionals and administrators, identify actions needed in the United States to emulate the successes that other countries have achieved.

The recommendations do not comprehensively address all aspects of U.S. traffic safety programs. The committee's recommendations concerning countermeasures address the areas of practice that are highlighted by the international comparisons and emphasize the areas to which the study charge refers: measures directed at driver behavior. All of the benchmark countries' safety programs acknowledge the necessity of a comprehensive highway safety strategy that reduces crash losses through improvements in vehicle design, road design, licensing requirements, and emergency response as well as through regulation of driver behavior.

LESSONS FROM THE INTERNATIONAL COMPARISONS

The United States is missing significant opportunities to reduce traffic fatalities and injuries. The experiences of other high-income nations and of the U.S. states with the best safety improvement records indicate the potential payoffs from more rigorous safety programs and point to measures that could lead to immediate improvements.

Most high-income countries are reducing traffic fatalities and fatality rates (per kilometer of travel) faster than is the United States, and several countries that experienced higher fatality rates 20 years ago now are below the U.S. rate. From 1995 to 2009, annual traffic fatalities declined 52 percent in France, 39 percent in the United Kingdom, 25 percent in Australia, and 50 percent in total in 15 high-income countries (excluding the United States) for which long-term fatality and traffic data are available, but only 19 percent in the United States. Some U.S. states have traffic fatality rates comparable with those of the countries with the safest roads; however, the typical speed of improvement in safety in other high-income countries is not matched in any state.

Researchers do not have complete understanding of the underlying causes of long-term trends in crashes and fatalities. Identifying the countries with the most effective government safety policies would require first sorting out the effects of demographic, geographic, and economic influences. For example, results of empirical studies suggest that changes in the following factors can affect the change over time of a country's traffic fatality rate: the median age in the population (an aging population experiences a declining fatality rate), the quantity and patterns of alcohol consumption in the general population, the overall level of road congestion (increasing average congestion slows speeds and may thereby reduce the fatality rate), and the quality of general medical services. Business cycles influence the fatality rate over short periods, with the rate declining during recessions.

In most instances, the committee was not able to verify fully the statements of the benchmark countries' safety agencies about the overall effects of their programs on crash losses compared with experience in similar circumstances in other jurisdictions with less developed safety programs or about the effectiveness of particular interventions that these countries used. The necessary data collection and analyses have not been conducted by the agencies or in some cases the analyses may have been done but were not examined by the committee. In reaching its conclusions, the committee relied on reports of the responsible safety agencies that appeared to be credible and for which empirical support was available.

This incomplete understanding does not prevent learning from the experience of other countries. It does mean that, to identify the keys to success, singling out the countries with the lowest overall fatality rates or the fastest aggregate improvements will not be sufficient. Instead, it is necessary to identify specific safety intervention programs for which quantitative evaluation shows benefits and then to isolate the elements of those programs that led to success.

The experience of the benchmark nations indicates that the successful national programs function effectively at three levels of activity:

- Management and planning: Transportation, public safety, and public health administrators systematically measure progress toward quantitative objectives, direct resources to the most cost-effective uses, and communicate with the public and with elected officials to maintain their support.
- Technical implementation of specific countermeasures: A range of measures is employed for regulating driver behavior, maintaining effective emergency response, and ensuring safe design and maintenance of roads. The techniques are generally of proven high effectiveness and often intensively applied.
- Political support and leadership: High-level political commitment ensures that resources are provided, administrators are held accountable for results of safety initiatives, and systems users are held accountable for compliance with laws and regulations.

Within these three areas, the most critical needs for action in the United States today may be in management and planning. Without effective management, neither elected officials' demands for progress nor advances in safety techniques will bring about sustained reductions in crash losses. However, improved management will ensure that the available resources are used to greatest effect and, over time, will foster political and public support by demonstrating that reduction in fatalities and crashes is an attainable goal.

State and local government executives and professionals responsible for highway safety are aware of potential solutions to safety problems. They are positioned to provide leadership by making concrete proposals to legislatures for comprehensive safety initiatives that promise specific results if the necessary resources and support are supplied. The development of aggressive safety programs in several of the benchmark nations (for example, in France and New Zealand) appears to have followed this path.

The effective use in the benchmark nations of countermeasures that are unavailable or little used in the United States (in particular, automated speed enforcement and high-frequency alcohol testing) has received attention from U.S. observers. However, there is experience to support the view that systematic management can produce safety progress with the tool kit of countermeasures that is available to the responsible agencies. The tool kit will vary among jurisdictions depending on legal constraints, community attitudes, road and traffic characteristics, and resources. For example, in a jurisdiction where the methods of rigorous speed and alcohol enforcement typical of the benchmark countries cannot be practiced, the benefits of conventional enforcement and of passive countermeasures such as safe road design are all the greater, and progress will be more dependent on investment in these kinds of countermeasures. Similarly, if the high-intensity enforcement methods used in the benchmark countries are not available, vehicle-based safety improvements become more valuable and their implementation more urgent. In contrast, without effective management, legal authorization of new enforcement methods or increased spending on safety would be likely to yield disappointing results. Management success will depend on political support that holds administrators accountable for outcomes and provides needed resources. The countries or U.S. states that make progress will be those with the best overall long-term management of their safety programs.

Any comparison of management methods in other countries with those of the United States must take into account the highly decentralized structure of U.S. government. The U.S. federal government regulates motor vehicle safety, but otherwise its involvement is indirect, exercised through rules imposed on state and local government recipients of federal highway and traffic safety grants. State governments build and operate intercity roads; state police enforce traffic regulations mainly on major roads; and state laws and courts govern driver licensing, vehicle inspection, speed limits, impaired driving, and other aspects of traffic safety. Local governments operate local streets and roads, enact local regulations, and provide local police and courts for enforcement of traffic laws within their jurisdictions.

In contrast, most of the benchmark countries' governments are relatively highly centralized; for example, a national police force may conduct most traffic enforcement. Australia's federal system has similarities to the U.S. structure, but no country's institutions match the thousands of U.S. entities with independent authority for public safety and for road maintenance and operation. This difference does not imply that the management practices of other countries necessarily are inapplicable in the United States, but it complicates the challenge of introducing them here.

The following sections present conclusions about effective practices in the benchmark nations and possible lessons for the United States at each of the three levels of activity, beginning with management and planning. Conclusions in each section are followed by recommendations for U.S. practices.

MANAGEMENT AND PLANNING OF SAFETY PROGRAMS

Management is the direction of resources to attain defined objectives. The senior managers of transportation, public safety, and health agencies are expected to define traffic safety program objectives and strategies, budget and allocate resources to interventions, coordinate programs across agencies and jurisdictions, monitor the effectiveness of interventions and progress toward objectives, and interact with elected officials and the public to maintain support and justify the commitment of the required resources.

Conclusions

The most characteristic features of successful national safety programs are to be found in the management of the programs. The case studies in Chapter 4 illustrate the value of systematic management and evaluation in the benchmark countries' safety programs. The following are essential elements of the management model:

- A systems perspective that integrates engineering design, traffic control, regulatory enforcement, and public health methods to identify and reduce risks. This approach requires collaboration across government agencies and levels of government.

- A plan that specifies goals and milestones, methods, schedule, and resource requirements. A jurisdiction's traffic safety plan constitutes a commitment for which legislatures may hold executive agencies accountable, and the public may hold accountable the government agencies responsible for delivery. The plan provides for long-term continuity in funding and in strategies. The most credible plans quantitatively specify the expected impact of individual planned countermeasure initiatives in order to demonstrate that aggregate casualty reduction goals are consistent with the means proposed.
- Regular monitoring to identify problems and measure progress toward goals and ongoing evaluation to determine effectiveness of the actions taken.

In most countries, adherence to the model depends on a recognized lead government safety agency with powers to manage resources and to coordinate efforts among agencies and levels of government.

The benchmark nations' safety administrators generally acknowledge these requirements and have taken steps to implement them, although not all have yet achieved fully satisfactory implementation in all areas.

In the United States, management practices in traffic safety programs typically are lacking in essential elements of this ideal management model. Meaningful goals and milestones are not published, data systems for monitoring effort and performance are inadequate, program impacts are not scientifically evaluated, and initiatives are reactive and episodic rather than strategic. Important differences between practices in the most proficient benchmark nation safety programs and common U.S. practice, as observed in the case studies in Chapter 4, are listed below.

Planning and Goals

The benchmark nations and all U.S. states prepare traffic safety plans that state goals for the jurisdiction's traffic safety program for a period of several years and describe the strategies for meeting the goals. U.S. state plans as well as those of the benchmark nations commonly declare a primary goal of reducing aggregate fatalities by a certain percentage by a certain year. Such a goal is likely to be useful only if it is backed up by a quantitative plan for attainment. Otherwise, it lacks credibility and does not entail accountability. A "stretch" goal (such as Sweden's Vision Zero program) can be constructive as a declaration of values in a high-level policy statement, but a state's safety plan should be thought of as a business plan, which must lay out practical means to reach the stated objectives.

Safety Plans   The safety plan can lead to realization of goals if it specifies

- Countermeasures to be used,
- The budget and other resources devoted to applying the countermeasures (for example, in the program to control alcohol-impaired driving, the annual numbers of roadside sobriety checks to be conducted and the resources required for the checks), and
- Projections of the expected intermediate outputs as well as the ultimate impacts of each countermeasure initiative. An intermediate output is a measure of the direct effect of an intervention—for example, the trend in median speed on a road is a measure of the effect of speed control measures over time, and the frequency of alcohol impairment among all drivers in a locale is a measure of the effect of anti–drunk driving initiatives.

Published plans of the benchmark nations do not all show this level of detail. However, the continuity and stability in strategies and effort of those countries' safety programs are evidence of substantial planning.

Analytical Tools in Planning   Lack of analytical tools for safety planning inhibits planning and weakens the case for safety spending in the competition for public resources. Safety planning and management require models analogous to those available to transportation administrators for air quality, pavement condition, and congestion evaluation. The necessary tools are systems for screening of road networks, diagnosis of crash causes, and selection of cost-beneficial countermeasures. Recently developed formal safety planning and management tools, as described in Chapter 3, promise benefits if the states devote the necessary resources to their proper use. Among them are the Interactive Highway Safety Design Model, an expert system to evaluate the safety of highways in the planning and design stage, and SafetyAnalyst, an expert system to screen the road network for high-hazard locations and assess costs and benefits of countermeasures.

These analysis tools also can contribute to safety planning. States can use them to set quantitative targets for their hazard elimination programs and for the safety performance of planned new construction, to help guide allocation of resources among roadway safety improvements and other safety programs, and to show how capital programs will contribute to the plan's overall safety goals.

Performance Monitoring and Evaluation
The benchmark nations have data systems designed to meet management needs with respect to content and timeliness (although deficiencies exist in most if not all systems). In the United States, state safety agencies lack the data systems necessary for efficient management of safety programs. The following are examples:

- U.S. jurisdictions generally do not have systematic data on the frequency, locations, and results of sobriety checks. States maintain data on sobriety checkpoints and targeted patrols funded with federal grants, but the portion of the total enforcement effort that these activities constitute is unknown. The benchmark nations' anti–drunk driving enforcement programs typically monitor all these statistics as measures of level of effort and to help in directing enforcement resources. Because of the lack of sobriety test data, U.S. data on the extent and patterns of impaired driving are incomplete and of uncertain reliability.
- Few U.S. jurisdictions maintain systematic speed data. Therefore, states are handicapped in allocating enforcement resources, cannot measure the effectiveness of their enforcement or improve their enforcement strategies, and cannot observe how speed affects crash rates. In contrast, several of the benchmark nations routinely monitor speed trends, which they regard as essential information for managing and evaluating their speed control programs.
- The 2010 *Highway Safety Manual* of the American Association of State Highway and Transportation Officials (AASHTO) and the new safety analysis tools developed by the U.S. Department of Transportation (USDOT) and AASHTO provide techniques for evaluation of the safety effects of infrastructure improvements. (See Box 3-7 in Chapter 3.) Many states will need new data systems to apply these tech-

niques. In general, states have not had either capabilities or standard procedures for routine monitoring and evaluation of the safety consequences of infrastructure improvements.

In general, the manager of a safety program, to supervise the program adequately, must track three kinds of measures:

1. Measures of enforcement or intervention effort, for example, numbers of citations issued for particular kinds of violations, numbers of alcohol tests administered, expenditures on public service advertisements, and audience ratings of advertisements: Accounting of expenditures and person-hours by safety program activity is essential in measuring cost-effectiveness and guiding resource allocation.
2. Intermediate output measures that indicate the immediate impacts of interventions: If an intervention targets driver behavior, then the behavior that it is intended to influence (e.g., average speeds and speed distributions on the roads targeted for enforcement, frequency of driver impairment as indicated by alcohol tests) should be measured so that the direct effects of interventions can be observed and as a guide resource allocation.

   Every intervention should have measurable intermediate outputs defined for it. If no intermediate output is monitored, management of the intervention must proceed by guesswork, and the likelihood of good results is reduced. Examples of intermediate output measures in a roadway hazard elimination program are the road protection scores assigned to roadways in the European Road Assessment Program described in Chapter 4 and counts of quantities of specific road improvements installed (e.g., as described in Chapter 3, France periodically reports the cumulative number of intersections replaced by roundabouts, and Sweden reports the miles of roads with median barriers installed). Surveys showing whether awareness of risks and attitudes toward high-risk behavior have changed among the target audience are intermediate output measures for safety advertising campaigns that are used in Australia and elsewhere. An example of an intermediate output measure for vehicle safety is the fraction of all cars on the road that meet the European Union's highest crashworthiness rating, which is tracked by Sweden. Although the committee did not observe them in use, intermediate output measures could be developed for

driver testing and licensing programs in terms of the fraction of all drivers meeting specified standards of skill, knowledge, or fitness.
3. Measures of safety impact: changes in the frequency of the categories of crashes that were targeted by the intervention (e.g., trends in speed- or alcohol-related crashes).

In a well-managed program, these measures are available promptly and at a level of temporal and spatial detail allowing managers to follow events. Assembly of these data would be the basis of a real-time management information system. In addition, periodic formal evaluations of program effectiveness would be conducted by using these data and possibly specially collected data. Monitoring would be public and easily accessible, because introducing accountability would be one of the main benefits of the information system.

The benchmark nations' safety programs appear to have most of these measures in some form, although probably all have gaps. In contrast, U.S. safety programs generally are not monitored in this way; capacities for tracking enforcement effort and behavioral responses appear especially weak. As described in Chapter 3, the states and the National Highway Traffic Safety Administration (NHTSA) have a plan for more systematic monitoring of certain measures of enforcement level of effort and for beginning work on developing speed monitoring systems. Attaining the capabilities of the benchmark countries to produce measures and to use them to improve safety program effectiveness will require a major state effort not only in data collection but also in implementing fundamentally new management practices.

Systems Perspective and Intergovernmental Collaboration

Traffic safety policies in several of the benchmark nations call for optimizing the performance of all components of the road transportation system, including infrastructure, vehicles, and drivers, by using the full range of available tools: regulation, enforcement, judicial penalties and offender supervision, engineering and technology applications to reduce road- and vehicle-related risk, and public information and education.

In the U.S. institutional setting, strong cooperation among government agencies and levels of government is a prerequisite for such a systems approach to safety. The centralized administrative structure of most of the benchmark nations allows government to act expeditiously and nationwide to coordinate activities among multiple agencies. In contrast, thousands of U.S. state and local agencies have responsibilities for public safety; for the courts; and for highway and street construction, maintenance, and operation. The states independently manage their traffic safety programs, with a degree of central control through federal-aid highway program rules and NHTSA regulations. This structural difference between U.S. institutions and most of the benchmark nations limits the transferability of management methods to some extent.

Integration of law enforcement with the planning and operation of the comprehensive safety programs of the U.S. states is needed. Collaboration must involve line officers as well as leadership. The practicality and effectiveness of measures such as automated enforcement, sobriety checkpoints, and corridor safety campaigns depend on recruiting cooperation of police at all levels. Law enforcement agencies will require capabilities for training and evaluation to support their participation in safety initiatives.

The U.S. federal system, although it can complicate administration, has been a source of innovation. Leadership by individual states has been crucial for safety progress and should be fostered. Examples are Tennessee's leadership on child safety seats and leadership from Florida, Michigan, North Carolina, and other states on graduated driver licenses for young drivers in the 1990s.

The U.S. federal government has used a variety of mechanisms to influence the safety policies of the states: mandates for the states to enact certain laws or be penalized by loss of a fraction of their federal highway aid or by transfer of grants from general highway construction to funds that can be used only for safety improvements; design standards for federal-aid highway projects; formula safety grants and incentive grants that reward states for enacting laws or programs meeting federal standards; and research, technical assistance, and demonstrations conducted by USDOT. These activities have had mixed success. A federal mandate has strengthened blood alcohol content (BAC) laws, but the federal speed limit and helmet use mandates met with opposition and were repealed. USDOT technical assistance programs are potentially of high value but operate with limited resources. The overall impact of federal grant programs has not been measured. Federal leadership has demonstrated its value in the past, but stronger national direction will be needed if highway safety progress is to be accelerated.

Recommendations

Initiatives of USDOT and AASHTO over the past decade have emphasized state and local traffic safety planning, management processes, and evaluation. These organizations have published guidelines and manuals outlining management practices that are consistent with the practices that have contributed to the successes of the benchmark nations and with the principles outlined above. Yet it is unclear that many states are making significant progress in critical elements of safety management: meaningful planning, monitoring and evaluation that support management decisions, or adoption of systems solutions to problems.

Overcoming the obstacles to implementing fundamentally new management practices will require capacity building and technology transfer in support of state and local government safety programs. Highway safety is primarily the responsibility of the state and local governments that operate the road system, but federal leadership is needed to stimulate reform. Therefore, **Congress should authorize and provide funding for three USDOT activities to be conducted cooperatively with the states:**

- A series of large-scale, carefully managed demonstrations of safety program management;
- Revision of the Uniform Guidelines for State Highway Safety Programs to provide practical guidance; and
- Development of a new model for state traffic safety planning.

In addition, in support of reform of safety management, **governments, universities, and professional organizations must strengthen the safety training of transportation engineers and other safety professionals and administrators.**

Large-Scale Demonstrations
Congress should authorize USDOT to cooperate with selected states in organizing, funding, evaluating, and documenting a series of large-scale demonstrations of important elements of safety management. Experience suggests that communicating the concepts of safety manage-

ment to the responsible jurisdictions will require a much greater level of effort than has been devoted to the task.

Objectives   The purposes of a demonstration would be (*a*) to document the functioning of a program conducted according to stringent and specific guidelines (e.g., the NHTSA Uniform Guidelines) and (*b*) to disseminate information widely on safety program management methods, problems, costs, and benefits to transportation agencies, officials, and the public through training, publications, and other media. A fully successful demonstration would show that an efficiently managed program can reduce crash losses; gain wide recognition of this potential benefit from elected officials, professionals, and the public; and stimulate adoption of the techniques as standard practices by transportation and public safety agencies.

The techniques for making highway safety progress are increasingly well attested, and initiatives are under way in the United States to promote their adoption. As described in Chapter 3, the initiatives include new requirements and guidance for safety planning, revisions of the NHTSA Uniform Guidelines, and dissemination of quantitative analytical tools. However, institutional and technical capacities required to apply these techniques are lacking. NHTSA's speed management guideline illustrates this need: it calls for painstaking monitoring of speed and evaluation of the effectiveness of local speed enforcement, but few state or local jurisdictions have the institutional capacity or resources to carry out these activities. The demonstrations would contribute to building the necessary capacity in participating states; in USDOT; and, indirectly, in nonparticipating states.

Finally, the demonstrations could be a means of introducing unfamiliar and potentially controversial safety measures in a manner that might mitigate concerns of the public, police, and transportation administrators. It would be understood that the measures would not be continued unless they proved effective; the federal government would endorse the demonstration, share in the cost, and provide technical support; and information about the demonstration and the evaluation would be readily available.

Research to evaluate the effectiveness of particular countermeasures would not be a primary purpose of the demonstrations (although the evaluation results would contribute to knowledge of effectiveness). They would use countermeasures whose effectiveness was reasonably well established. Trials specifically designed to evaluate countermeasure effectiveness are a valuable research technique, but this recommendation does not address the conduct of such trials.

Design Requirements The requirements for a demonstration that would be useful for these purposes are the following:

- A plan containing a specific and detailed statement of goals and methods.
- Scale and resources adequate to meet the goals and identified in the plan. The demonstration should be of a magnitude to allow measurement of safety impacts.
- Use of state-of-the-art interventions. The plan should present a quantitative estimate of the results expected from the interventions to be used.
- Provision for real-time monitoring and for scientifically rigorous independent evaluation. Demonstrations with multiple participants should use uniform evaluation methods in all jurisdictions. Monitoring must measure level of effort and intermediate outputs as well as ultimate safety impacts.
- Arrangements to provide the public and officials with information about the demonstration's objective, methods, and results in accessible form at all stages of its progress.
- Provision for technology transfer; that is, ensuring that the demonstration will be useful to jurisdictions that do not participate. Documentation, full and prompt publication of results, and preparation of a variety of training and publicity materials would be required.

A demonstration would concentrate on specific components of a state's safety program, which could be a category of countermeasure (e.g., a speed management program or corridor improvement program) or a management process (e.g., monitoring and evaluation). Demonstrations involving areas of state programs that are covered by the NHTSA Uniform Guidelines for State Highway Safety Programs should be designed to show how states can use the guidelines effectively. Similarly, demonstrations involving the activities that states must conduct to prepare the federally required Strategic Highway Safety Plan should show methods and results of these planning activities.

The minimum necessary scale for the proposed demonstrations is suggested by examples of past demonstrations: the Minnesota 2005 speed management demonstration (described in Chapter 4), which covered major portions of the state's road system, involved multiple local jurisdictions, had a duration of 1 year, and cost $3 million; and the Gloucester (United Kingdom) Safer City project (described in Chapter 3), which was a 5-year urban traffic safety demonstration partially funded with a £5 million competitively awarded grant from the national government. USDOT conducts demonstrations today, but they are of relatively small scale, and provisions for evaluation have been incomplete. Small-scale demonstrations with narrowly defined objectives can be useful if they are carefully designed, but they are not addressed in this recommendation.

Organization To participate in the large-scale safety management demonstration program, a state would submit a proposal in response to a USDOT request. Costs would be shared by the state and the federal government. The state would operate the program, and USDOT would ensure that standards were followed and proper evaluations conducted. External technical assistance from USDOT and other expert sources would be available to participating state and local governments.

USDOT would support only proposals that met minimum requirements with regard to administration, organization, resource commitment, and monitoring and evaluation. The grant program should be constructed to attract strong proposals from motivated state and local governments through the offer of substantial aid and the prospect of visible results. Strong proposals would most likely come from states in which the commitment to safety of the highest levels of government, including elected officials, was evident.

Most demonstrations would entail recruitment of local government cooperation and the training of local highway departments and police. Demonstrations also would require intensive collaboration among the government agencies with safety responsibilities [police, highway agencies, emergency medical services (EMS), and the judiciary]. Certain of the Uniform Guidelines propose organizational arrangements for collaboration, for example, the speed management working groups that the guideline on speed management calls for.

To help it evaluate the organizational arrangements proposed for the large-scale demonstration projects, USDOT should refer to the World Bank's 2009 *Country Guidelines for the Conduct of Road Safety Management Capacity Reviews*. The checklists in that document provide a practical test of the adequacy of arrangements for attaining the demonstrations' dual goals of building capacity in state and local safety agencies and showing that evidence-based interventions can produce sustainable and cost-effective safety benefits.

To help ensure quality and credibility of results, an independent advisory and review board should observe each demonstration. Inclusion of experts from other countries on the board would add valuable perspectives. The board should be independent of the agencies conducting the demonstration, have access to all relevant information and receive regular reports from managers of the demonstration, and publish its advice and reviews. It should advise throughout the course of the demonstration and review evaluations for technical soundness.

Revised Guidelines and Safety Plans
USDOT should work with the states to revise the Uniform Guidelines for State Highway Safety Programs to ensure that these documents provide directly applicable and practical guidance for development of state programs.

USDOT, in cooperation with the states, should develop a new model for state Strategic Highway Safety Plans that is more rigorous than present practice. Plans should be required to contain meaningful goals expressed in terms of quantitative measures of level of effort and of intermediate outputs (changes in driver behavior or changes in road conditions) as well as changes in frequencies and rates of crashes and injuries, specific strategies for attaining the goals that specify the countermeasures to be used and resources required, provisions for monitoring progress toward goals, and concrete provisions for interagency coordination. The more specific and detailed the plan, the more accountable officials will be for their performance.

As described in Chapter 3, parts of the present guidelines are impractical because state and local governments lack necessary technical and organizational capacities. NHTSA recently has revised several of the guidelines. The experience of the demonstrations recommended above would aid NHTSA's efforts in making the guidelines more useful and influential and would help state and local governments in strengthening the capacities needed to benefit from the guidelines.

Future revised NHTSA Uniform Guidelines should make clear the priorities for action within each of the guideline areas and define the minimum requirements for an effective program. They should provide officials and the public with a benchmark for judging the adequacy of state and local resources. In addition to their present focus on process, they should emphasize measuring the impacts of safety measures. They should identify sources of detailed technical guidance for each of the recommended program elements. Each guideline should have enough detail to allow the guideline's use as a checklist to grade a state's program according to its degree of compliance.

Direction for improving planning is provided in the Governors Highway Safety Association (GHSA) 2009 recommendations to Congress for revision of the federal highway safety programs authorized in the expiring federal surface assistance transportation act, the Safe, Accountable, Flexible, Efficient Transportation Equity Act: A Legacy for Users (SAFETEA-LU). Four of the recommendations relate to planning. In them, GHSA proposed that Congress

- Encourage states to apply performance-based planning (i.e., to use a minimum, standard set of performance measures in their planning) and fund development of performance measures,
- Increase federal aid to the states to fund safety data improvements,
- Strengthen state Strategic Highway Safety Plan requirements, and
- Authorize development of a National Strategic Highway Safety Plan.

Enactment of these provisions in the successor legislation to SAFETEA-LU would be consistent with the committee's recommendation above for action to strengthen state safety planning capabilities.

Independent Evaluation and Research Capability

Congress should consider designating and funding an independent traffic safety evaluation and policy research organization. This entity would have three charges: (*a*) to provide technical support in development of interventions and management methods, (*b*) to advise senior executives and elected officials on policy, and (*c*) to reinforce accountability of the operating agencies to legislators and the public through independent performance evaluations. The entity would have independent authority to review and advise federal programs and could offer services to a state at the state's request. This charge could be given to an existing organization (e.g., a university-based research organization) or to a newly created entity.

Organizations with these functions have made important contributions to safety progress in the Netherlands, Australia, France, and the United Kingdom. Their objective evaluations have strengthened the position of the safety agencies interacting with elected officials and the public by showing that the agencies' actions and proposals are evidence-based and can be expected to produce results.

Several U.S. organizations now perform some of these functions at the national level, including USDOT, the National Transportation Safety Board, and the Government Accountability Office. However, none of these organizations has both independence from transportation program administrators and the broad charge to review safety performance on a regular basis and from the point of view of the entire system.

Professional Development

Transportation agencies should take into account demonstrated competency and professional qualification in highway safety in their hiring and promotion decisions. Engineering schools and state engineering accreditation associations should set standards for safety competencies of engineers practicing in areas that affect highway safety. It was noted above that overcoming the obstacles to implementing fundamentally new safety management practices will require substantial effort toward capacity building in government agencies responsible for safety. This effort should encompass professional training.

Professional training in road safety management is lacking in U.S. engineering schools. The 2007 report of the Transportation Research

Board's (TRB's) Committee for a Study of Supply and Demand for Highway Safety Professionals in the Public Sector (TRB *Special Report 289*) noted inadequacies in education and training programs and recommended that state government safety agencies and USDOT directly engage universities to advocate and promote development of comprehensive education programs for road safety professionals. The National Cooperative Highway Research Program (in Project 17-40) has defined a set of core competencies for traffic safety professionals and is developing and testing a model curriculum to impart these competencies.

Administrators in state and local government traffic safety programs are not all engineers but may have professional training in public administration, public safety, or an applied social sciences field. Outside engineering schools, few specialized education programs would have a sufficient concentration of future transportation professionals among their students to justify a traffic safety curriculum. Therefore, in addition to training in university curricula, in-service training programs are needed, especially short courses designed for local government public works engineers.

TECHNICAL IMPLEMENTATION OF COUNTERMEASURES

A countermeasure is a law, regulation, enforcement method, or engineering technique intended to reduce a specific targeted risk. Emergency response capabilities, adjudication practices, and public information programs also are forms of countermeasures.

As explained above, the committee examined the application of selected categories of countermeasures as case studies to compare safety practices internationally. The case studies provided the basis for the conclusions and recommendations presented below. The study did not survey the use or results of all countermeasures employed, and therefore the recommendations are not intended as a complete catalog of opportunities for improving the effectiveness of countermeasures.

Conclusions

Safety officials in the benchmark nations have attributed progress to their implementation of comprehensive safety programs, which include improvements in road design and traffic management; regulation of vehicle safety; regulation of driver behavior with regard to speed, alcohol and drug use, and seat belt and helmet use; restrictions on younger and older drivers; and reliable emergency response. These programs require consistent actions by lawmakers, road authorities, the justice system, and public health officials. Within this comprehensive framework, countries that have sought rapid declines in casualty rates have emphasized curbing high-risk driver behavior, especially speeding, drunk driving, and failure to use seat belts, by means of stringent laws, intensive public communication and education, and rigorous enforcement.

Two enforcement techniques aimed at driver behavior and widely credited with contributing to fatality reductions in the benchmark nations are automated enforcement of speed limits and high-frequency roadside sobriety checks to enforce laws against alcohol-impaired driving. The objective of these techniques is general deterrence, that is, to make the risk of detection and punishment high enough to change the driving behavior of the population. The deterrent effect is reinforced with social marketing.

Neither technique is in common use today in the United States. Because of the constitutional protection against unreasonable searches and seizures, U.S. police cannot legally require a sobriety test without probable cause (i.e., a reasonable suspicion that a violation has occurred). Automated enforcement has proved to be controversial and politically unpopular in some U.S. jurisdictions that have applied it, although progress has been made in gaining acceptance of the technique.

Despite these differences, the benchmark nations' enforcement practices provide important lessons applicable in the United States. They demonstrate that sustained and intensive enforcement, rationally organized and managed, can alter driver behavior sufficiently to produce worthwhile systemwide safety improvement. Enforcement probably is more expensive in the United States because of restrictions on the techniques used; therefore, resources must be employed judiciously. However, benefits ought to be attainable in the United States by using the available enforcement techniques to their best effect.

The subsections below present conclusions with regard to five kinds of countermeasures: prevention of alcohol-impaired driving, speed control, motorcycle helmet use, seat belt use, and highway network screening and corridor safety improvement programs. The conclusions include estimates of the order of magnitude of reductions in annual fatalities in the United States that might be practically attainable with application of certain of the countermeasures described. Such estimates are highly approximate. Outcomes would depend strongly on the level of effort and expenditure devoted to the countermeasures and the quality of management of safety programs. The benefits of implementing multiple countermeasures would not necessarily be additive; for example, if improved enforcement caused the frequency of impaired driving to decline, then the fatality reduction benefits of programs to increase seat belt use might decline because crashes became less frequent or because sober drivers are more likely to use seat belts.

Prevention of Alcohol-Impaired Driving

Several of the benchmark countries (including Germany, the United Kingdom, Sweden, and the Netherlands) have reported lower rates of alcohol involvement in crashes than has the United States consistently for many years. To what extent these differences result from differences in impaired-driving laws and programs rather than from differences in patterns of alcohol use or other social differences is unknown. The United States and many other countries, including Great Britain, Australia, and Sweden, have experienced slowdowns or reversals of progress in reducing alcohol-related traffic fatalities since the 1990s. Again, the causes are not well understood.

The two most evident differences between drunk driving countermeasures in the benchmark countries and those in the United States are the legal maximum BAC limits and the intensity of enforcement efforts. Research supports the effectiveness of lowering the BAC limit and of high-frequency testing (by means of sobriety checkpoints) in reducing alcohol-related motor vehicle fatalities.

The BAC limit is 0.8 g/L (0.08 percent) in the United States and 0.5 g/L (0.05 percent) or lower in Australia, Canada, Japan, and nearly every country in Europe except the United Kingdom and Ireland. The rate of roadside alcohol testing is 1 test per 3.6 registered drivers per year in France and 1 test per 2.6 drivers in Sweden. In the Australian state of

South Australia, the rate is 1 test per 1.6 registered drivers per year, and other Australian states maintain similar rates. Most European countries and Australia conduct random roadside alcohol checks. In the United Kingdom, where testing restrictions are similar to those in the United States (although more permissive), the rate is 1 test per 56 drivers annually. No systematic U.S. statistics on testing frequency exist, but the U.S. rate probably is well below the British rate. A 2003 survey found that only 11 U.S. states operated sobriety checkpoints as often as once a week.

Roadside sobriety checkpoints, operated by most U.S. states following protocols dictated by court decisions and state laws, make heavy use of police resources. To apply this technique effectively, there is need for design and evaluation of alternative strategies for deploying checkpoints; demonstration of the value of the best strategies to legislators, police officers, and the public; and provision by legislatures of budgets and personnel required to maximize the cost-effectiveness of the technique. Research in the United States has shown that frequent use of small-scale checkpoints (staffed by three to five police officers) can effectively reduce alcohol-related crashes.

All countries recognize that enforcement is only one aspect of the program required to combat alcohol-impaired driving. The program must include public health measures to prevent, identify, and treat alcohol abuse; public education programs on the costs of drunk driving; and judicial procedures that allow efficient adjudication of alcohol-impaired driving cases and intensive follow-up on offenders and penalties. For follow-up, ignition interlocks (devices installed in vehicles to prevent operation by any person with BAC over a specified level) recently have been recognized as an effective means to reduce recidivism.

In countries that have instituted sustained, high-frequency programs of preventive (i.e., not exclusively subsequent to a crash or violation) sobriety testing, including Australia, Finland, and France, reductions of 13 to 36 percent in the annual number of alcohol-involved fatal injury crashes have been achieved. Evaluations of intensive campaigns of selective testing at sobriety checkpoints in U.S. jurisdictions (following procedures now legal in most states) have reported reductions of 20 to

26 percent in fatal injury crashes involving alcohol use. In the United States in 2007, 13,000 persons were killed in crashes involving a driver who was alcohol-impaired. Therefore, widespread implementation of sustained, high-frequency sobriety testing programs in the United States at sobriety checkpoints could be expected to save 1,500 to 3,000 lives annually.

There is evidence to indicate that lowering the legal BAC limit to 0.5 g/L (0.05 percent), combined with more intensive enforcement, would reduce U.S. fatalities further. Evaluations of the effects of reducing the limit from 0.8 g/L (0.08 percent) to 0.5 g/L (0.05 percent) in the Netherlands, Austria, France, and Australia found that the change reduced alcohol-impaired driving and crashes and that at least part of the effect was independent of any concomitant changes in enforcement.

Speed Control

Governments in several countries today place high priority on speed control in their safety strategies on the premise that reducing speeding can immediately reduce the frequency of fatalities and injuries and therefore is a necessary element of national plans that specify demanding road safety targets.

Successful speed management initiatives in other countries are of high visibility (through public outreach and endorsement of elected officials), are long term (planned and sustained for periods of years), target major portions of the road network, sometimes use intensive enforcement methods (for example, automated enforcement and high penalties), use traffic-calming road design features in urban areas, and monitor progress toward publicly declared speed and crash reduction objectives. No U.S. speed management program in operation today is comparable in scale, visibility, and high-level political commitment to the most ambitious speed management programs in other countries.

Traffic safety experts in the United States have advocated a more selective initial application of automated enforcement than has been the practice in the most ambitious safety programs in the benchmark nations. Automated speed enforcement may be most readily introduced in locations such as work zones, where a need can be demonstrated and public acceptance is easier to gain.

The evidence from numerous research studies, synthesized in several credible reviews, is that reducing the mean speed on a road reduces injuries and fatalities in crashes on the road, when traffic volume is controlled for (i.e., speed reductions reduce casualty risk). Methodological difficulties in such research imply that estimates of the relationship between speed and casualty frequency have considerable uncertainty. Nonetheless, the assumption that decreasing mean speed will reduce casualty rates is one of the foundations of traffic safety programs in the benchmark countries, and the success of these programs in France, Australia, and elsewhere adds credibility to the assumption.

The cost-effectiveness of conventional speed enforcement strategies in the United States is uncertain. The most ambitious enforcement method commonly applied is the high-visibility enforcement campaign, which combines increased frequency of police patrols on a targeted portion of the road system with a publicity campaign to inform the public that speeders are likely to be ticketed. These campaigns typically are short term and do not use automated enforcement. Evaluation to measure the costs of alternative enforcement strategies and their effects on speed and casualties should be a research priority.

In countries that have implemented sustained, wide-area speed control programs using automated enforcement, including France and Australia, reductions in average speeds in free-flowing traffic on the order of 3 mph have been attained, and the incidence of speeding more than 6 mph over the limit typically has been reduced by about half. In the United States, a 1-year trial speed management program in Minnesota attained average speed reductions on the order of 1 mph on rural roads and urban expressways and substantial reduction in the frequency of speeding by using available personnel (diverted to speed enforcement from other duties). Standard methods of patrol and speed measurement were used, but more intensively; the trial did not involve automated enforcement. Syntheses of research on the effect of changes in average speed on crash rates have concluded that a 1 percent reduction in average free-flow speed on a road system can be expected to yield about a 4 percent reduction in crash fatalities (although the body of research on this relationship is not definitive). These data suggest that systematic speed control programs applied nationwide in the United States could save 1,000 to 2,000 lives annually at a feasible cost and with standard enforcement techniques (i.e., without use of automated enforcement). Programs with greater resources or that improved cost-effectiveness by using automated enforcement could achieve better results.

Motorcycle Helmets

Laws in every benchmark country require motorcycle riders to wear helmets. Only 20 U.S. states have such laws. Research has demonstrated that helmet laws substantially reduce the risk of death or injury from riding a motorcycle. Historically in the United States, enacting a helmet law has led directly to safety benefits; that is, implementation of the law has not been an obstacle. In contrast, in other areas of highway safety, such as speed control and roadway hazard elimination, effective implementation poses great management challenges and is critical for success.

Well-organized grassroots advocacy by motorcyclist groups opposing helmet laws has been highly effective, as such advocacy often is in the United States on issues that most affect a single well-defined group and that do not attract strong interest in the general population. The importance of advocacy groups may be a significant difference between the process of forming safety policy in the United States and that in many other countries.

NHTSA studies of the consequences of changes in helmet laws suggest that if all states had universal helmet use laws, on the order of 450 motorcyclist deaths per year would be avoided.

Occupant Restraint Laws

France, Germany, the Netherlands, Sweden, the United Kingdom, Canada, Australia, and some U.S. states all report seat belt use rates by front seat occupants exceeding 90 percent. The U.S. average in 2010 was 85 percent; 47 percent of passenger vehicle occupants killed in crashes in 2009 were belted. If U.S. belt use were increased by 5 percentage points, about 1,200 lives would be saved annually. State enactment of primary seat belt laws is among the measures that have proved effective in the United States in raising the use rate. Nearly every high-income country requires rear seat occupants to wear seat belts; only 20 U.S. states have this requirement.

Highway Network Screening and Corridor Safety Improvement Programs

State hazard elimination programs, funded by federal-aid funds earmarked for the purpose, have tended to operate in isolation from other state highway and safety functions. The effectiveness of these programs has never been adequately evaluated. Recently, efforts have been made to integrate these programs more closely with mainstream state transportation and safety activities. The new federal Highway Safety Improvement Program increased funding and required that the state hazard elimination program be developed within the framework of a state Strategic Highway Safety Plan to ensure broad collaboration in forming the program and consideration of the full range of countermeasures.

Two evaluation practices in use in the benchmark nations, road safety audits and road assessment programs, are bringing greater attention to the problem of upgrading the inherent safety of road infrastructure. Road safety audits are formal, independent examinations of the safety of the design of new road projects. (Similar procedures have been developed for roads already in use.) Audits originated in the United Kingdom, are practiced in Canada, Australia, and New Zealand, and are beginning to be conducted in the United States. Road assessment programs, in operation for several years under the sponsorship of automobile clubs in Europe and Australia and under development in the United States, are an important experiment in highway safety action. They are nongovernmental efforts that aim to increase public demand for safety and make public officials more accountable for the safety performance of highways by revealing and publicizing the differences in crash risks among roads.

Safety corridor programs, now in operation in several states, constitute a more comprehensive and systematic approach to reducing the risk of travel on a particular road than the traditional infrastructure-oriented hazard elimination program. These programs identify highway corridors that demand high priority for crash reduction. Corridor treatments are designed that combine enforcement, publicity, engineering improvements, and EMS improvements. Coordination is required with local governments on enforcement and EMS and with the state's capital programming process where capital improvements are called for.

The corridor program will be most effective if it is guided by a systematic analysis of the state's highway system that selects corridors and designs improvements with crash risk and cost-effectiveness as the basis for decisions. The risk maps of usRAP (the U.S. Road Assessment Program) and the corridor screening method in SafetyAnalyst (see Box 3-7 in Chapter 3) are two tools that can be used to identify corridors in greatest need of improvement. The safety corridor approach, combined with the safety planning and analysis tools now becoming available to the states, hold the promise of integrating safety improvement goals into highway planning and management far more effectively than the traditional hazard elimination programs.

Road safety audits, road assessment programs, and safety corridor programs all represent a positive, systematic approach to infrastructure safety. They actively and continuously seek opportunities to avoid casualties, in contrast to the reactive perspective of traditional hazard elimination programs.

Recommendations

If state and local governments seek to match the performance of the benchmark nations, they should recognize that additional resources for enforcement will be required. The level of enforcement can be increased by managing existing resources more effectively; increasing funding for conventional enforcement methods; and adopting more cost-effective enforcement methods, in particular, automated enforcement. Cost-effective enforcement methods maximize the impact on crashes and fatalities for a given amount of law enforcement resources. Enforcement budget data were not available to the committee; however, high-intensity enforcement programs like the alcohol and speed control programs of the benchmark nations evidently have high costs in personnel and other resources. The experiences of the benchmark nations as well as research on the effectiveness of interventions suggest that greater investment in enforcement can be cost-effective if the effort is guided by appropriate management techniques. Increased resources for enforcement would necessarily entail increased resources for the essential supporting activities of training, management information systems, and evaluation. Increased resources will be needed at the federal level for USDOT research, training, and technology dissemination functions that can be valuable aids to state efforts to upgrade enforcement techniques.

The states and USDOT should give high priority to initiatives to encourage adoption of camera enforcement and regular use of sobriety checkpoints. The needs include research to design and evaluate methods for using these enforcement techniques effectively (for example, the small-scale sobriety checkpoints whose use is promoted by USDOT); definition of detailed guidelines for their application; evaluations that document the value of these techniques as elements in an overall enforcement strategy; communication to inform elected officials, police officers, and the public of the value of the techniques; and training programs for police in their application. Evaluations should ensure that the safety benefits of the techniques adopted justify their costs in agency resources and in road user delay and inconvenience. Application guidelines should be developed with the active cooperation of the International Association of Chiefs of Police. Federal safety grant programs dedicated to these enforcement techniques would aid in their promotion. NHTSA grant program rules should explicitly highlight these techniques as eligible for funding in all existing programs where they are allowable expenditures.

Police in all states should have authority under state law to operate sobriety checkpoints and to use speed cameras.

State officials and the federal government should act to preserve the existing universal helmet use laws by communicating the health, safety, and economic costs of repeal to legislators. NHTSA and the state safety agencies also should place high priority on design, evaluation, and implementation of effective motorcycle safety measures other than helmet use laws. Such measures may include speed enforcement, training and licensing requirements, more effective enforcement of licensing requirements, fees commensurate with public costs, insurance requirements, publicity campaigns, and reforms in penalties for violations and in follow-up monitoring of offenders.

Each state should ensure that local police receive regular and substantial training in enforcement against impaired driving, speeding, and

other high-risk driver behaviors. The experience of NHTSA demonstration programs shows that local police often lack the level of training necessary for successful enforcement. Training also should impart to police officers the value and importance of safety enforcement.

The states and USDOT should refine the traditional practice of the hazard elimination program into a corridor safety improvement program that systemically identifies high-priority corridors, designs comprehensive safety improvement strategies for each corridor encompassing physical improvements and enforcement, and routinely evaluates the impacts of the strategies implemented. Road safety audit reviews would be a component of such a program.

POLITICAL LEADERSHIP AND PUBLIC SUPPORT

Successful safety initiatives in the benchmark nations that the committee examined have had the advantage of genuine and active support of elected officials in almost all cases, although elected officials were not necessarily the originators. In addition, sustaining the initiatives has depended on eventually gaining the trust of the public.

Conclusions

Although no universal prescription can be offered for earning political and popular support for ambitious traffic safety interventions, the international case studies and the experiences of U.S. states that the committee examined suggest the following observations on how support came about:

- Building support commonly is a long-term process. Gaining support for seat belt regulations and changing public and official attitudes toward impaired driving in the United States have been matters of slow progress over decades. Similarly, safety programs in the benchmark countries have long histories of evolutionary development and learning through experience.
- Creating new high-level institutional structures has been a vital step in the evolution of programs in certain of the benchmark nations. For example, a ministerial-level committee in France oversees and directs the national traffic safety program. These groups meet regularly and

interact with public administrators and professionals. Such arrangements reinforce accountability of managers to the legislature and of the legislature to the public. In contrast, legislative interest in the U.S. states tends to be episodic (for example, when a controversial law is proposed), and the continuing and routine aspects of safety programs seldom receive legislative oversight or high-visibility political support.
- The programs have emphasized transparency with respect to goals and in public communications. Public statement of specific and credible goals is essential for accountability. In several of the benchmark countries, prominent independent research centers evaluate and publicize progress toward goals. Making public the motivation and expected benefits of enforcement campaigns can help reduce skepticism in the community.
- In at least some of the benchmark countries, regular communication channels exist among the road safety agency, police, and researchers, and forums exist for interaction of legislators with professionals and researchers. The Australasian College of Road Safety is an example of an organization providing opportunities for multidisciplinary interaction. The benefit is a common understanding of safety problems and solutions.
- Public administrators and professionals often have been the initial leaders in educating and developing support among elected officials and the public. The evolution of policies in France, Australia, New Zealand, and several U.S. states illustrates this pattern. It has been necessary for safety programs to pull themselves up by their own bootstraps; that is, to build public and political support over time through transparency with regard to goals and methods, public communications efforts, and demonstrated results.
- Most programs have used sustained, large-scale, and sophisticated social marketing (that is, the application of business marketing techniques to promote a social welfare objective). The objectives of publicity campaigns have been to amplify the deterrent effect of enforcement and to influence public attitudes toward high-risk behavior. Publicity campaigns have been scientifically designed and evaluated.

Social marketing of safety programs is highly developed in Australia, New Zealand, the United Kingdom, Ireland, France, and other benchmark countries. The benchmark nations' publicity campaigns serve dual functions: they directly affect driver behavior, amplifying the effect of enforcement, and in the longer term they affect public attitudes toward unsafe driving and rigorous enforcement. The programs share a number of key features: a repeated theme is the consequences of failure to obey the law; advertisements use emotion and realism; funding is sufficient for high production values and prime time broadcasting; each campaign has a single, focused message; publicity is synchronized with enforcement; and the effectiveness of the activity is scientifically evaluated. Safety advertising campaigns in the United States usually lack some of these key features. In general, U.S. campaigns do not show awareness of the lessons learned in other countries with extensive experience and evidence of success.

Recommendations

Each state legislature should require the responsible executive agencies to report regularly to it on progress on fulfilling the state's safety plan and success in meeting the plan's goals. The legislature should expect agencies to report up-to-date summaries of each of the three kinds of program measures defined in the section on management: measures of level of effort and resources expended, measures of intermediate impacts of efforts (for example, changes in the frequency of speeding and of alcohol-impaired driving), and the final impact on numbers of crashes and casualties related to the risks that state programs are targeting. The agencies should be required to publicize these reports. Legislatures should consider linking their reviews of agency performance to the budget process; that is, requiring programs seeking continued funding to report on their past effectiveness.

As a preliminary step to strengthening U.S. capabilities for application of social marketing to traffic safety, USDOT should conduct an in-depth review of methods and outcomes in other countries. Then one or more pilot campaigns should be conducted to test and demonstrate social marketing methods at the level of the international state of the art, ideally as components of some of the large-scale demonstrations recommended above, with partial federal funding and federal oversight of evaluation.

The national organizations of transportation and public safety officials, state legislators, and safety researchers should take every opportunity for organization of forums that bring together administrators, legislators, and researchers for exchange of information and views on traffic safety. Cultivation of working relationships among these groups will be necessary for implementation of long-term, systematic traffic safety strategies.

Public agencies should cooperate in the development of usRAP, but the program must maintain independence, which is necessary for its effectiveness. The road assessment programs in Europe and Australia are important examples of an innovative technique to engage the public in safety, to increase understanding and support of public agencies' safety programs, and to reinforce public agency accountability for safety.

All states should enact the minimum framework of traffic safety laws that has been instrumental in achieving the safety improvements that the most successful benchmark country safety programs have attained. According to ratings of state laws applied by the Insurance Institute for Highway Safety, only 16 states have adequate laws (rated "good" or "fair") in as many as five of six key areas of traffic safety (strict impaired driving enforcement, meaningful restrictions on young drivers, primary enforcement of seat belt use, strong child restraint requirements, mandatory helmet use, and authorization of camera enforcement at red lights). In addition to the laws on this list, all states in which existing law impedes its application should enact enabling legislation for automated speed enforcement. Safety professionals in the states and at USDOT can promote improvements in traffic safety laws by conducting evaluations that show the benefits of enacting the laws and by thoughtfully planned efforts to communicate information on benefits to elected officials, senior agency administrators, and the public.

Study Committee Biographical Information

Clinton V. Oster, Jr., *Chair,* is Professor in the School of Public and Environmental Affairs, Indiana University. His research centers on aviation safety, airline economics and competition policy, and environmental and natural resource policy. He chaired the Transportation Research Board's (TRB's) Committee on Education and Training for Civilian Aviation Careers and the Committee on the Federal Employers' Liability Act, and he was a member of the Committee for Guidance on Setting and Enforcing Speed Limits. Professor Oster received a PhD from Harvard University, an MS from Carnegie-Mellon University, and a BSE from Princeton University.

Tony Bliss is Road Safety Advisor and formerly Lead Road Safety Specialist in the Transport Division of the Energy, Transport, and Water Department of the World Bank. His work concerns the development and promotion of multisectoral strategies to improve road safety results in low- and middle-income countries. He produced a strategic framework to guide World Bank road safety initiatives and assists in the preparation of road safety projects in client countries throughout the World Bank regions. He also led the creation and establishment of the World Bank Global Road Safety Facility, which is funding global, regional, and country capacity-building initiatives. Previously he was the General Manager of the Strategy Division, Land Transport Safety Authority, New Zealand. He has a BA and an MA in economics, both from Canterbury University, Christchurch, New Zealand.

William A. Bronrott is the Deputy Administrator of the Federal Motor Carrier Safety Administration of the U.S. Department of Transportation. From 1999 until his appointment as Deputy Administrator in 2010, he was a Democratic member of the Maryland House of Delegates for District 16 in Montgomery County. In the legislature he focused on highway safety and environmental issues. He has served as a member of the Board of Directors of the Metropolitan Washington Council of Governments and chaired the Montgomery County Blue Ribbon Panel on Pedestrian and Traffic Safety from 2000 to 2002. He has received awards from Mothers Against Drunk Driving, the National Commission Against Drunk Driving, the Institute of Transportation Engineers Maryland–District of Columbia Region, the American Automobile Association, and the Maryland Public Health Association. Mr. Bronrott received an MA and a BA in communications from the University of Maryland.

Troy E. Costales is Administrator of the Transportation Safety Division of the Oregon Department of Transportation. He manages driver education and highway safety programs on safety belts, alcohol and other drugged driving, work zones, pedestrians, and bicyclists. Before joining the Transportation Safety Division in 1997, he supervised the statewide crash data system. He is a member of the Standing Committee on Highway Traffic Safety of the American Association of State Highway and Transportation Officials (AASHTO) and Chair of the Task Group on the AASHTO Strategic Highway Safety Plan. He participated in the Federal Highway Administration's 2002 scanning tour on Managing and Organizing Comprehensive Highway Safety in Europe. Mr. Costales received a BS in management from George Fox University in Oregon.

Kent L. Cravens is a Republican member of the New Mexico Senate representing District 21. He has been a member of the legislature since 2001. He serves on the Senate Judiciary Committee and has sponsored legislation on enforcement of regulations on drunk driving and underage drinking. Senator Cravens is a member of the National Conference of State Legislatures' committees on transportation and health. He is the owner of a small business in the printing industry in Albuquerque.

John J. Cullerton is a Democratic member of the Illinois Senate representing the 6th Legislative District in Cook County and is President of the Illinois Senate. He has been a member of the Senate since 1992. He was a member of the Illinois House of Representatives from 1980 to 1992. His focus in the legislature has been on the issues of traffic safety, gun control, and criminal justice reform. He has received awards from

Advocates for Highway and Auto Safety and from the Illinois Association of Chiefs of Police. Senator Cullerton received a JD and a BA from Loyola University, Chicago.

Joseph A. Farrow is Commissioner of the California Highway Patrol, the state's lead traffic safety agency. He was appointed chairman of the Vehicle Theft Committee and the Law Enforcement Stops and Safety Subcommittee of the International Association of Chiefs of Police and is a member of the TRB Committee on Traffic Law Enforcement. Commissioner Farrow was a 2006 recipient of the International Association of Chiefs of Police J. Stannard Baker Award for career contributions to traffic safety. He received a BA from California State University, Sacramento, and an MA from California State University, San Diego.

Patrick S. McCarthy is Chair of the School of Economics in Ivan Allen College at the Georgia Institute of Technology. His areas of research include transportation economics, regulation, industry studies, and infrastructure. His research has included studies of the effects of speed limits and alcohol regulation on highway safety and he has received research funding from the National Institutes of Health and the AAA Foundation for Traffic Safety. Professor McCarthy earned a PhD in economics from the Claremont Graduate University and a BA in economics from the University of San Diego.

Alison Smiley is President of Human Factors North, Inc., a Toronto-based human factors engineering consulting company founded in 1982. She is an adjunct professor in the Department of Mechanical and Industrial Engineering at the University of Toronto. She has carried out research on driver behavior using simulators and instrumented vehicles, participated in road reconstruction and design projects, and developed and taught human factors and road safety courses to engineers, police, and other transportation professionals in Canada and the United States. She has served on a number of TRB committees and serves on the board of the journal *Accident Analysis and Prevention*. She was the 1997 recipient of the A.R. Lauer Safety Award given by the U.S. Human Factors and Ergonomics Society for outstanding contributions to the human factors aspects of highway safety. She received an MASc and a PhD in systems design engineering specializing in human factors from the University of Waterloo and a BSc from the University of Western Ontario.

John S. Strong is CSX Professor of Business Administration, Economics, and Finance at the College of William and Mary. His research is on transportation economics and safety, particularly in the airline industry, and on economics and finance in developing countries. He has worked on airport, air navigation, and regulatory issues in the United States, Asia, Latin America, Africa, and the former Soviet Union for governments and private organizations. He was a member of the TRB Committee for the Study of the Regulation of Weights, Lengths, and Widths of Commercial Motor Vehicles. He received a PhD and an MS from Harvard University and a BA from Washington and Lee University.

Richard Tay is Associate Dean (Research) and Chair in Road Safety Management in the Faculty of Law and Management of La Trobe University in Bundoora, Australia. Until 2010, he was Professor and Research Chair for Road Safety in the Department of Civil Engineering and Adjunct Professor for Injury Prevention in the Department of Community Health Sciences at the University of Calgary in Alberta, Canada. He is also an Adjunct Professor in Road Safety at the Centre for Accident Research and Road Safety in the School of Psychology at Queensland University of Technology in Australia. He has lectured at Nanyang Technological University in Singapore, the Chinese University in Hong Kong, and Lincoln University in New Zealand. His research and teaching involve the application of engineering, health, economics, marketing, psychology, and statistical models to analyze road crashes and evaluate road safety policies and programs as well as the development, implementation, and evaluation of measures to improve road safety. He has a PhD in economics from Purdue University, an MS in engineering economic systems from Stanford University, and a BS in electrical engineering from Texas Tech University.

Allan F. Williams retired in 2004 as Chief Scientist at the Insurance Institute for Highway Safety (IIHS). Before he came to IIHS, he was Project Director at the Medical Foundation, Inc., in Boston, Massachusetts, and Alcoholism Research Analyst at the Massachusetts Department of Public Health. Dr. Williams is the author and coauthor of numerous journal articles and publications in the field of highway safety. He received a PhD in social psychology from Harvard University and an AB in psychology from Wesleyan University.